UNIVERSITY OF KNOWLEDGE

GLENN FRANK, B.A., M.A., Litt.D., L.H.D., LL.D., *Editor-in-Chief*

PRINTED AND BOUND IN THE UNITED STATES
OF AMERICA BY THE CUNEO PRESS, INC.

Every Branch of Knowledge Man Possesses May Be Applied To Some Good Purpose

THE HEAD OF KHAFRE

UNIVERSITY OF KNOWLEDGE

GLENN FRANK, EDITOR-IN-CHIEF

THE DAWN OF CIVILIZATION

AND LIFE IN THE ANCIENT EAST

BY

ROBERT MARTIN ENGBERG, Ph.D.

of the Oriental Institute of the
University of Chicago

FAY-COOPER COLE, B.S., Ph.D., Sc.D., Editor

Chairman Department of Anthropology
University of Chicago

•

UNIVERSITY OF KNOWLEDGE INCORPORATED

CHICAGO

GLENN FRANK
Editor-in-Chief

INTRODUCTION

The first volume in this series told the story of the earth's beginning. It set the stage for the entrance of man as the actor in the human drama. The second volume told the story of man's beginning. With stage and actor brilliantly and authoritatively set before the reader in these two volumes, this third volume tells the story of the play's beginning.

The physical earth is the stage.

Man is the actor.

Civilization is the play.

These three volumes together give us perspective on the whole human venture. They tell us of the darkness out of which we and our world came. They trace, with fascinating and illuminating detail, the struggle of the human race toward the light. We can never understand as we should how and why we are as we are,

[VII]

think as we think, and act as we act here and now unless we know the inheritances and age-old habits that still live in us from the long past recorded in these volumes.

This volume deals, as I have said, with the human drama of civilization. It tells how man the actor played his part in the morning hours of civilization. It paints the background against which man is playing his part in these later hours of civilization. It is grounded in research of a high order. There is nothing of hasty journalism in this volume, and yet it has much of the freshness, much of the news value, of a five star final edition of the day's newspaper because it reflects the newest and most recent findings of archaeological excavation and interpretation.

For a long time our knowledge of ancient civilization was more or less static, but in recent years research has converted the dead past into a living past. And that sense of life pulses through this volume. This is the useful distinction of this volume—it carries the latest news from the research front where patient and painstaking investigators are perfecting our knowledge of the dawn of civilization, its early fruits, and the interactions between the cultures of ancient peoples.

In reading the manuscript of this volume, I had the sense of being actually on the scene with the excavators as they unearthed the records which illuminate for us the miseries and glories of the ancient world. Dr. Engberg, the author, has written this volume in the light of his own participation in excavations that have thrown up discoveries which change important dates and alter long-held conceptions of ancient civilization. It is fresh and accurate and records findings that have not yet found their way into any of the major encyclopedias or works of reference.

This volume tells you of the men of yesterday that you may better understand the men of today.

GLENN FRANK

FAY-COOPER COLE
Editor

PREFACE

Until a few years ago ancient history was supposed to start with Greece and Rome. Then archaeologists began to uncover the buried records of Egypt, Babylonia and Crete and it was soon recognized that these lands had exerted a profound influence on the early development of the Classical Nations.

Further excavations made it clear that the great cultures of the Near East did not develop in isolation, but that Crete was in intimate contact with Egypt and both, in turn, traded and had many relations with Syria and the great city states of the valley of the Euphrates. Now the ever widening horizon of our knowledge carries the contacts of these peoples to India, across Turkestan to China.

War, trade, and mass migrations carried the advances of one period and region to distant lands. The nations of antiquity borrowed liberally from one another, conservatism was broken and rapid progress was made toward civilization.

The deciphering of these records of the past has been due to the work of many institutions and scholars. Among this brilliant group of investigators Dr. Robert Engberg, the author of this volume, occupies a recognized place.

After three years of work in American archaeology, Dr. Engberg joined the field staff of the Oriental Institute of the University of Chicago and for four years carried on excavations at Megiddo (Armageddon). In Egypt his researches have placed him among the foremost students of the Hyksos period. He is co-author of several books dealing with the archaeology of Bible Lands and other portions of the Near East.

The record of life in the ancient East, told in these pages, is a story of the rise and fall of nations and peoples; of achievement and social decay; of invention and of cross fertilization of ideas. Out of this background comes our own civilization. It is a story delightfully told by a master of the subject.

October 1, 1937   FAY-COOPER COLE
                                                   University of Chicago

ROBERT MARTIN ENGBERG
Author

ACKNOWLEDGEMENT

In recent years interest in the more remote history of man has increased greatly, and people speak with considerable familiarity of some of the figures and movements of our newly recovered antiquity. Each year new facts, buried for thousands of years, are uncovered, thereby adding to our previous store of knowledge. When the key to decipherment of Egyptian hieroglyphic writing was found a little more than a century ago, a new historic vista was revealed, stretching back some five thousand years. Shortly thereafter, when the cuneiform inscribed records of Babylonia began to tell their story, the veil was lifted on a similar span of time in the land of the Tigris and Euphrates. Concerning other parts of the ancient world, like discoveries took place, all of them tending to recreate long lost civilizations that flourished and faded before the dawn of our era. Archaeology has played an important part in this development, and an attempt has been made in this book to present some of the more important and interesting discoveries of recent years, giving at the same time a sequence story of historical events.

The dates that are used will not agree in all cases with those the reader may find in encyclopedias and older histories. The yearly discoveries of which we have spoken have greatly refined our knowledge of the dates of ancient men and events, and in the following pages we have attempted to incorporate the most recent information.

In presenting this short history of the ancient world it is hoped that the reader will find not only a story of interest in itself but will leave it realizing that Greece and Rome, our cultural ancestors, owed much to that older world which had taken the first significant strides toward civilization.

In the preparation of this book the writer has had the benefit of much friendly assistance and criticism. The editors have read the entire manuscript, and large portions have been examined by George G. Cameron and Waldo H. Dubberstein of The Oriental Institute of the University of Chicago.

John A. Wilson, Director of The Oriental Institute, made available its photographic files, and in the selection of illustrations Miss Doris Fessler gave splendid assistance. The writer's familiarity with Oriental Institute excavations accounts for the choice and number of photographs selected from that organization.

Much appreciated has been the contribution of Herrlee G. Creel of the University of Chicago, through whose book, *The Birth of China*, the writer has been materially aided in the treatment of the early historical periods in China. Harald W. Jacobson of the Oriental Institute has generously checked and improved the Indian and Chinese chapters.

A number of maps were specially prepared for this volume by Walter W. Romig, and for the others we gratefully make acknowledgement to Robert J. Braidwood and The Oriental Institute. Lastly, as is usual, the writer wishes to admit a heavy indebtedness to his wife, Irene Nugent Engberg, who has been of assistance in numerous ways too difficult to relate in detail.

Acknowledgement is also made to the following individuals and institutions for the pictures they generously provided: James Henry Breasted, Jr.; J. Bradford Pengelly; Field Museum of

Natural History, Chicago; The Art Institute of Chicago; Museum of Fine Arts, Boston; University Museum, Philadelphia; Metropolitan Museum of Art, New York; British Museum, London; Louvre, Paris; Cairo Museum; and to many others, acknowledgements to whom appear with the illustrations.

To all these, whose help and cooperation have been inestimably valuable, the author expresses his sincere appreciation.

ROBERT M. ENGBERG

Chicago
October 15, 1937

TABLE OF CONTENTS

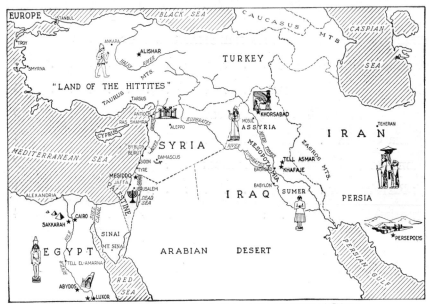

Courtesy of Robert J. Braidwood and The Oriental Institute of The University of Chicago

THE NEAR EAST

INTRODUCTORY STATEMENT

VIEW OF THE FOURTH CATARACT OF THE NILE

IT IS a trait of human nature to take things for granted, to ignore the fact that hundreds of generations of human development lie behind us, and that to these generations we owe our present civilized condition as much as we do to our own. Civilization does not grow full-bloom over night nor in the mind of any one man. It is like a snowball which, starting as a small sphere, gradually becomes a thing of tremendous size when rolled along a path of freshly fallen snow. Such is our civilization, each day adding something new, with each day's accomplishments becoming possible only because of that which was discovered or observed the day before.

Likewise no age is independent of that which preceded. To-day we accept the alphabet and its uses in almost the same way that we take breath into our lungs. But there is a long story behind the invention and development of the alphabet. To appreciate its importance we must project ourselves back to the time when people somehow got along without it. To understand its development we should know that the Greeks borrowed their alphabet from the Phoenicians, and that the Phoenicians in turn

[17]

—at an earlier date—learned of this important instrument of our everyday life from a source directly related to Egypt. Progress has been slow, but perhaps because of that very fact we are able to follow many of its painful steps through the centuries.

Ancient history, to many, used to begin with the Greeks. Now, thanks to the rapidly increasing knowledge of the really ancient languages, which by their age almost suggest that Greek and Latin are modern tongues, we may survey the ancient oriental kingdoms and empires that have contributed so greatly to the development of the world as it is today. Greece learned much from the Orient, although she called the foreigners barbarians. At an earlier date Egypt had applied the same term to the Greeks before the Greeks became civilized.

We speak of civilization but what is it? It is that condition upon which man embarked when first he began to live in groups. Civilization became more advanced when man ceased being purely a hunter and began to cultivate his food. In time he required an organized government to regulate the town or city or state in which he lived. Presently writing was discovered and soon there were systems of credit and banking by which ever-growing commerce could be more easily handled. These are all elements of civilization, due to the social being called man.

The study of man, and as a consequence the study of civilization, cannot be properly treated unless we go back to the earliest evidence of man. In this book, the story takes us through the great days of Egypt, Mesopotamia, Iran (Persia), Palestine and Syria, Anatolia (Turkey) and Crete, and the early but extremely important periods of China, India, Greece and Rome. So much information has been uncovered in recent years that this volume is hardly sufficient to do credit to the deeds and thoughts of ancient man. Let us, therefore, hasten into our story.

PART I

THE ANCIENT NEAR EAST

THE LAND

DURING untold ages the mountains, valleys, streams, and coast-line of the Near East have changed innumerable times. Seas have covered the land, and mountains in turn have been pushed out of the water. New rivers have started, and volcanoes have poured out their molten lava over the surrounding land. But by the time our story begins, the Near East had taken pretty much the same shape that it bears today. The Nile flowed down from its two main sources in central Africa to the point where the White and Blue branches meet, near the city of Khartum. The same cliffs bordered the course of the Nile when it reached Upper (southern) Egypt, and the Delta had already been formed. The land was prepared for the development of civilized man.

The same was true in the other great cradle of civilization, the plains bordering the Tigris and Euphrates—in the country now called Iraq, but which is better known to us as Mesopotamia. The two rivers flowed southward from their mountain sources and watered the fields of the earliest man known in this territory.

It is because land features have played such a great part in directing the course of man's development that we devote the next few pages to a rapid visit through the Near East.

[19]

Courtesy The Oriental Institute of The University of Chicago

LANDSCAPE ALONG THE TIGRIS

THE LAND OF THE NILE

Trade follows the highways. A glance at the map will make it quite clear that the highway in Egypt lies along the narrow thread of the Nile. As the river flows northward from Khartum it passes through the arid Nubian Desert, where vegetation is frequently restricted to a strip twenty feet in width. Lower down, it passes Aswan and the last of six cataracts. It is here that much of the finer stone, including granite, was quarried for the Nile temples. The valley widens to some extent as we proceed northward, but nowhere, except in the Delta, is the cultivable land more than fifteen miles wide. Relics of Egypt's oldest civilizations are found in the valley bottom near the river, many hundred feet below the cliffs that rise to the west. The Delta lies to the north of Cairo, and today the Nile has essentially two mouths, although ancient sources indicate that there have been at least seven.

We thus see Egypt as a long and winding strip of green with far-reaching deserts on both sides. There are in addition the Fayum, a relatively large fertile area southwest of Cairo, and a few oases which dot the bleak Libyan Desert which extends westward from the Nile.

The reason that Egypt, of all the countries on earth, has such a queer physical form lies in the fact that practically no rain falls except in the extreme north. The Delta partakes of the typical Mediterranean wet and dry seasons, but Upper Egypt depends for moisture on the Nile. A shower in Upper Egypt is the cause of considerable excitement, and no little wonder. The Nile, then, is the life blood of Egypt and the season of inundation is the most important of the year. Without this constant supply of water Egypt would become a desert.

The Blue Nile, which rises in the highlands of Ethiopia, is supplied by the heavy rains which fall during the summer months. The waters arrive at Khartum about the middle of May, heavily laden with mud, and two weeks later the river at Aswan begins to rise. The Nile reaches its maximum height at these places about

Courtesy The Oriental Institute of The University of Chicago

VIEW ALONG THE EUPHRATES
Native row boats moored to the shore.

INUNDATION OF THE NILE
Camels in a palm grove.

a hundred days later. When the waters subside, they leave an even film of mud in which the crops for the next year are sown. This process, happening over and over, is the secret of the fruitfulness of the Nile valley and has been from the time we first see primitive Egyptians as farmers. The White Nile, which comes from the Equatorial regions of central Africa, has much less volume than the Blue Nile but is effective in keeping up the water level in Egypt during the months when the Blue branch has run practically dry.

A natural consequence of the heavy load of mud carried by the inundation is that the bed of the Nile has risen steadily. It is estimated that the bed of the river has been raised four inches every century. Temples which, when built, were well above water level are now covered during the inundation, and in the Delta the foundations of many ancient structures are perpetually wet.

Trade in Egypt developed between the different settlements, and, since these were mainly on the Nile, it was the river which became the national highway. Much of the trade was done by boat, and early in its history Egypt became conscious of this second benefit of the Nile. There were also roads which led to the Red Sea, but these never assumed the importance of the Nile which is still the artery of the country.

Early in the history of Egypt, the Mediterranean became a highway of tremendous importance. Many Egyptian products have been excavated in the island of Crete, and these of course could have traveled by ship only. Trade by sea was also carried on with the Syrian coast from whose nearby mountains came the cedar of Lebanon. This was carried back to Egypt to be made into coffins, sacred ships, and other things for which good wood was necessary.

There was likewise a land road leading to Asia which went across the barren flats of northern Sinai and led in time to the rich markets of the Levant, Anatolia, Mesopotamia, and Iran.

PALESTINE AND SYRIA—THE CORRIDOR BETWEEN EGYPT AND MESOPOTAMIA

Palestine and Syria are small countries and never in ancient times attained the world position of the oriental powers. Nevertheless, they have always occupied an extremely important position, lying as they do on the direct road between Egypt and her Asiatic competitors. This geographic position has been unfortunate at times, but it has never lacked importance. If Egypt, in a time of national strength, aimed at the subjugation of some of the "upstart" Asiatic countries, perhaps that of the Hittites or of Mitanni in the bend of the Euphrates, she sent her armies across the Sinai highway and then through Palestine and Syria. In other cases transport ships were sent direct to the Syrian ports—this of course at a time when the ports were under Egyptian control.

On the other hand, there were times when the situation was reversed. Assyria, Babylonia, or Persia, when at the height of their

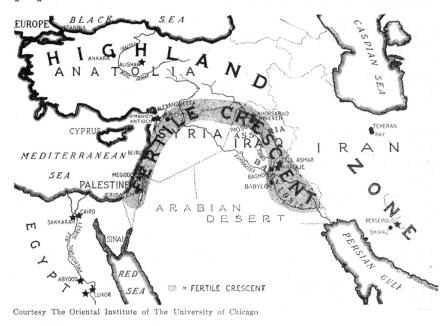

Courtesy The Oriental Institute of The University of Chicago

THE NEAR EAST

power, sought to add Egypt to their empires; but to do so they had first to conquer or pacify the land that lay between. That land was Palestine and Syria, always the corridor between the eastern and western powers. The direct route between Babylonia and Egypt lies across the Syrian Desert, but the hardships in crossing this desert have been experienced by many who will never tell their tales. The easiest and therefore the most sensible route for steady travel lay along the watercourse of the Euphrates, up into the Mitanni country, and thence across to the valley highways of Syria and Palestine. Dr. Breasted, the foremost American Orientalist of his day and the organizer of the Oriental Institute at the University of Chicago, aptly termed this route the "Fertile Crescent".

It was natural that the Syrian and Palestinian cities of the Fertile Crescent should learn much about the high civilizations to either side of them. The greatest Egyptian influence was generally felt in Palestine and southern Syria, territories nearest Egypt.

Courtesy James Henry Breasted, Jr. and The Oriental Institute of The University of Chicago

AIR VIEW OF THE JORDAN RIVER

Courtesy The Oriental Institute of The University of Chicago

A HARVEST SCENE NEAR MEGIDDO

Mesopotamian culture, on the other hand, permeated the life of northern Syria. But throughout Palestine and Syria there was a deep-seated knowledge of both countries.

Phoenicians have always suggested sailors to the western world, and they were that indeed; but how often does one stop to ask why the Phoenicians became sailors? The answer lies, to a large extent, in the formation of the country occupied by them. Phoenician territory lay on the Mediterranean coast from Acre, in northern Palestine, to the northern end of this same Levant coast, and included the famous cities of Tyre, Sidon, Beirut, and Byblos. Nearness to the sea is necessary for a country to have a seafaring people, but the real reason that the Phoenicians took so naturally to the sea is that they possessed no land to develop. The several high mountain systems come practically to the water's edge. In spots there are a few miles of good agricultural land, but in other places the roots of the ranges are washed by the sea. The mountains, then, acted as a barrier to development inland and naturally caused the Phoenicians to become conscious of the great body of blue water that made them famous. In addition, the Syrian coast possesses a number of good harbors which were put to natural use in very early times.

Courtesy The Oriental Institute of The University of Chicago

BEDOUIN CAMP NEAR MEGIDDO, PALESTINE

JAFFA AND THE MEDITERRANEAN SEA

Contrast this with the nature of the Palestinian coast which is practically straight and possesses few harbor possibilities. In ancient times the only natural harbor lay behind the dangerous reefs of Jaffa. In consequence of this, as well as the fact that most of the Palestine coast is flanked by a broad fertile plain, the coast dwellers tended to remain agricultural. It is true that there were a number of coast cities, but they lacked natural advantages. Indeed, we may believe that the Phoenicians themselves would not have become the marvelous sailors and navigators that they were had historic accident placed them in Palestine.

THE LAND OF THE TWO RIVERS

In ancient times the country through which the Tigris and Euphrates flow had taken practically its present form. The Euphrates rose in the mountains of Armenia and started for the Mediterranean, but on reaching northern Syria it was deflected to the lower land leading to the Persian Gulf. The Tigris lies to its east and parallels it for the most part. The two almost touch at Bagdad but do not meet until they reach a point about two hundred and fifty miles southeast of the city of the Caliphs. From there they flow for another hundred miles through the delta and at last empty into the Persian Gulf. The delta is the one land feature that has changed appreciably in historic times. Our first glimpse of the country five thousand years ago shows the coast line almost two hundred miles above the present mouth of the rivers. Former coast towns have been left high and dry by river mud which was deposited on reaching sea level. The rivers are still working to fill up the head of the Persian Gulf.

The Syrian or Arabian Desert lies to the west of our territory and forms an effective barrier to direct intercourse with the countries beyond. As we have seen, the Euphrates became the important route for trade with the Mediterranean area. To the east of Mesopotamia lie the Zagros Mountains which separate it from Iran. The Zagros range swings down from the same mountains that give rise to the Tigris and Euphrates.

Iran is essentially a high plateau, highest on the side near Mesopotamia, to which access is had through a number of valleys which drain into the Tigris. In the northern and northeastern parts of the country the land drops off to the Caspian Sea and Russian Turkestan which is flat and low.

TURKISH PEASANT'S HOUSE IN VILLAGE NEAR ALISHAR

OXCART IN MODERN ANATOLIA

THE LAND OF THE HITTITES

Anatolia, the home of the Hittites, is largely an upland plateau which slants gradually toward the Black Sea. In the southeast there are two high mountain ranges, the Taurus and Antitaurus, which have been effective all through history as barriers to approach from Syria and Mesopotamia. The famous Cilician Gates lie between these ranges and lead out to the broad Cilician plain on the Mediterranean. The mountains continue into Armenia, southeast of the Black Sea. This territory has always been most inaccessible, and contacts with Europe have been made only with difficulty. There is a coast road around the east end of the Black Sea, and a few passes across the Caucasus exist, but the region has been naturally sheltered from time immemorial.

We can thus understand that the geography of the Near East has always been important in the fashioning of its history. Mountain barriers are cultural barriers. Open and connected areas tend more naturally to form political and cultural units. We shall see further, as we go on, that the configuration of the land has been of the greatest importance in the development of the Near East.

Courtesy The Oriental Institute of The University of Chicago

TELL ASMAR, MESOPOTAMIA
Twenty-six stages of the Fertility God's temple, covering about 1000 years, excavated to a depth of 40 feet. Original shrine in the foreground.

THE STORY OF ARCHAEOLOGY

I N REVIEWING our present knowledge of the ancient Near East we observe that a tremendous debt is owed to archaeology. A great deal of our information regarding the ages before the discovery of writing has necessarily come from observations made from the burials and debris left behind by early man. Among the most fruitful sources of information are the buried cities which only recently have begun to tell their story by means of the spade of the archaeologist.

HOW A CITY GETS BURIED

One of the questions most frequently asked an archaeologist is, "How does a city get buried? Do the desert sands simply sweep in and cover everything in sight?" Actually most ancient cities in the Near East are miles away from deserts which, moreover, are not always sandy. The typical ruin, called a "Tell" or "Tepe" by the Arabs and "Hüyük" by the Turks, usually lies in fertile territory and is overgrown with grass and wild flowers. It is a mound with a rather flat top which towers above the surrounding plain. The ruins of a large city may cover several square miles; the average Tell covers only a few acres.

The archaeologist digs systematically into this artificially formed mass of debris and may find, when he has reached rock or virgin soil, that he has cut through a dozen or more strata or levels. These are the buried cities one hears of, each one perhaps no deeper than a yard or so. Very seldom do the walls of the buildings attain any real height, and almost never is a roof found.

This is what has happened to the living cities of long ago. The first one, the one now at the bottom of the pile, was built on a

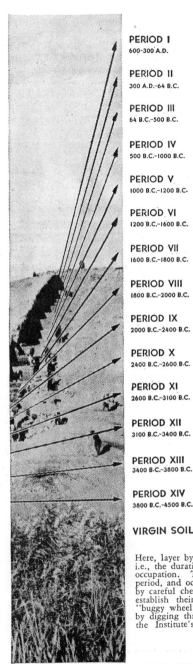

PERIOD I
600-300 A.D.

The level of an early Christian church, with its chapel and close. Byzantine coins and bronze crosses of the priests.

PERIOD II
300 A.D.-64 B.C.

A village partly contemporary with St. Paul and early Christian missionary activity in Antioch. Coins of the Caesars and Roman lamps.

PERIOD III
64 B.C.-500 B.C.

An occupation of the period of the Persian Empire, showing also traces of the Hellenization of the Orient under Alexander the Great.

PERIOD IV
500 B.C.-1000 B.C.

Layers of the Syrian Hittite kingdom, contemporary with the later Assyrian Empire and the Babylonian Nebuchadnezzar. Hittite hieroglyphs.

PERIOD V
1000 B.C.-1200 B.C.

Ceramic traces of the "Peoples of the Sea," some of whom are known as the Philistines, others as the Achaeans who sacked Troy.

PERIOD VI
1200 B.C.-1600 B.C.

A period of ethnic movements and extensive pottery importation. Infiltration of *Habiru* into Palestine and Joshua's capture of Jericho.

PERIOD VII
1600 B.C.-1800 B.C.

Evidence of cultural relations with the east, attested by cylinder seals of the Hurrian peoples of northern Mesopotamia, identified as the Horites of the Bible.

PERIOD VIII
1800 B.C.-2000 B.C.

Small painted bowls related to the pottery of the Hyksos or "Shepherd Kings" of Egypt. Time of the Patriarchs.

PERIOD IX
2000 B.C.-2400 B.C.

The beginning of a series of clay figurines of the "Mother Goddess" type, which are remarkable for their intentional grotesqueness.

PERIOD X
2400 B.C.-2600 B.C.

An occupation by the makers of goblets with fork-scratched decoration: an evidence of trade with northern Mesopotamia and central Syria.

PERIOD XI
2600 B.C.-3100 B.C.

Importation of cylinder seals from Abraham's city, Ur of the Chaldees; and fine red and black polished pottery from Asia Minor and the Balkans.

PERIOD XII
3100 B.C.-3400 B.C.

Earliest general use of metal, rapid mastery of the technique of casting figures in copper. Decline of flint and bone tools.

PERIOD XIII
3400 B.C.-3800 B.C.

Painted hand-made pottery as fine as any subsequent painted style. Flint and bone implements, with earliest traces of copper.

PERIOD XIV
3800 B.C.-4500 B.C.

The earliest Syrian village life, with the same material culture as found in near-by caves. Hand-made pottery, bone and flint tools, no traces of metal.

VIRGIN SOIL: SIX FEET UNDER THE PRESENT WATER LEVEL.

Here, layer by layer, are five thousand years of history. Each "period", i.e., the duration of one particular culture, may contain several levels of occupation. The sketches show objects which are typical for their period, and occur only sporadically, if at all, in any other period. Thus by careful check of the objects from a given floor, the archaeologist can establish their sequence, just as one might differentiate between the "buggy wheel" and the "automobile tire" periods in American history by digging through a city dump. The step-trench shown above enabled the Institute's Syrian Expedition to establish, for the first time, a complete chronology for North Syria.

Courtesy of Robert J. Braidwood and The Oriental Institute of The University of Chicago knoll or rocky prominence. The fact that there was spring water nearby undoubtedly had much to do with the selection of the site. Then, too, the seeming preference for raised ground in country where there were hills indicates that defence was not overlooked. The city was built accordingly. There were sections where the people lived, others in which the shops were located. Normal life went on for a period, and, except for the addition of a house here and there, the city remained much the same. But at length catastrophe overtook the place. Perhaps an enemy captured it and set it on fire. An earthquake may have shaken the loosely built houses until all that remained was a desolate field of foundations. Malaria or some other scourge may have visited the town and caused its desertion. It is often impossible to tell why a town was deserted, but the fact is clear that some compelling reason emptied the town of its inhabitants. With no one there to take an interest in the maintenance of the place, no one there to repair the ravages of the winter rains or to stop the stealing of ready cut building stone, the city soon was flattened to the ground and became covered. But there remained the foundations of buildings, and on top of them, the scattered debris of fallen roofs and walls. This is what the archaeologist finds when he digs into an

Courtesy The Oriental Institute of The University of Chicago

THE INSIDE OF A ROCK CUT TOMB AT MEGIDDO
Showing pottery and scattered human bones.

Courtesy The Oriental Institute of The University of Chicago

MEGIDDO

Excavating houses and plotting the position of objects in rooms.

Courtesy The Oriental Institute of The University of Chicago

EXCAVATION IN PROGRESS ON THE MOUND OF MEGIDDO

Courtesy Charles Breasted and The Oriental Institute of The University of Chicago

AN AIR VIEW OF JERUSALEM
Show the Mosque of Omar (right middle foreground) with the Garden of Gethsemane a
little beyond to the right, and the Mount of Olives in the upper right hand corner.

ancient site. He finds the foundations for sure, and in addition there are the many small articles that were either lost or left in the buildings when they were destroyed. If evacuation had taken place suddenly, the chances are that most of the household furnishings remained where they stood. If these were of a nature to withstand the effects of winter rains and summer suns, the archaeologist finds them too, and is able to tell much about the life of the times.

The process we have described for the establishment and destruction of an ancient city was repeated many times over. Perhaps because of the nearby source of water, a second city was built upon the ruins of the first. Tradition, always tremendously important in the Near East, may easily have added its force to selection of the site for the second city. When the second group of people decided to build there, they simply leveled off the ground and erected their houses. At the same time the height of the city had been raised a few feet by the accumulation of the first city. The settlement on top existed for a time when finally it, too, met a fate similar to the first. It was deserted, and its crumbling ruins added a few more feet to the steadily growing mound. This, repeated over and over, has been the history of most ancient cities in the Near East. Jerusalem today lies above many ancient Jerusalems.

PREHISTORY IS THE STORY OF ARCHEOLOGY

If we were to imagine our world of knowledge as based only upon what the ancients have written, we should know only a small part of the life of early man. Most of that picture, moreover, would deal with matters and thoughts that had taken place after 3000 B.C., since it was about then that writing reached the point where it was used generally. But what about the facts of existence prior to that time? It is the excavator who provides us

American Colony Photo

THE DAMASCUS GATE, JERUSALEM

with the information we seek. Careful observations made in the course of digging tell us of the types of houses that were used, of the defenses thrown up around the cities, of the kinds of weapons that were the fashion, or the pottery that was used daily in the preparation of meals. From these excavations we know that most countries have gone through a series of very definite cultural changes. At first stone and flint were the principal materials from

Courtesy The Oriental Institute of The University of Chicago

VIEW LOOKING NORTHWEST FROM MODERN JERICHO TO THE MOUND OF ANCIENT JERICHO (left center) AND THE MOUNT OF TEMPTATION

which tools and weapons were made. Then, because of the wonderful discovery that there was copper in the ground, weapons came gradually to be made of smelted metal. A further stage is represented by bronze, superior in many respects to copper. The addition of tin to copper, made perhaps accidentally at first, brought about advances in civilization that are difficult for us to appreciate. At a still later time came the discovery that iron ore could be smelted and cast into objects which were even more serviceable than those made of bronze. The next major step carries into our own age of iron and steel.

Jericho is an example of a site which has given us a complete sequence dating from a time when stone and flint were materials of extreme worth and continuing through the copper, bronze, and iron ages.

Troy is another site among many that year by year add to the store of information concerning early man. Homer spoke of the city that fought the Greeks. Archaeology tells the story of many Troys, one built upon the other. From the records of excavation over the entire Near East we gradually obtain a pretty full picture of cultural development, and we learn that each area was different from another. Each area developed specialties which can be distinguished in the same way that we tell whether a product is French, or Chinese, or Mexican, or American; and just as foreign products come to our shores today, so in ancient days there was much trade and shipping between countries. It is a matter of almost daily occurrence in an excavation in Palestine to find pottery which came from the island of Cyprus in the Mediterranean. One knows that it came from Cyprus because experience has shown that it is native to the island. In Palestine, on the other hand, this pottery is entirely out of character when compared with the multitude of pots which experience has taught are native to the mainland. Clearly we have here an indication of trade by sea with a neighboring land. At the same time products from Palestine are found in Cyprus or Egypt, and Egyptian articles are uncovered on the neighboring islands or in Palestine and Syria. At Troy, Mycenaen pottery is revealed, and on the Greek mainland Minoan products from Crete are found. Simply by way of illustration, this is what was happening in the busy world of the Mediterranean. Trade is old, older than writing, and we learn of it by uncovering the ancient cities.

POTTERY FOSSILS

If one of our modern buildings should be destroyed, and nothing remained but the cornerstone deposit containing a coin, we might be in a position to date the building approximately. If the coin were dated 1900, we could at least say that the structure had

Courtesy The Oriental Institute of The University
of Chicago

Courtesy The Oriental Institute of The University
of Chicago

HYKSOS POTTERY FROM MEGIDDO

EGYPTIAN MENDING POTTERY
FOUND IN THE EXCAVATION
OF MEGIDDO

not been erected before that year. To a certain extent archaeologists employ the same principle with pottery, just as geologists
make use of fossils in the rock for dating purposes.

Pieces of pottery do not bear dates, but they possess other
characteristics which are practically as valuable. When an excavator has dug down through an entire mound, he will perhaps
have tapped a dozen levels; and from each of these he will have
specimens of all sorts of things including numerous examples of
pottery. Some of these may be whole, but most of them will be in
small pieces. Fortunately for us, the ancient housewife was not
too orderly in the matter of broken pots. If one dropped in the
dirt street, it was allowed to lie there if it disturbed nobody.
The same thing happened if a pot broke on the dirt floor of the
house. The pieces remained and were gradually covered with dirt
and dust and still more broken pots. This is the reason that most
of the materials found in an excavation consist of pottery.

We have spoken only of pots as pots. What makes them valuable for the reconstruction of history is the fact that there were fashions in pots. These did not change as rapidly as do styles in hats, for instance, but the same principle was in operation. New methods of manufacture were discovered, a new shape took the fancy of the community, or different designs were considered more pleasing. Perhaps these designs were made by impressing the clay with a sharp instrument before the pot was placed in the oven. Possibly colors applied with a brush made their appeal to the buyers of pottery. The archaeologist comes to know the peculiarities of the pottery of the various periods and can tell at a

POTTERY FROM
   MEGIDDO,
  PALESTINE
(1200-1400 B.C.)

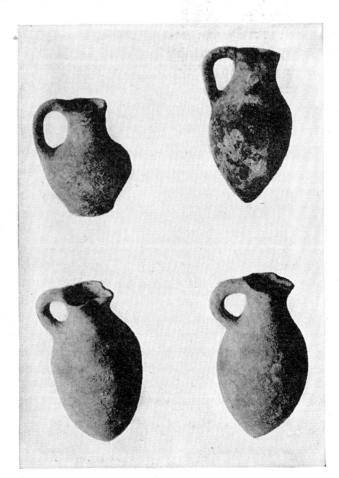

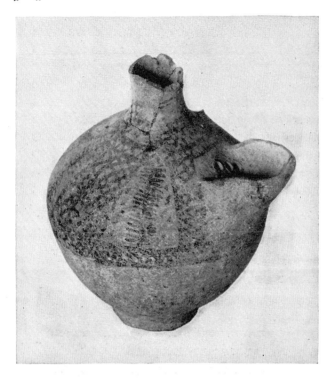

JUG FROM
MEGIDDO,
PALESTINE
Twelfth Century
B. C.

Courtesy The Oriental
Institute of The
University of Chicago

glance the general age of the deposit with which he is dealing. He may be able to say that it is within a century or two of 3000 B.C. In other cases he will be able to date the pottery to a century or less.

The value of pottery as an aid in piecing together ancient history is thus apparent. It gives a general date to many things found with it. Our picture of the time of the Philistines, for instance, becomes much fuller when we add to the written record the picture of actual cities lived in by Philistines. The study of pottery can be extremely interesting in itself, but its real value lies in its application to the larger problems of ancient history.

ARCHAEOLOGY FROM THE AIR

While the real work of excavation is done on the ground, the archaeologist has frequently received much help from observations made from the air. Quick trips by plane have on a number of

Courtesy The Oriental Institute of The University of Chicago

PHOTOGRAPHING EXCAVATED AREA AT MEGIDDO
FROM EXTENSIBLE LADDER

occasions made it possible to locate the numerous ruins of a district. Mounds can be spotted from the air and marked on maps. This serves the same purpose as many days of laborious travel by land, some of which can be most difficult if modern roads are lacking. All this, of course, is preliminary to the real investigation of the sites themselves.

Air observation and photography have filled a need that no other agent could have accomplished. Old roads and building foundations, completely covered with earth in such a way that they were not recognized from the ground, have actually been photographed from the air. The answer lies in the fact that the structures were but a short distance below the surface, and the ability of the structures to absorb ground water, being different from that of the earth to either side, caused a difference in the moisture in the dirt that covered them. This is something hard to detect from the ground, but to an observer in an airplane the contrast is marked. As a result the archaeologist knows exactly where to dig without losing a great deal of time. In this manner miles of Roman road and numerous buried camps on the flat Syrian Desert have recently been photographed, adding much to our knowledge of the eastern Roman Empire. Even when a site is known, a photograph from the air may be the means of locating important buildings still covered with earth.

Certain archaeologists have used balloon photography with considerable success. The plan here is to send up a small captive balloon controlled by two strands of stout twine with a camera suspended from the bottom of the balloon. The wind supplies the third point of support. When the camera has reached the proper height, perhaps one hundred yards, the picture is taken by sending an electric current up a third strand, this one being of wire, which is connected with the shutter of the camera. A small battery on the ground supplies the current. The balloon is then hauled down, another plate inserted, and the camera elevated over another area.

This type of photography is particularly useful in making a record of the city after it has been uncovered. Almost completely lost outlines of streets and houses will stand out as they cannot

Courtesy Charles Breasted and The Oriental Institute of The University of Chicago

AIR VIEW OF MEGIDDO

Right: BALLOON RISING
WITH CAMERA
TO PHOTOGRAPH
THE EXCAVATIONS
AT MEGIDDO

Courtesy The Oriental In-
stitute of The University of
Chicago

Courtesy The Oriental Institute of The University of Chicago

INCOMPLETE AIR MOSAIC OF MEGIDDO SHOWING METHOD OF
PIECING TOGETHER INDIVIDUAL BALLOON PHOTOGRAPHS

possibly do for the man on the ground. And although plans of the
same areas will be drawn on a larger scale, the photograph produces a much more realistic impression of the ground plan of a
city.

There are technical matters of real difficulty involved in piecing together the various air photographs of a site. When all the
pictures are developed and printed, it will be seen that some were
taken at greater heights than others, with the result that scales
differ. Then, too, a sudden gust of wind may have tilted the
camera just at the moment of snapping the picture. All these
matters are straightened out on the enlarging board in the photographic laboratory, and finally there are a number of rectangular
pictures that collectively represent the uncovered city. There remains, however, a great deal of overlapping; so the next step con-

sists in cutting the pictures to remove the overlap. At length all pieces fit together and are mounted to form what is called an air mosaic. From it one sees the old houses, streets, gates, and fortifications as one would if hovering at a height of about three hundred feet.

THE ARCHAEOLOGIST IS NOT A TREASURE HUNTER

The archaeologist is always interested in the possibility of turning up something of rare value that will add vividness and instant interest to the exhibits of the museum to which he contributes. A hoard of gold will accomplish these purposes, as will the contents of a rich unplundered tomb. But the archaeologist is fully prepared to forego these pleasures, in the belief that a basic understanding of mankind lies in learning the everyday life of the everyday kind of man. A visitor from Mars would get a very incorrect impression of our world if he saw only the interiors of palaces or the homes of the wealthy.

The selection of a site to dig presents many problems. History will be best served if one uncovers a site whose ancient name is known; but most ruins in the Near East have native names which bear no relationship to known ancient names. The problem is difficult, yet at times can be solved. We may illustrate with an actual case.

The city of Megiddo, famous as Armageddon, is mentioned frequently in the Bible and also in Egyptian and Assyrian texts. It was clearly an important city of northern Palestine, but for a long time no one knew exactly where it was located. However, it at last occurred to those interested in the problem that the account of a siege of Megiddo which appears in the annals of a famous king of Egypt, Thutmose III, might contain the solution. We shall speak of this siege at greater length later on, but here we note that the king crossed the Sinai Desert and traveled thereafter up the coastal plain. He was headed for Megiddo where a large anti-Egyptian force had gathered. The account tells further of several passes leading across the hills to Megiddo and of the one that was finally selected. Then we are told of the position of

Courtesy The Oriental Institute of The University of Chicago

THE MOUND OF MEGIDDO FROM THE WEST
Young Arab and flock of goats in foreground.

Megiddo with regard to this pass and of the watercourse near by. The description of the physical features of the country was so perfect in its details that each can be recognized on the spot to-day. Under such conditions the site, which at present is called Tell el-Mutesellim by Palestinians, must be the Megiddo of ancient times. Assured of this, the Oriental Institute began operations there in 1925, and while no inscription has been uncovered telling that the name of the place was Megiddo, there is sufficient evidence that the identification is correct.

But such detailed geographic descriptions are rare in ancient literature, and as a result many cities, famous from the writings that are preserved, have not been identified on the ground. Until recently such a city was Lachish, which played an important part in many biblical, Egyptian, and Assyrian stories.

In a number of cases native names of the present day reflect names of an older day. The Hebrew Beth Shan has become Arabic Beisan. The ancient seaport of Jerusalem was Joppa. To-day it is Jaffa. In Roman times a small town near Megiddo was called Legio, while at the present time it is an Arab village named

Lejjun. Queer things happen to place names when new people come in. The town of Shechem, near which "Jacob's Well" can be seen, was renamed Neapolis around the time of Christ. On the arrival of the Arabs it became distorted as Nablus.

Once a site has been selected for excavation, a series of operations is set in motion. The ground must first be plotted so that things found can be labeled as to location. This is usually done by setting out stakes at regular intervals, so that the mound is finally covered with a series of markers which form squares. The stakes may be ten, or even twenty-five yards apart. After the surface earth has been removed, one comes to the first level consisting of house foundations, floors, roadways, gates, and other structures which have escaped the ravages of time as well as of the plundering peasant on the lookout for ready-cut stone. All recognizable structures are given numbers so that materials found in and around them may be kept together for study later on. The archaeologist's chief concern is to see that things belonging to a certain city do not become mixed with those from another. And this is not as easy as it sounds when one realizes that the old builders, just as our own today, paid little attention to what lay beneath the surface. If they wished to sink a foundation in a certain spot, it did not matter if they dug into a tangle of old walls. These walls might once have belonged to a temple, but they were only old walls, useless to the new builder. This may serve to indicate some of the problems which the archaeologist has to face. He deals with a mound of rubbish in which holes have been dug and filled up again numberless times, in which countless disturbances have taken place, but in which, nevertheless, certain things have remained stationary over thousands of years. He tries to make such things intelligible and selects from them the matters of importance to history.

The archaeologist should have a command of the sequence of pottery types for the district in which he is working, in order to know the centuries involved in his work. He should know the material of things which are uncovered, whether they are ivory, bone, bronze, iron, carnelian, or amethyst. This knowledge is necessary that the record may be made correct and complete

THE EXCAVATION OF ONE OF THE UPPER LEVELS AT MEGIDDO
Basket carriers and a narrow gauge railway combine to remove the debris.

when the objects come down to the field house from the top of the mound. He must know how to treat things which may spoil or corrode under the influence of the moisture in the air. If materials are found which cannot be recognized until cleaned, he must know the proper method of treatment. Otherwise, precious evidence may be lost forever. When the first level has been completely uncovered and every possible notation of importance taken, the archaeologist says to himself, "Is there any more information that I can get? Have I forgotten anything? Have I answered all problems that have been raised? If not all of them are answered, I have little right to strip Level I and go down to Level II."

THE ARCHAEOLOGIST SOMETIMES FINDS TREASURE

While the aim of most archaeologists is to extract whatever information may be uncovered during the course of excavation, no matter how dreary the result at times may be, there are few who at some time or other have not experienced the joys of finding something spectacular. It may be the palace of a king, a hoard of royal jewelry, a foundation deposit of an important building, or a group of objects bearing an absolutely unique type of art. Or, again, it may be a statue of a king or god inscribed with statements not before suspected, or the discovery of an unrifled royal tomb. Certainly one of the most spectacular events in the entire history of archaeology was finding the tomb of King Tutankhamon in 1922. Never before had a king's tomb in Egypt been found in such an unplundered state.

When Howard Carter and Lord Carnarvon came upon the tomb, they had already spent six seasons in its search. They knew it existed and that it was in the Valley of the Kings, the great burial place of the kings of the Empire period. But the seventh season was to be their last in the Valley if they were unsuccessful in their objective. As fate would have it, the steps leading down to the tomb, which is cut in the rock, were discovered a week after Carter arrived in Luxor to begin his last season's work. Hope was high, but as yet it could not be certain that this was actually the tomb of King Tutankhamon. That fact was not established until the staircase had been cleared down to the doorway which had been blocked up, plastered, and sealed. Among the seals were those of the king, but others indicated that the tomb had been entered after the body had been deposited. It seemed likely that robbers had been in the tomb within fifteen years of the death of the king. The cemetery inspector's seal indicated this. It therefore remained to be seen whether this was just another rifled tomb similar to many that had been found before.

The outer doorway was at last removed, and it was seen that the passage continued downward leading to a second doorway. This had been blocked, plastered, and sealed in the same manner as the first and showed the same signs of disturbance and resealing. The archaeologists were still not certain that they would find a furnished or an empty tomb.

But when the hole at last was made in the upper part of the blocking, there was revealed a mass of glittering objects. The hole was enlarged and Carter squeezed through. He realized fully that treasure had been found. Before his eyes lay a confused jumble which included gilt couches, gold-plated chariots, alabaster vessels, numerous delicately made coffers, and two statues of the king. A side chamber was similarly filled, but there was no coffin. Could this possibly be but a storage place?

Further examination revealed the presence of a sealed doorway between the statues of the king. The first rooms had therefore been but antechambers, and the king himself lay in all his glory beyond the closed door. At this point the excavators showed remarkable restraint, for they decided to take care of the materials already in sight before opening the closed doorway. The mass of material was so great and unique that extreme care had to be taken in getting the necessary data, and it was almost three months later that the door was broken through.

Then came the most astounding surprise of all. The first glance through the opening revealed what appeared to be a solid wall of gold. The opening was steadily enlarged, and at last it was apparent that the object in the chamber was actually a complete funeral canopy—the first one seen by modern man. It was eleven by seventeen feet and nine feet high and practically filled the burial chamber. The canopy was covered with gold and paneled with blue fayence, which is a peculiar kind of hard glassy paste made from early times in Egypt. One end of the canopy was closed by two doors, but these opened easily and disclosed another canopy inside. This too was of gold and was draped with decorated linen. There were doors in this canopy also, but they were bolted and sealed, and with that discovery it became certain that Tutankhamon himself would be found inside. Further progress was stopped at that point so that attention might be given to the additional large quantity of material that had been found scattered through the burial chamber and an annex.

Courtesy James Henry Breasted, Jr. and The Oriental Institute of The University of Chicago

Above: THE VAL-
LEY OF THE
KINGS AT
THEBES IN
WHICH IS LO-
CATED THE
TOMB OF TUT-
ANKHAMON

Right: REMOVAL
OF A CHEST
FROM THE TOMB
OF TUTANKH-
AMON

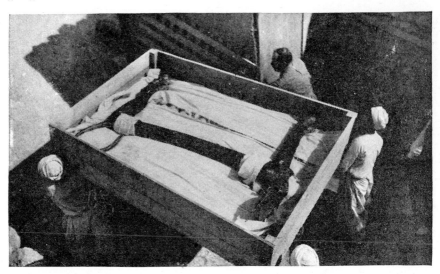

BOXES WERE SPECIALLY PREPARED FOR THE REMOVAL OF OBJECTS IN
TUTANKHAMON'S TOMB

International Newsreel Photos

A BED BEING TRANSPORTED FROM THE TOMB OF TUTANKHAMON

Courtesy Cairo Museum and Howard Carter

GOLD MASK OF TUTANKHAMON

The next season revealed the fact that there were four canopies, the last of which covered a fine, decorated sarcophagus, or coffin. When the stone lid had been lifted, there came to view the first of the inner coffins. It was a magnificent piece of work, bearing the likeness of the dead king, and was covered with gold, rare stones, and glazes. The second coffin was equally wonderful and lay nested closely to the first. But the climax had not yet been reached. The third and last coffin proved to be of solid gold, the estimated value of which is around $250,000. It ranks among the world's masterpieces in art because of its delicate engraving and setting of semi-precious stones. The mummy of Tutankhamon was badly preserved and had decomposed, but enough evidence remained to show that the king had been about eighteen when he died. He was truly a boy king.

The discovery of Tutankhamon's tomb caught the imagination of the world and it was rightly judged one of the most marvelous, spectacular, and astonishing discoveries that archaeology had ever made; but sober thought compels us to ask what it has taught. We have learned of the splendor of an Egyptian pharaoh's tomb, and a minor king's tomb at that. But what historical value is contained in it? It is a fair statement to say that many a strip of poor-looking papyrus or a dirt-covered clay tablet has contributed more real information concerning events and thoughts than the whole of the tomb of Tutankhamon.

PAPYRUS AND TABLET SPEAK

Papyrus, from which our word paper is derived, grew abundantly at one time in the marshes of Lower Egypt. It has now disappeared from Egypt proper but still grows in the Sudan and in the district north of the Sea of Galilee.

The plant belongs to the sedge family and has a triangular stem, an outer rind, and a pithy center, in addition to the root and flowering top. It was the soft center which was used in making sheets for writing. The rind was stripped off and lengths of the pithy interior were placed side by side on a flat surface. On top of these were placed other strands at right angles. The mass was

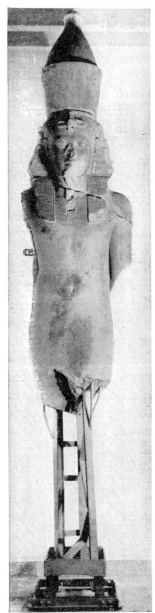
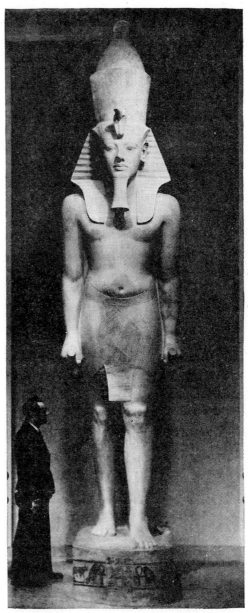

STATUE OF TUTANKHAMON AT THE ORIENTAL INSTITUTE

Left: Showing portions that were recovered during the Institute excavations at Medinet Habu. This statue was usurped by two later kings. Right: The same statue after restoration.

then beaten and rubbed until it was of the consistency of thick paper, after which the sheet was dried and trimmed to the required form. Recent experiments indicate that it would have been unnecessary to add any adhesive material to the raw stalks. Their own juices seem to have taken care of that problem.

The last step necessary to make the material suitable for writing may have involved rubbing the surface to give additional smoothness. After this, numerous small sheets were fastened together to form a roll. Many of these measure ten and twenty feet in length, while others are as long as a hundred feet. The scribe began writing at the right end of the roll and carried his lines across the first segment. This might be twenty-four inches or so. He continued writing, line under line, until the first segment was filled to his satisfaction. Then he went on to the second segment, and so on until the document was completed.

Papyrus rolls and scraps of papyrus have been found in tombs and in the rooms of ruined houses hidden away in pottery jars. Others, a great number of them, have been purchased in the shops of antique dealers. But by far the greater number of papyri have come from ancient Egyptian dump heaps where the garbage, refuse, and waste paper of another day were thrown. These include letters, business accounts, fragments of classical writings of the Greek authors, and even copies and fragments of the Gospels. These documents have been of immense aid in reconstructing the past and furnish us, moreover, with a side of Egyptian life that is truly fresh and lifelike. The people threw away, but we suppose they also had read, the poems of Sappho, Pindar, and others; and, in the Græco-Roman dumps, the commonest author of all is Homer. Many of the finds are trifling, such as the letter of a boy whose father had gone to Alexandria and left him behind. This youngster wrote that if he were not sent for he would neither eat nor drink. Another letter from a husband to his wife instructed her to keep the baby if it proved to be a boy, but to throw it out if it was a girl.

There are hundreds of papyri which deal with the more human side of life. The knowledge of these is essential if one truly is to appreciate ancient life on the Nile. State records and

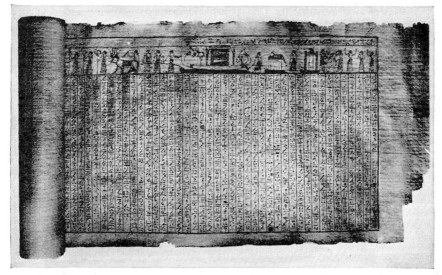

Courtesy The Oriental Institute of The University of Chicago

A PARTIALLY UNROLLED PAPYRUS AT THE ORIENTAL INSTITUTE

religious texts form a necessary part of the story, but the real flavor of the life must come from the intimate evidence that remains. The stories and folk tales that were constantly repeated are as certain an indicator of personality and taste as they are today. Few will deny that we may be judged by the literature that we read. An interesting tale which has much in common with our own fairy tales was being repeated in the thirteenth century before our era.

It concerns a son of a king who was born in answer to prayer to the gods; but this son was destined from birth to die either by the crocodile, the snake, or the dog. To avert any of these disasters the king put the child away in a stone house in the desert where he had all the comforts and privileges of the palace. When he was grown he went up to the roof one day and saw a man and his greyhound walking below. The youth asked his servant what the animal was and learned that it was a greyhound. Thereupon the boy petitioned the king that he too might have a dog like it and was given a small greyhound, the king perhaps thinking that a small animal could do no harm.

When the boy was full-grown he became restive and wished to move about. Again he petitioned his father and told him that he was doomed anyway and ought to be allowed to do as he wished. The king consented and gave him a fully equipped chariot. Thereupon the young prince left his lonely abode in the desert and accompanied by his servant and dog journeyed to the country of Naharin, which is in the bend of the Euphrates.

Now it happened that the prince of Naharin had an only daughter whom he kept locked in a house specially built for her, and the window in it was high above the ground. The sons of all the princes of a neighboring land had been summoned and told that whoever succeeded in reaching the window, behind which the daughter sat, should have her as his wife. The Egyptian prince at length joined the others and succeeded in reaching the window where he was welcomed happily by the princess. They then went to the prince of Naharin to tell him the glad tidings, but he was angry since the successful one was an imposter—one not invited. For some reason the prince of Egypt refused to disclose his true identity, choosing rather to masquerade as the son of an Egyptian officer. But the father's wrath could not withstand the determination of the princess who threatened to die if she could not have the stranger. The father withdrew his objections and brought the two before him and blessed them. They were given a house and lands and everything that they desired.

After many days had gone by, the youth told his wife of his three destinies, "I am doomed by the crocodile, the snake, and the dog". She wished him to kill the greyhound, but he refused, so thereafter she guarded him very closely and never let him go out alone.

At length the prince and his wife returned to Egypt where they lived near a lake in which dwelt a crocodile which was under the influence of a water spirit. Some time afterwards it happened that the youth fell asleep with his wife watching by his side. A snake came out of its hole to bite the sleeper but was given beer which made it helpless. The faithful wife then killed it with an ax. When the prince awoke he was told that one of his destinies had been thwarted and that his god would take care of the others in the same way.

Time passed happily for the pair; but one day the youth went out for a stroll with his dog, and the two came to the lake in which lived the crocodile. The prince was seized and carried into the waters where the crocodile said, "I am the destiny which follows you".

At this point the papyrus is damaged, but we learn later that the prince was freed. A few more words indicate that another episode of the story has begun, but the rest of the tale is completely lost, and we may only guess regarding the sequel. The end of the story probably told of the death of the prince by the hand of the faithful dog.

Courtesy The Oriental Institute of The University of Chicago   Painting by Nina De Garis Davies

THE PROCESSION TO THE TOMB OF RAMOSE, VISIER OF AMENHOTEP III
Showing papyrus plants.

It is exasperating indeed to get this much of a story but not its end; but we may continue to hope that another copy of the tale will some day be uncovered. A number of important but interrupted stories have been completed by chance finds.

The common material on which things were written in Mesopotamia and surrounding territories was not papyrus but clay. Early in history it was found that clay, which was abundant everywhere, could be baked so that impressions made on the surface were preserved. There evolved the peculiarly shaped and roughly rectangular object which is called a tablet. The clay was first fashioned into the size necessary for the amount of writing necessary. If only a few lines were needed, a small tablet was used, for it was important to reduce as much as possible the bulk of the records. A longer amount of writing called for a larger tablet. This, then, was the process. An unbaked tablet of the proper size was selected by the scribe, who with his pencil-shaped stylus impressed the characteristic wedge-shaped characters called cuneiform into the soft clay. When his copy had been completed, the tablet, if important, was placed in an oven, and heat baked the written impressions until it was hard. Contracts and documents which might be needed for reference in years to come were usually baked. Scientific works were also treated in this manner because they were textbooks and would be used repeatedly. On the other hand, exercises by the schoolboy were not baked. Even so, numerous tablets which were not treated by heat have come down to us, and in many cases can be read if the surface is not too badly damaged. Thus has the writing of Asia been preserved in clay.

Writings in clay have produced most of our knowledge of detailed history for the early period in western Asia. From them we have learned of the major political and social changes that from time to time rocked the ancient world. But we have also been told of smaller events, those human occurrences and deeds that are so important to the individual. History is still interested in battles and dynasties, but it also recognizes that the conditions of everyday life are at the bottom of all real history.

A group of most interesting tablets was recently uncovered at the site of Nuzi in Upper Mesopotamia which does much to fill in the picture for the period around 1500 B.C. We read, for instance, that a man acknowledged receipt of thirteen donkey-loads of grain, thirteen sheep, and one horse, as the bridal price for his daughter. Another tablet tells that a labor contractor agreed to furnish twenty laborers to a certain man for the period of the harvest. If he failed in his agreement, he was to pay a certain sum.

In another case a man mortgaged his field for a period of five years in return for a donkey. We must assume that the field was a poor one since donkeys were of little value. Another peasant who mortgaged his field agreed to pay the exorbitant annual interest rate of thirty per cent. Another document tells that the

Assyrians raided Nuzi and carried off large numbers of sheep and cattle as well as their shepherds. Among this group of tablets are some which give slave lists, while others give the details of real estate trades and law suits. We have hardly touched on the complete list of topics treated in the Nuzi documents, but another subject of considerable interest deserves attention.

There was a law in Nuzi which sought to make it impossible for a man to sell land that he had inherited. The purpose was to protect the small landowner from the greed of the wealthy. There was apparently also a desire to keep family holdings intact. But a serious loop-hole existed in the law and as a result it served only to defeat its own purpose. The tablets from Nuzi show clearly that a man outside a family who wished to acquire family property could do so with little trouble. He had simply to come to an agreement with the holder of the property as to what it was worth, and then have himself legally adopted into the family. Adoption was legal although hardly intended in the first

Courtesy The Oriental Institute of The University of Chicago

CLAY TABLETS FROM MESOPOTAMIA
Records of business dealings in cuneiform writing.

Courtesy The Oriental Institute of The University of Chicago
A CLAY TABLET FROM ANCIENT NUZI
Record of mortgage on a field. About 1500 to 1400 B. C.

place for anything but adoption of children. Nevertheless, there was no law to prevent one man from adopting another. As the thing worked out, the adopted "son" received the property and in return gave his adopted "father" a gift which generally consisted of money, grain, or cattle. The "father" remained on the land and did the farming but had no title whatsoever. Certain documents provided that the younger man would take care of the older man and his wife as long as they lived and would give them decent burial.

Much deciphering and study is necessary before all the Nuzi tablets become available, but enough has already been noted to make them one of the best sources for information on the family life of the people of Iraq around 1500 B.C.

A SYRIAN PORT GAVE US OUR WORD "BIBLE"

The origin of words is a very interesting subject and at times leads one back through Roman and Greek times to the Orient. The word "admiral," for instance, can be traced to an Arabic source. Perhaps the word of greatest general interest in our language is "Bible," which has had an extremely curious history indeed.

Egypt was the homeland of papyrus, and it was there that it was transformed into sheets for writing purposes. But other countries also had a use for the finished rolls. Many of these were

Courtesy M. Dunand, *Fouilles de Byblos* I

VIEW OF THE ANCIENT RUINS AT BYBLOS ON THE SYRIAN COAST
From very early times Byblos was in communication with Egypt by sea.

sent by sea to Byblos, on the Syrian coast, for use on the Asiatic mainland. Greece was another country which had a great need for writing materials and accordingly sent to Byblos for her requirements. In consequence of this the Greeks came to call papyrus "byblos." In time the Greeks coined the word "biblia" which they applied to books in general, and from this there arose the very specialized term which we know today as "Bible."

A PAPYRUS DISCOVERED IN A MUSEUM

In the middle of the last century Leopold II, then Duke of Brabant, picked up in his travels a group of Egyptian souvenirs. Early in 1936 they were transferred from the Royal Palace to the Brussels Museum. The present king, Leopold III, felt they would be more useful on public display. Accordingly, the curator of the Egyptian section of the museum, M. Capart, arrived at his work early one morning to inspect the new additions to his department. He had seen them before in a glass case at the palace but had never handled them. Now he was able to inspect closely a number of fayence statuettes, bronze figures of gods, and a curious plaque of inlaid bronze which had once been set into a piece of furniture. In due course M. Capart picked up a small wooden statue which he had not noticed before. He observed that it was a funerary statuette of poor workmanship with a painted inscription, and that the hollow base had been plugged with a piece of old linen. This he pulled out slowly and there appeared a roll of papyrus, about eight inches high and in excellent shape. Capart thought at first that he had found a common funerary papyrus, but on raising the outer edge of the roll he saw that he was wrong. To those gathered for the occasion he read aloud the date, Year 16 of Ramses IX (about 1126 B.C.). This was truly exciting, for that year is famous in the annals of Egyptology as the year in which the celebrated but incomplete Abbott papyrus now in the British Museum was written. Here perhaps was a missing portion.

The roll of papyrus was prepared for inspection by placing it upon sheets of moist blotting paper. In a short while the first layer became pliable and was unrolled. Capart glanced hurriedly over the neatly written lines and suddenly saw the name of a

Courtesy J. Capart, A. H. Gardiner and B. van de Walle   Photo by Raeburn Rohrbach

PORTIONS OF THE PAPYRUS LEOPOLD II

king known from another well-known document, the Amherst Papyrus. The published edition of the latter was quickly brought from the library of the museum, and, to Capart's complete surprise, one of the Amherst pages made a perfect fit with the unrolled portion of the newly discovered roll. The Amherst is torn along the top, while the Leopold II papyrus, as it is now called, is torn along the bottom. The written characters which were missing in one were completed when the two were placed together.

In this strange manner the story of the tomb robberies around Thebes in the twelfth century B.C. has been greatly enlarged. The corruption of officials, who in that day accepted bribes at one time and practiced third-degree methods at another, is brought to light, striking a curiously modern note.

Having noticed some of the things done by archaeologists, we shall proceed to view the various countries of the Near East as they were in prehistoric times.

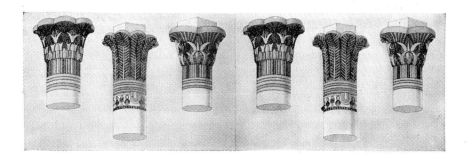

A FEW years ago it would have been difficult to tell the story of the prehistoric peoples of the Near East. To-day, although the picture is far from complete, we can view the main features of cultural advance during those momentous years when man ceased being a hunter and took to the soil. Excavations on sites representing the period before writing came into use have been so numerous that we can now distinguish between successive phases of that ancient world to which the better known civilizations owed their beginning.

EGYPT BEFORE THE FIRST DYNASTY

The point at which we take up the story of man may be dated for the sake of convenience somewhere between four and five thousand years before the beginning of the Christian era. No one knows for certain, and probably never will, because there was no writing at that time. However, dates are not everything, and furthermore there are several kinds of dates. The exact number of years represented by the prehistoric civilizations of Egypt escapes us, yet we can derive a very good idea as to which civilizations preceded others. The fact that some can be called older, or perhaps be regarded as having existed at the same time as others in a different part of the country, is a matter of considerable interest and importance.

In Stone Age times the deserts on either side of the Nile were fertile and supported wild game, for while Europe was living under glacial conditions northern Africa was having rains. But gradually these ceased and people were driven to the valley of the Nile where there always was water. Early in this period somebody made the brilliant discovery that wild grains such as wheat and barley could be cultivated, a disclosure that rocked the world of that time. Therefore, instead of subsisting chiefly on hunting and fishing, the people turned to farming for a livelihood. Where before they had been parasites they now became productive. It is quite likely that the first stages saw a thorough combination of these occupations, for it is not likely that the habits of generations were instantly dropped. But the tendency to adopt the more secure way of living offered by farming increased, and with it came the development of settled communities, the earliest of which have apparently been found. In Middle Egypt they are called Tasian because the first clear-cut evidence of this civilization came from Deir Tasa. The type of culture that existed at about the same time in Lower Egypt has been found at two places, in the Fayum and at a site in the Delta called Merimde. For this reason the northern cultures are called Fayumic and Merimdian.

Aside from farming, hunting, and fishing the Tasian folk may have made food-gathering trips to the Red Sea. At home they discovered the secret of pottery making, and, although their products were poor when compared with later pottery, it constituted a very important step forward. Before that time vessels for holding liquids were made of stone, leather, wood, or gourds. It is in Tasian times, too, that we note the earliest traces of linen, but the form of the finished costume has yet to be discovered. Paint palettes have been found which suggest that the Tasians painted their eyes and faces in a manner similar to that of the later Egyptians. It causes no surprise to learn that a people, thus advanced, wore shells and bone and ivory beads. When the Tasians died they were laid away in simple pit graves, wearing their finery and accompanied by vessels containing food and drink for the life hereafter. It was the custom in Tasian villages to compose the body of a dead person in a certain set manner, with arms and legs drawn up closely to the body.

The Tasian stage of civilization was low in comparision with that of later times, yet it was far above any which had preceded. It must represent for us that important stage when

THE FAYUM SHOWING A BEACH FORMED IN MIDDLE PALAEOLITHIC TIMES

THE FAYUM

A prehistoric straw-lined granary, showing a wooden sickle as found.

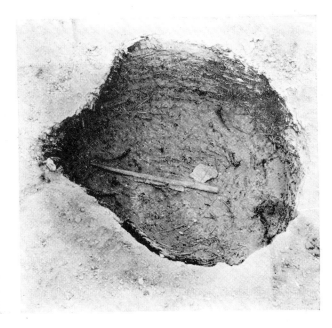

man ceased being purely a hunter. He had come in from the chase and was ready to settle on a farm watered by the bountiful Nile. Communities developed, and when that step had been taken the most important ingredient of civilization was already present. Without communities, the development of Egypt and the rest of the ancient world would have been retarded just so much longer.

At about the same time a similar development was taking place in northern Egypt. The first agricultural villages were being formed, but in a somewhat different way. The two districts were widely separated and customs varied considerably. We are not to suppose that the territory lying between was a blank as far as population is concerned, for there is little doubt that farming began along the Nile at many points at about the same time. We simply lack evidence for the unknown territories, and for that reason the differences between the cultures of Upper and Lower Egypt seem very distinct.

The type of civilization which is called Fayumic has been discovered along the edge of an ancient lake that once filled the Fayum depression. Wheat, barley, and flax were grown, and the farmers cut their grain with crude saw-toothed sickles. These people also hunted and fished, but they had succeeded in domesticating certain animals, including the pig, cow, sheep, and goat. The men did much of their fishing with harpoons, and it was perhaps while they were thus occupied that the women made the excellent baskets that have been found. The making of pottery was an important industry, and although the vessels were crude they were an improvement over earlier ones. The people of the Fayum dressed in linen to some extent but it is likely that they used skins as well.

Merimde, which lies on the western edge of the Delta where it gives way to the desert, has produced a type of culture closely related to that which we have seen in the Fayum. These people, too, were clearly at a stage when they were giving up hunting as a major aspect of life and were taking to the cultivation of grains. Storage bins and threshing floors have been found, and even a street has been uncovered. The Merimdian people had numerous minor peculiarities that distinguish them from the other folk we have seen, but their principal difference consisted in the way they

Courtesy The Oriental Institute of The University of Chicago

PREDYNASTIC EGYPTIAN STONE JARS AND VASES

buried their dead. Here the dead were placed among the dwell-
ings and no food or drink was placed in the graves.

One negative characteristic of these three contemporary cultures is that they show no traces of the use of metal; the benefits
of copper were still to be discovered. It can well be said that the
Tasian, Fayumic, and Merimdian civilizations represent the Neolithic stage of human development.

In the south the Tasians were followed by another people, the
Badarians, so called for the town Badari where their culture is
well illustrated by the excavations. These people were shorter
than their predecessors, being not more than five and a quarter
feet tall, and having at the same time more slender and delicately
built bodies. Although the Badarians were of a different stock,
they adopted Tasian culture, developing it along established lines.

Progressive steps taken by these people included the extension
of trade relations. Products were brought from the Red Sea and
Nubia, and fragments of cedar wood suggest that trade with

Syria, which was to become so famous, had already begun. We are left in the dark on many points of interest, but one fact is clear: by Badarian times Egypt had entered the age of metals. Beaten copper beads have been found, and while not numerous they nevertheless testify to knowledge of some of the properties of copper, though it remained for a later people to discover that copper could be smelted and cast into objects of diverse form.

Passing again to the north, we find that a related civilization followed on the collapse of the Merimdian. It is called the Maadi culture from the name of a town near Cairo where its ruins have been discovered. The Merimdian way of living was continued and improved, while copper became plentiful, much more so than in southern Egypt. At the same time trade relations were extended and included contacts with Palestine.

The southern cultures which were in existence at about the same time have been called Amratian, Gerzean, and Semainean. The Amratian followed the Badarian, and the Semainean brought the predynastic period to a close. Culture traits which had been in use in the Badarian period were continued in the next, but at the same time there was an influx of ideas which point to the introduction of North African customs. These appear to have been related in some way to the late Paleolithic culture called Capsian.

Slaves existed by Amratian times, and personal property of another sort is indicated by distinctive marks impressed on pots. Copper became more abundant, but the principle of smelting remained unknown. Merchants had greatly extended their sphere of interest, copper coming from Sinai, gold from Nubia, and wood from Syria. It is even possible that emery was imported from the far-off islands near Troy and Greece. Already the Mediterranean was giving promise of busy days to come.

There are indications of the role which religion played in the lives of the people. Dogs were often buried with their masters, as were small models of cattle and other desirable things. These suggest the Egypt of better known times when articles were placed in the grave for the use and comfort of the deceased. The models of cattle in this case surely represented real animals which were to serve the dead person in a magical way in the life hereafter. Weapons, pottery ornaments, and food were placed in the grave for the same reason. The predynastic Egyptian believed that after death he would hunt, plough his field, sail the Nile, and do all the other things that had occupied him in life.

The Amratian people were followed by the Gerzeans who continued and improved many traits already established while a number of new features made their appearance. New types of weapons, dress, and pottery, as well as different burial rites, indicate that a new strand of humanity had made its presence felt. Some of the pottery types came from Palestine while others suggest relations with the Delta. Copper remained rare, but flint work reached a state of perfection never again attained in Egypt.

It is in the Gerzean period that we see the emergence of centralized power that at length culminated in the union of the country. There had always been chieftainship of a sort, even before the stage represented by the beginning of organized villages, but in the Gerzean period we gain a fleeting glimpse of power

PREDYNASTIC EGYPTIAN POTTERY VESSEL ON WHICH IS PAINTED A NILE SHIP

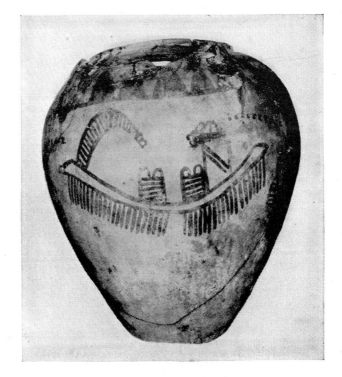

Courtesy Quibell, *Hierakonpolis* II

TOMB PAINTING OF THE GERZEAN PERIOD

tremendously increased. We are allowed to view the tombs of a few men which in all respects are far superior to the hundreds of other tombs known for the period. One of these was lined with mud brick which had been plastered over and then washed with a coat of yellow ochre, and on this an artist had depicted a scene which combined incidents from the chase, dances, and combat on ships. This was the tomb of a wealthy and powerful man, one distinguished in his day. His civilization may seem barbaric until we look over our shoulder at earlier times. On facing about, we dimly discern the First Dynasty rising above the horizon.

The final predynastic period, the Semainean, prepared Egypt for the coming of Menes, first historical king of united Upper and Lower Egypt. Villages grew into cities, and local chiefs assumed the grandeur of divine kingship. Tombs of the common people remained much as they had been, but the wealthy demanded burials that were finer than ever. These were of considerable size and at times were partially dug out of the rock which lay beneath the sand, and were then covered with a wooden superstructure. Stairs led down to the chambers for convenience of pallbearers and those who bore offerings. Indications are clear that wealth was being concentrated.

During this period trade relations with surrounding territories increased on both land and sea, the most interesting new "billing" being with Mesopotamia. The exact nature of this contact is not known, but that there were influences back and forth cannot be doubted, for a number of objects found in Egypt bear artistic representations characteristic of the Tigris and Euphrates regions. The stone on which they were carved is Egyptian, but the ideas are clearly eastern. The precise meaning of these things is not fully realized, but that there was communication of ideas between the valley of the Two-Rivers and the Nile is apparent.

We have now reached the point in the history of Egypt when the land was divided into a number of powerful nomes, or states, each ruled by a prince. Before the end of the predynastic period these had been combined into two large kingdoms, Upper and Lower Egypt. The two vied with each other for prestige and influence, property and wealth, and each was ruled by a man whom we may now call a king. Fortunes shifted, and on a number of occasions it must have appeared that one of the kings would gain power sufficient to unite the entire country under one head. At length the inevitable happened, and about 3000 B.C. a southern king who has come down in history by the name of Menes became the first historical king of Upper and Lower Egypt.

MESOPOTAMIA BEFORE THE FLOOD

While Egypt was taking her first long strides toward civilization, a comparable development was taking place in the valleys of the Tigris and Euphrates. The earliest settlements were in the north where a very respectable type of culture was evolved. The people were farmers for the most part, but they also hunted. Their pottery shows a high degree of artistic development in both form and decoration which is astonishing even to the modern eye. Trade was carried on between districts and with distant countries. Indeed, many of the essentials for the development of civilization were present in the northern part of Mesopotamia at a

Courtesy H. R. Hall and C. L. Woolley *Ur Excavations*

PREHISTORIC FRIEZE FROM MESOPOTAMIA
Milking scene at right.

time which was perhaps not far from 5000 B.C. Yet it was southern Mesopotamia which went ahead to become the leader of culture and progress for several thousand years.

At the time of which we have been speaking, however, southern Mesopotamia which came to be called Sumer was still under the waters of the Persian Gulf. At this time the heavily laden rivers were carrying down mud and silt to deposit in the sea. Thus the land of Sumer was composed entirely of new land, and on these marshy flats there settled foreign people who probably came from the north or northeast.

The remains of this earliest civilization have been found and are known today as the Al Ubaid culture. As is usual in matters dealing with prehistoric material, names are given after sites which have proved typical. At Al Ubaid we find this culture fairly well represented, although other places have since yielded a more complete picture. Because the Al Ubaid people were the first ones to settle in the country, their towns and cities now lie buried at the bottom of mounds, often some distance below ground-water level. As in the valley of the Nile, the accumulation of mud and silt has caused the water to reach a higher level.

The Al Ubaid people may have been drawn to the marshes at the head of the Persian Gulf by the fresh water lagoons and swamps which were becoming a haven for wild life driven from the north by increasing aridity. These people built reed huts and cultivated their cereals. Perhaps to preserve as much ground as possible for farming they set foundations for their huts in the water. At any rate at Uruk, which is the biblical Erech, there have been found platforms of rushes set between the marsh bot-

tom and the floor levels of huts. The huts were chiefly of reed
matting plastered with clay or dung and bitumen, which is a
tarlike substance found naturally in Mesopotamia. Bricks were
also made by throwing clay into a mold and then drying them in
the sun. Some of the houses even had doors which pivoted in a
stone socket.

Rough stone hoes were used to till the fields, and cereals were
harvested with saw-toothed chert or obsidian flakes set in a clay
frame shaped somewhat like the jawbone of a cow. The grain
itself was ground on stones. Another source of food was the date
palm which to this day provides much nourishment for the inhabitants of the district.

There is evidence that these people had domesticated animals.
Perhaps among the latter were cattle, sheep, and pigs; but we
know of them only from the dung-plastered huts in which the
people lived.

Slings and perhaps bows and arrows were used to bag game,
and fish were caught in nets. Boats were an early necessity because of the marshy conditions, and as proof of their existence the
archeologist has found clay models which are surprisingly like
boats still used on the Euphrates.

Practically nothing is known of the physical form of the Al
Ubaid population, but some idea has been gained of their habits
of dress. The evidence for clothing comes from spindle whorls
which were used in the preparation of thread and from painted
figurines of baked clay. The latter suggest that skins as well as
textiles were utilized for dress. The men wore long beards, and
their long hair was put up in a bun at the back. The men's upper
lips were shaved, and the women wore wigs.

Copper was probably known by the first inhabitants of the
region, but has not been found until late in the Al Ubaid period.
We can understand how the uses of copper might have become
known earlier in Sumer than in Egypt when we recall that lower
Mesopotamia possessed practically no flint or stone with which
to make tools, weapons, and vessels.

The Al Ubaid people came into the country with a developed
type of living and adapted themselves thoroughly to their en-

vironment. Some aspects of their culture are related to that of the highlands of Iran and Elam to the east, but the actual homeland of these people cannot yet be located with certainty. Future excavation may settle this most interesting point; meanwhile we simply know that they were foreigners who located on the newly made land at the head of the Persian Gulf.

The Al Ubaid people were succeeded in time by those known by the name of Uruk, which we have seen was the Babylonian name for the biblical city of Erech. The clearest evidence for the Uruk culture has come from that ancient city, although traces have been found generally. There are strong suggestions that a new people came in at the beginning of this period. For one thing, a completely new type of pottery with distinctive features was at this time added to the old. Transportation was entirely revolutionized through the introduction of the wheel. Furnaces of an advanced sort came into use and were employed either for baking pottery or smelting copper. It is possible that each of these innovations was invented on the spot, but there is a greater likelihood that a roving population brought them when they settled in Sumer.

It is quite clear that at this early period the necessities of the church were successfully met by some form of taxation to which the farmers, fishermen, and traders of the country contributed. Wealth was needed and found for the erection of huge structures in honor of the state gods. At the same time other state income was used to dig canals, thereby providing for necessary drainage and irrigation. Thus, with water drawn off, villages became cities, marshes became fields, and in the city of Erech a monumental temple was erected.

This temple was built upon a huge pile of mud, the forerunner of the ziggurat and the "Tower of Babel." The foundation platform, which consisted of lumps of mud, reached a height of about forty feet. On this rested the temple, measuring about twenty by twenty-five yards. It was built of large whitewashed mud bricks and consisted of a long central court surrounded by chambers. A stairway, down which the god might descend, led from the top of the mound. But this was not the entire temple com-

Courtesy The Oriental Institute of The University of Chicago

MODEL OF THE TOWER OF BABEL, AS CONCEIVED BY UNGER,
NOW IN THE ORIENTAL INSTITUTE

plex, because it is likely that a larger temple existed at the foot
of the ziggurat.

A tablet apparently inscribed with numbers was found in the
temple atop the mound. This was, perhaps, a record of some
sort kept by a servant of the temple, as was so common in later
days.

The temple, of which we have spoken, fell into ruin long before the end of the Uruk period and was succeeded in turn by
two others. The art of building progressed with rapid strides in
this period, and we now know that vaults with true arches were
being constructed. It is difficult to date this achievement with
any precision, but perhaps it was not far from 3500 B.C. At

a much later date the Romans borrowed this important architectural feature from the Orient.

As far as we know, it was in the Uruk period that pictographs were first employed to record ideas. However, the fact
that no earlier examples exist by no means precludes the possibility that this form of expression was not older. Quite likely it
was. The story of the development of cuneiform, or wedge-writ-
ing, from pictures will be told later. Now we pause to record the fact that writing had begun, but the figures represented
ideas and not sounds. The numeral system was also being developed, and it is known that two types were in use. One was the
sexagesimal system, which simply means that counting was based
on the numbers 1-10-60 and multiples of six. The other was the
decimal system, quite familiar to us, which employs 1-10-100 and
multiples of ten. It was the first which later became typical of
the territory and is responsible for our division of the circle into
three hundred and sixty degrees, the hour into sixty minutes, and
the minute into sixty seconds.

Culture was clearly progressing at a rapid rate, but we see
that even greater strides were made in the Jemdet Nasr period
which followed.

At Jemdet Nasr, a large fortress over a square block in size
was found, which towered above the flat plain. A new type of
brick was used in the construction of buildings in this area. They
were thin, rectangular, sun-dried mud bricks. A stairway led up
to a building of considerable size. This gives one an idea of the
extent to which community living had progressed. But there was
progress in other matters as well.

Writing was strongly developed during the Jemdet Nasr period. The pictorial symbols which were impressed into the soft
clay of tablets now had a phonetic, or sound, value. In the preceding period the pictures had stood only for ideas, but now spell-
ing was coming in. The words seem to be early Sumerian, the
language of the period following Jemdet Nasr. As regards numbers, the two systems that we have already noticed were still in
use. The sexagesimal system did not become dominant until the
following period. Among the still primitive written records, that

BOAR CARVED
IN STONE
Jemdet Nasr period.

Courtesy Bagdad
Museum

have been preserved from Jemdet Nasr times, are school texts and temple accounts.

A new animal, "the ass of the mountains," was introduced to the plains of Babylonia at this time, but whether it was the true horse is still uncertain. At any rate the same term was used in historical times to designate the horse.

The artist kept stride with the times. Among other things, brought to light by the excavator, is a boar carved in stone. Pottery was pleasantly decorated in color, and seal designs characteristic of the period reveal a wealth of artistic ability.

PREHISTORIC
POTTERY FROM
MESOPOTAMIA

Courtesy H. R. Hall
and C. L. Woolley,
Ur Excavations

ASSYRIAN
GLAZED
VESSEL
The decoration is
in several colors.
Now in the Uni-
versity Museum,
Philadelphia.

Courtesy University
Museum,
Philadelphia

The metal-smith made many things of copper, and that metal became more plentiful than ever before; but we may believe that it still was a luxury.

During this period the Jemdet Nasr people expanded north-ward; perhaps the land of Sumer was becoming too crowded. The region to which some of the people went is called northern Babylonia. By about 2500 B.C. it became famous as the land of Akkad.

But what of the "Flood" of Babylonian tradition that has come to us in the story of Noah and the ark? We can only say that there must have been many floods along the lower courses of the Tigris and Euphrates, many more than have been exposed by excavation. At Ur there was a flood in the Al Ubaid period. During early historic times, at Kish there was another flood of considerable proportions. Was this the overflowing of waters that loomed so large for later generations? For a number of reasons it is unlikely. The Babylonian myth tells of kings with lives of supernatural length who ruled before the flood, and Noah and his forefathers also lived lengthy lives; but in both stories those who followed existed for periods more within our understanding, and those in the Babylonian tale are to some extent historical and appear to belong to the period following 3000 B.C. It happens that there was a flooding of the ancient towns of Uruk and Shuruppak at about that time, but the difficulties persist. This flood was by no means general and did not affect many of the principal cities of the time. There remains, then, only the persistent and world-wide tradition that there was a flood of tremendous size. But floods leave records, and archaeology fails to support the tradition.

By the end of the Jemdet Nasr period, about 3000 B.C., the stage had been set for the advent of true history. All preparations had been made, as in Egypt at about the same time. Thereafter, in both countries we are able to follow developments by means of the written word.

It was the Sumerians, a people whose origin is by no means clear, who were the actors during the next scene and who accepted and improved the cultural advances that had taken place so laboriously through the centuries. Through them Babylonia was carried into the full light of history.

THE DIM PAST OF ANATOLIA

Meanwhile other regions were not dormant if not as progressive. Anatolia, which is the name given to the Turkish possessions on the great peninsula of Asia Minor, had passed out of the Stone Age directly into the Metal Age. There are some questionable Neolithic sites in this region, but recent excavation indicates that copper was used in the earliest organized villages. The city at the bottom of the ruin of Troy used copper, as did the first community at the site in central Anatolia which is now called Alishar. These earliest communities represent the Chalcolithic period, a term indicating that both copper and stone were in use at the same time. But Asia Minor covers an immense territory and possesses varied geographic outlooks, and we are not at all surprised to learn that there were several types of culture represented in the Chalcolithic period.

We have seen that geographic differences caused a variation between the cultures of Upper and Lower Egypt. Thus there were three main types of development in early Anatolia. The one to the west is well illustrated by the lowest city at Troy, which appears to have been related to the ancient culture of the Balkans. On the other hand, the inhabitants of the first city to be built on the site of Alishar made use of a type of pottery whose forms and decoration seem to tie it to the "Black Earth" culture of the lower Danube and southern Russia. The third culture area, which shows still other variations, is located in southeastern Anatolia and may be related to northern Syria, or to Cilicia which borders on the Mediterranean.

Excavation is being continued in Anatolia, and in time we may know the answers to many of the riddles that now cloud the picture for the period which lasted from about 3500-3000 B.C.

SUCCESSORS OF THE CAVE MAN IN PALESTINE AND SYRIA

Because of the influence of better climatic conditions men were leaving their caves even before the new Stone Age and were discovering that wild grains could be cultivated. We know this because flint sickles, which had been set in bone holders, have been found in cave debris of the later Stone Age. But pottery had not been invented and the age of metals was a long way off. Grain had been added to the diet, but the essential elements of civilization had not been conceived.

It is likely that the discovery of grain cultivation led directly to the development of communities. Farming areas lay in the

Courtesy The Art Institute, Chicago

GENERAL VIEW OF THE JUDEAN HILLS FROM JERICHO

open fields, and the people had to be nearby in order to till them. But to a man living with his family on his plot of land there were dangers that had never beset him in his cave. He was open to attack from all sides, and for this reason alone the community idea was bound to develop. In a village, man had mutual protection as well as other advantages.

The earliest village known in either Palestine or Syria is Jericho. It may have had another name at that early time—that we may never know; but it stands out today as perhaps the oldest town in the world. An agricultural people lived there soon after the close of the Stone Age, but flint and stone continued to be the principal materials from which tools and weapons were made. Pottery had not been invented, and liquids were kept in other types of vessels. We know of these people from the ruins of a number of superimposed floor levels which were found at the bottom of a deep excavation a few years ago. Before that, knowledge of the period was entirely lacking.

The whole Near Eastern world appears to have learned of the benefits of pottery at about the same time, and at Jericho, too, the invention was presently made known. This important event cannot be dated with precision, but for a number of reasons it seems likely that it happened sometime between four and five thousand years before our era.

The first pottery was crude, but for certain purposes it had great advantages over stone and skin containers. The potters developed styles and gradually improved the quality of their product. Metal was still unknown, but flint and bone were put to good use.

Jericho is the only site in Palestine that has produced the type of culture of which we have been speaking, but undoubtedly there were other villages that existed at the same time. A number of cities in Palestine have been explored to the bottom and have not exposed a comparable culture, but the sites are not exhausted by any means. Ruins in the Jordan valley, in which Jericho is situated, possibly cover the remains of villages that were in communication with the first towns at Jericho.

Settlement of other fertile parts of Palestine and Syria was made at last, and contacts with surrounding countries assumed importance. By Gerzean and Maadi times in Egypt trade was carried on with Palestine. Pottery with a distinctive Palestinian character has been found far afield in Upper Egypt as well as

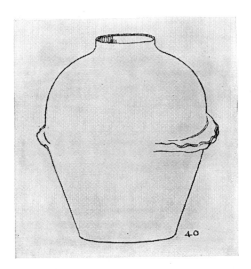

AN EXAMPLE OF PALESTINIAN POTTERY FOUND IN PRE-DY-NASTIC EGYPT

Courtesy Sir Flinders Petrie. *Corpus of Prehistoric Pottery and Palettes* on the Syrian coast. Egypt seems also to have discovered by this time the value of cedar of Lebanon. The world was still young as far as civilization was concerned, but trade for necessities had already assumed a position of importance in the lives of the people who lived around the Mediterranean.

The pottery vessels which have been found in Egypt probably got there by donkey pack. Perhaps they were filled with olive oil which has always been an important product of Palestine. Caravans also crossed the Sinai Desert, going east, bearing things from Egypt. Among these were pots, filled no doubt with desirable things from the valley of the Nile. Some of them had been made in Upper Egypt. The liquids and foods were consumed, but the pots remained. Moreover, their different shapes were admired by the foreigners, and so the local potters began copying the shapes that were most appreciated. The potter on the Nile reproduced vessels from Palestine, and the potter in Palestine did likewise. But the inevitable happened; neither could make a perfect copy since each shaped the clay by hand, and the product was a mixture of two distinct pottery traditions.

By a time shortly before 3000 B.C., Palestine and Syria were closely linked by excellent trade routes to both Egypt and Babylonia. We can visualize the first hardy merchants who were ready to risk much that they might become enriched. Seals and seal impressions of a distinctive Jemdet Nasr character have been found in both Syria and Palestine and testify to a relationship which must have been of real importance.

Syrian ships carried cedars to Egypt, but they also sailed to the islands of the Mediterranean, even as far as Malta. Their masters were really the first Phoenicians, but we cannot give them names. These may be gone forever because writing lay in the future.

Toward 3000 B.C. we find that considerable progress had been made on the road to civilization. Cultures had become specialized according to regions. The people of North Syria used pots that were quite distinct from those made at Byblos on the coast. The latter, in turn, were somewhat different from the pots and pans of Palestine. And within Palestine itself there were smaller regional differences. Each community, as well as each series of communities, was working things out for itself. The best was adopted by all, but each retained its own character and individuality.

The world was becoming national. Languages had already done much to further this distinction, but accumulated wealth and the widening gap of custom were also playing their parts. Soon the countries on the borders of the Mediterranean and the people of inland countries who were attracted to the sea were to become much more conscious of the national groups that lay about them. Writing, by means of which the greatest strides toward civilization have been made, played an important part in this process, and with it we enter the realm of true history.

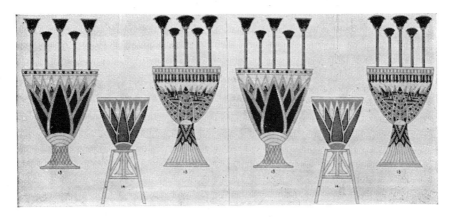

OLD KINGDOM EGYPT

HENCEFORTH we shall be able to speak of Egyptian history in terms of dynasties. Dynasty is simply a convenient term to designate the various royal houses in the same way that we refer today to the House of Windsor or the Hapsburg House. Manetho, an Egyptian priest who lived around 300 B.C., wrote a history of Egypt and arranged the rulers from Menes of the First Dynasty to Alexander the Great. He stated that there had been thirty dynasties, and this has been accepted by writers of history. The latter have in addition regrouped certain dynasties on the basis of major trends in Egyptian history. Thus the first six dynasties can be conveniently examined as a whole and are given the name Old Kingdom.

It was about 3000 B.C. that Menes brought Upper and Lower Egypt together to form a united kingdom. The date is not certain by any means; perhaps it is a couple of hundred years off. But around 3000 B.C. the south conquered the north and set the machinery of centralized government into motion. The capital was at Thinis, near Abydos, and for this reason the first two dynasties which ruled from there are called the Thinite dynasties.

THE PYRAMID OF ZOSER AT SAKKARAH

Eighteen kings are known to have reigned during this period which lasted about 480 years. No sharp cultural lines can be drawn between late predynastic and dynastic Egypt. Progress continued along initiated courses, but there were no real changes. Sculpture and stone work gradually improved and led naturally to the great structures and works of art of the Pyramid Age.

The first king of the Third Dynasty was Zoser who chose Memphis, which is not far from Cairo, as his capital. He represents for us another family and tradition, that of the north, and it was he who built the first pyramid. His step pyramid, so-called because it was erected in tiers, stands at Sakkarah on the edge of the desert south of the great pyramids at Gizeh. The first extensive stone work in Egypt began with Zoser who kept large numbers of men busy at the quarries. The masonry of the times shows clearly that stone work was relatively new to the Egyptian mind, for stone blocks were laid in mud-brick fashion, and wood and reed architecture was imitated. The earliest known stone columns in Egypt were erected during Zoser's reign in imitation of bundles of reeds.

Courtesy Cairo Museum

STONE COLUMNS OF ZOSER AT SAKKARAH

Courtesy Charles Breasted and The Oriental Institute of The University of Chicago

AN AIRVIEW OF THE PYRAMIDS AT GIZEH

Courtesy The Oriental Institute of The University of Chicago

AN EGYPTIAN OFFICIAL, NANUPKAU, AND HIS WIFE,
who lived toward the end of the Old Kingdom. They were buried
at Gizeh

Courtesy The Oriental Institute of The University of Chicago

ABOVE: MODELS OF DRUMMER
AND HARPERS FOUND IN THE
TOMB OF NANUPKAU

RIGHT: STATUE OF KING MEN-
KURE AND HIS QUEEN

Courtesy Museum of Fine Arts, Boston

STATUETTE
GROUP OF TWO
YOUNGSTERS
PLAYING LEAP
FROG
Found in the tomb
of Nanupkau.

Zoser had an extraordinary man as his grand vizier. Later Egyptian tradition regarded him as the inventor of hewn stone. We know that this was not the case, but it is altogether likely that he had much to do with the development of stone masonry. This man was Imhotep, and in history he is better remembered than many a king. He illustrates admirably the attitude of Egypt, from his time on, toward higher learning. His reputation as a wise man, priest, maker of proverbs, man of medicine, architect, and patron in general, only increased as time went on, and by the time of the Ptolemaic successors of Alexander he had become a full-fledged god.

The Third Dynasty lasted but sixty years or so, coming to an end about 2720 B.C. It was followed by the Fourth Dynasty group of kings whose tombs are bywords the world over as symbols of durability and power. These are the great pyramids which

Courtesy The Oriental Institute of The University of Chicago

THE GROUP OF SMALL FIGURES FOUND IN THE TOMB OF NANUPKAU
Some of the figures are seen grinding grain, cutting up meat, and preparing food.

were built to house the earthly remains of the wealthy king-gods. Kings had long since ceased to be merely human in the eyes of their subjects. The kings of the Fourth Dynasty, especially Khufu who was called Cheops by the Greeks, were among the most powerful persons who ever lived. At no later time would it have been possible for a single man to order the erection of a tomb like the great pyramid.

Khufu was the second king of his dynasty, and he was followed by four others. Two of these are well remembered by their pyramids which stand next to that of Khufu. Khafre built the second pyramid at Gizeh, and Menkure the third, but these were smaller and poorer than the first although they too stand for untold wealth. Looking up the Nile from the top of the great pyramid, one can see still other pyramids, including the one built for Zoser. They stand along the edge of the valley like attentive sentinels observing the march of events. The greatest of them saw the end of the Fourth Dynasty which came to a close about 2560 B.C.

The Fifth Dynasty lasted for about 120 years and included nine kings. The royal family had changed, but Egypt prospered as before. These kings, however, lacked the complete power of those who had preceded them, for by now the nobles had attained a higher position in the affairs of the nation. Nevertheless the Egypt of this period was able to invade foreign territory and maintain the country in a state of unity.

The last dynasty of the Old Kingdom, the sixth, lasted from 2420-2270 B.C. and included five kings. One of them, Pepi II, held the throne for over ninety years, the longest reign of any Egyptian king. Egypt prospered as a unified nation, developing commerce with Nubia and the coasts of the Mediterranean, improving the arts, and creating a considerable ethical standard. But as the country grew, so grew the necessity for greater governmental care. Districts were allotted to the favorites of the king. These became more powerful day by day and at length created themselves hereditary princes. The end of the Old Kingdom was in sight. The time came when the king could no longer maintain discipline and respect among the nobles. It was a matter of each man for himself and the spoils to the most clever. Finally the Sixth Dynasty came to an abrupt end, terminated by an invasion of foreigners from Asia. For 170 years Egypt was prey to these people and to ambitious Egyptian nobles who contrived to gather together a following. This period is little understood and is appropriately called a Dark Age, but out of it there again came unity which developed into the classical age called the Middle Kingdom.

THE SCRIBE

The scribal profession is as old as the transmission of ideas by writing. The first scribes drew pictures to convey the ideas that they had in mind. This stage of writing occurred long before the First Dynasty, for by that time the system of hieroglyphic writing had been well formulated, although it cannot be read with assurance. Pictures were quite satisfactory for certain things and gave the intended idea, but we can all appreciate the difficulty we would have if we tried to tell a story in picture form. We might find it fairly successful thus to relate that a dog was chasing a man. Such a picture is easily drawn. Or perhaps it would not be too difficult to depict men fishing in the Nile, or others paying their respects to one of the numerous Egyptian gods. But these are action pictures. How, with the primitive equipment which we for the moment possess, could we make clear the idea that we were tired of the place where we were and wished to go home as soon as possible; or that we were undecided as to the best course to follow under the circumstances?

The Egyptian could probably have explained all these matters with the greatest fluency and surely did if he was anything like his modern descendant, but to send a written message was different. Pictures served for a while, yet these lacked complete effectiveness. At length someone whom we shall never know conceived of the idea of syllable writing. The method can be well illustrated in English. The picture of a *bee* can be placed

AN EXAMPLE OF EGYPTIAN FIRST DYNASTY HIEROGLYPHS

Courtesy Sir Flinders Petrie, *Royal Tombs*.

Photo by R. Rohrbach

Courtesy The Oriental Institute of The
University of Chicago

PORTRAIT STATUETTE OF AN EGYP-
TIAN SCRIBE
Third Dynasty.

Courtesy Metropolitan Museum of Art

SCRIBE READING A PAPYRUS ROLL
Eighteenth Dynasty.

next to the representation of a *gun*, the resultant word being
begun. This is called phonetic, or sound, writing. Of course the
bee and the *gun* have lost all of their true picture meaning and
stand for an altogether different idea. In the same way a *bee* and
a *leaf* can be combined to indicate the word *belief*. This system
was continued in Egypt until all the syllable sounds in the language could be represented by pictures which had a sound value.
In addition there came into being an alphabet of twenty-four
letters from which our own was in time partially descended.

Thus equipped, the scribe recorded things that could never
have been described with pictures. But to a busy scribe it became
laborious and impractical to draw all the details of the many
hieroglyphs, so he developed a system which we may compare to
our handwriting. Thenceforth the capital letters, the hieroglyphs,
were used mainly for monuments, public inscriptions, sacred
writings, and the like, while the longhand, or hieratic, was employed for letters, documents, and state and business records.

Courtesy Cairo Museum
AN OLD KINGDOM SCRIBE WITH HIS EQUIPMENT
From a tomb at Sakkarah.

Scribes held an honorable position throughout Egyptian history and well they might, since there were relatively few people who could read and write. To this day one can see scribes gathered together in the market places of the Near East waiting for their illiterate customers. In ancient times in Egypt the scribe carried his small box with its ink and reed containers. Today he uses a bottle of ink and a pen. In many ways the Near East is still in the days of Abraham.

THE DECIPHERMENT OF HIEROGLYPHIC WRITING

Until a little over a hundred years ago nobody in modern times had been able to read the ancient Egyptian records. These had ceased to be written shortly after the beginning of our era, and, since it was the priests who had perpetuated the use of Egyptian, it soon was claimed that the strange-looking pictures had only a mystical meaning. Many fantastic theories arose and colored the labors of numbers of scholars.

And then there was found the most famous key to the decipherment of hieroglyphic writing, the Rosetta Stone. One of Napoleon's engineers had accidentally dug it up while working at Rosetta in the Delta in 1799. Later it passed into British hands and is now in the British Museum in London. It is roughly 2½ by 3 feet and is a dark volcanic rock called basalt. Parts are missing but there remain three divided registers, each containing a different kind of writing. Each gives the same information, in hieroglyphic, demotic, and Greek—demotic being the conventionalized script of the time when the stone was carved (196 B.C.).

Thomas Young, the famous English physicist, made the first important step toward solving the puzzle of hieroglyphs by reading on another inscription the names of Ptolemy and Berenice.

JEAN-FRANCOIS
CHAMPOLLION

Courtesy Maspero, *Lettres de Champollion Le Jeune*

But it remained for Champollion, a brilliant young Frenchman who from youth had been interested in oriental languages, to make the important discovery that hieroglyphic was composed of alphabetic and syllabic signs. He identified the names of Ptolemy and Cleopatra on an obelisk shaft and from them had learned the sound value of twelve letters. It was at this point that he was at last able to make full use of the Rosetta stone. The Greek of the inscription was clear to him, and that, with a knowledge of other oriental languages, enabled him to add to his list of known signs and discover the meanings of words and the construction of the language.

Champollion made the first announcement of his discoveries to the French Academy in 1822, and before he died ten years later at the age of forty-one, he had published a grammar and dictionary of hieroglyphic. The first correct steps had been taken but they were only a foundation. Many eminent scholars have followed in Champollion's footsteps, adding gradually to our store of knowledge of the language and things Egyptian. Yet even today Egyptian is not completely understood, although the sense of most inscriptions can be grasped.

The world owes Champollion a debt of gratitude, for without his keen insight we might yet be without real knowledge of the marvelous achievements and happenings on the Nile which had been taking place for almost three thousand years before Greece and Rome came on the scene.

THE EGYPTIAN CALENDAR

All early calendars possess difficulties that arise from the fact that a day does not evenly divide the lunar month or the solar year. There are roughly 365¼ days in the year and about 29½ days in the moon month. The Egyptians seem to have had a moon calendar to begin with, but they had also observed that a conspicuous star in the Egyptian sky, called Sirius or Sothis, appeared again over the horizon just before sunrise at about the time that the Nile began to rise. The beginning of the flood was the big event in the Egyptian year, and we can well understand why the calendar-makers chose the reappearance of Sothis to mark the first day of the year. The Egyptian year thus included the time between the days when Sothis appeared again, after having for some time been invisible, just before sunrise.

This year was divided into three seasons of four months each, one representing the inundation of the Nile, another the winter or sowing season, followed by the summer or harvest period. The months were considered to be 30 days long and twelve of these totaled 360 days. A five-day period devoted to feasting was added to these and brought the days of the year to 365.

The difficulty with this system is that the solar and star years, which are practically identical, measure roughly 365¼ days. Thus every four years Sothis rose a day later, and as a result the calendar year and the solar year fell out of gear. The Egyptians must have noticed that a discrepancy had come into the system, but they did nothing with it until much later when a day was added for Leap Year. This uncorrected error meant that New Year's Day became a day later every four years. After 1460 years, however, it came back to the time when the Nile began to rise. This period of 1460 years is known as a Sothic cycle.

It is known from a Latin source that the Egyptian New Year's Day coincided with the appearance of the Sothic star in 139 A.D. It is evident then that the same thing had happened in 1321 B.C., 2781 B.C., 4241 B.C., and so on, all these dates being 1460 years apart. Now it must have been on one of these dates that the calendar came into use, but 1321 is eliminated because the calendar was definitely in use before that time. Of the remaining possibilities it seems most likely that the year 2781 B.C. marks the event, but we cannot yet be absolutely certain that the Egyptian calendar did not come into being in 4241 B.C. In any case it is over 4500 years old and is the calendar which Julius Caesar introduced to Rome with some modifications and which with further changes has become the instrument by which we adapt our days, nights, weeks, and months.

MUMMIES

The date of the first mummification in Egypt is not known, but it seems to have been no later than the Second Dynasty, or soon after 3000 B.C. A number of tombs from that dynasty contained bodies that had been bandaged in mummy fashion. After this early period the evidence for the practice increases and continues into early Christian times when it was discontinued.

It seems likely that mummification came about through a wish to preserve the form and identity of the deceased. Details of the treatment varied from period to period and according to the wealth of the person, but the following description may be regarded as general. After death the body was sent to the embalmer's establishment where it was placed on a board. The brain was removed through one of the nostrils, after which the face was covered with a resin-like pitch. The next step involved the removal of the viscera through an incision which had been cut in the left side. All the vital organs were removed except the heart and sometimes the kidneys. The parts that had been taken out were placed in special containers. Then the body was immersed in a salt bath, only the head remaining out of the solution. This process removed the outer skin and disintegrated the fatty tissues of the body. The body was then dried and treated with spices, oils, and resin. Sometimes the brain and abdominal cavities were stuffed with linen, and a number of mummies contained onions, for what reason is not known. In other cases the legs, arms, and parts of the trunk were cut out and stuffed with linen with the probable intention of making the form more lifelike. Preliminary to wrapping the whole mummy in a linen shroud, the nostril through which the brain had been drawn was stuffed with a linen plug, and pads of the same material were placed over the eyes. After these preliminaries, the mummy was tightly bound with yards and yards of linen bandages, and they in turn were covered with a coating of linen, glue, and plaster. This coating is usually quite colorful, for at the head of the mummy appears a painted human face, while brightly colored paint-

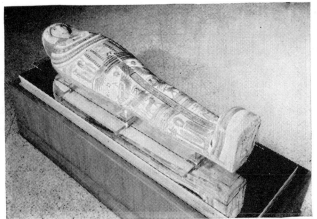

A PAINTED COFFIN OF A THEBAN LADY DATING FROM THE TENTH CENTURY B. C. Her mummy lies inside.

Courtesy The Oriental Institute of The University of Chicago

PARTIALLY UNWRAPPED MUMMY OF AN EGYPTIAN WOMAN, DATING FROM THE SEVENTH CENTURY B. C.

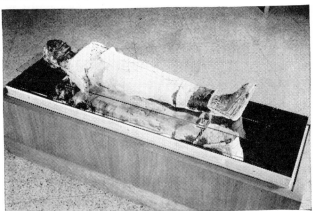

Courtesy The Oriental Institute of The University of Chicago

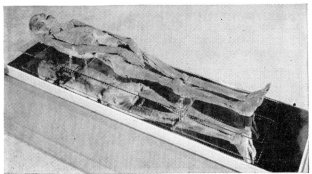

Courtesy The Oriental Institute of The University of Chicago

UNWRAPPED MUMMY OF AN EGYPTIAN WOMAN, DATING FROM THE SEVENTH CENTURY B. C.

ings and hieroglyphs appear on the body. It is usual to find at least a prayer for the dead inscribed on the outer casing. The body was then ready for the rites at the grave.

THE GREAT PYRAMID—ONE OF THE WONDERS OF THE ANCIENT WORLD

The Greeks regarded the pyramid tomb of Khufu as one of the seven wonders of the world, and it still remains an object for deep consideration by both the historically and mystically minded. But we need not dwell on those who see in the pyramid and its measurements the explanation of life's mysteries; our purpose is to tell what the pyramid was and what it stood for.

The Great Pyramid was a tomb built for Khufu, second king of the Fourth Dynasty, who reigned around 2700 B.C. and was one of the most powerful men who ever lived. He had at his command all the resources of the country, and it seems clear that the principal event of his time was the building of the pyramid. It was to be a structure which could be penetrated by no human being, and which would house forever the remains of the king. Herodotus, who lived in the fifth century B.C., related the Egyptian tradition that a hundred thousand men were engaged in its construction for twenty years, and we can well believe that such was the case.

The immense size of this largest of ancient stone structures will be gathered from the following figures. The area covered by the pyramid is about thirteen acres, the base being 755 feet on a side. The ground plan is practically square, and its accuracy and that of the pyramid as a whole arouses our greatest admiration for the mechanical skill of the architects of this early period. The pyramid towered to a height of 480 feet, which is equivalent to that of a modern skyscraper 48 stories high. It is composed of a solid mass of yellow limestone blocks and at the time of its completion was covered with an outer layer of fine white limestone. Shining in the sun, it must indeed have pleased the soul of the great king.

Courtesy James Henry Breasted, Jr. and The Oriental Institute of The University of Chicago

THE GREAT PYRAMID AT GIZEH, TOMB OF KING KHUFU
The entrance is in the side lying in the shadow.

Not the least remarkable aspect about the pyramid was its method of construction. In that day there were no pulleys and little in the way of mechanical assistance to ease the labors of the multitudes. The lowest courses were dragged into place by brute force, while those in the courses above were hoisted by means of a sloping ramp of mud brick which had been thrown against the completed portions of the pyramid. When the building was finished, the ramp was removed. About 2,300,000 blocks of limestone went into the construction, and the average weight of each was two and a half tons. Considering these immense weights, it is all the more astonishing that the work was so perfectly done. Joints of only one ten-thousandth of an inch between blocks were apparently normal in the outer limestone casing.

The tomb entrance—which is in the eighteenth masonry course above the ground on the north side of the pyramid—leads to several chambers, in one of which the body of the king was placed. But for all the care and precaution taken in building the tomb it was entered by thieves, and the mummy of Khufu has never been found. It once was thought that the queen also had been buried in the pyramid, since there was more than one burial chamber. It appears, however, that Khufu, at different periods during construction of the pyramid, changed his plans for the size that he wished and accordingly had it enlarged several times. This seems to account for the number of chambers and for the passages leading up to them. After Khufu had been laid away in state, stone plug blocks were dropped into place in the various passages in order to keep intruders away, and the entrance on the north side was closed with the same white limestone that covered the surface of the pyramid.

Members of the family and favored nobles built their tombs around the pyramid of their king and near the pyramid temple which had been erected just to the east facing the Nile. Food, drink, and other necessities were placed here for the use of the dead king in the after-life. The pyramid complex was completed by a covered causeway which led from a temple at the edge of the cultivation up to the pyramid temple.

We have seen that Khufu was defeated in his principal purpose, which was to preserve for all time the body that had been a great and magnificent king. But his monument still stands as a symbol of his age. Untold powers and wealth lay in the hands of the king; the entire land of Egypt was dominated and made to obey the word of a single man.

THE IMMUTABLE SPHINX

The Great Sphinx, which stands in front of the second pyramid at Gizeh, exists because quarrymen for the first pyramid found a mass of limestone which they considered too poor in quality to be used. Thus the good stone on all sides was quarried away and the poor stone remained. When Khafre, builder of the second pyramid, was erecting his tomb and the temples that were associated with it, attention was called to the huge stone knob which lay to the east of the pyramid. Forthwith it was decided to shape it in the form of a sphinx with the head of a king and the body of a recumbent lion. Thus two accidents, one geologic and the other human, conspired to give the world a monument which has been little less famous than the pyramids themselves. This, too, is a huge structure, being about 66 feet high and 240 long. The ear alone is 4½ feet in length and the mouth 7½ feet wide.

The Sphinx, like the pyramids, stands at the edge of the desert and has always been subject to the shifting sands which tended to cover it up. The first known excavator of the Sphinx was King Thutmose IV who set up a slab (about 1420 B.C.) recording the fact. Others since his time have freed the monument of its quilt of sand and built walls as a preventive measure, but all to no avail. It requires constant attention to keep the Sphinx above ground. Aside from sand the colossus has suffered from natural cracking of the poor rock, and in addition has been wilfully mutilated in recent times. Several hundred years ago it was used as a target by the Arabs. But the Sphinx still stands with face toward the east bearing with unchanged expression the marks of a long life.

Courtesy The Oriental Institute of The University of Chicago

THE SPHINX AND PYRAMID OF KHAFRE AT GIZEH

Courtesy Underwood & Underwood Photo

THE TRADITIONAL MT. SINAI TOWERING ABOVE THE PLAIN OF ASSEMBLY

THE MINES OF SINAI

Before the time of Menes, Egyptian expeditions had made the treacherous journey to Sinai in search of copper, turquoise, and other desirable materials which nature had imbedded in its rocks. This we know from materials which have been found in the ruined villages and towns of predynastic Egypt. From the First Dynasty on, the kings of Egypt began to leave inscriptions on the rocks of southern Sinai where the mining was carried on. The earliest inscription tells of the punishment of wild tribes that had dared to attack the king's workers.

CHISEL CUTTINGS AT AN ANCIENT MINE IN SINAI

RELIEF IN SINAI
An Egyptian King of the First Dynasty smiting a native chief.

Zoser, the first king of the Third Dynasty (about 2780 B.C.) and builder of the first pyramid, also sent expeditions to the mines, as did Snefru who introduced the Fourth Dynasty (about 2720 B.C.). In fact, Snefru left in Sinai such a strong impression of his might that in later years he became a patron god who would aid and protect officials sent to the wilds in search of riches for their pharaohs.

Inscriptions were also left by Fifth and Sixth Dynasty kings and others who doubtless gained revenues from the rich rocks of Sinai. It was necessary at all times to have an adequate armed guard because of depredations by the roving Semitic natives of the country who were related to the later Hebrews and Arabs. One may doubt whether the officials, delegated to conduct the work and transport the copper and semi-precious stones back to Egypt, actually relished the honors that were bestowed upon them. Sinai never became quite civilized, yet it is a curious fact that by way of Sinai the alphabet was passed on to Palestine and Syria and at length to Greece and ourselves.

SHIPS TO LEBANON

Even before dynastic times there had been trade by sea with the Syrian coast, but the record comes only from materials uncovered in excavation. However, by the time of Snefru (about 2720 B.C.) we are told in so many words of such an expedition. The king sent forty ships which returned laden with cedar logs from the slopes of Lebanon, at that time blanketed with trees. Quite likely the trade in timber was carried on through Byblos where an Egyptian temple had been erected as early as the Second Dynasty. In fact, objects of the First Dynasty have been found in the ruins of Byblos.

With favorable winds, the voyage from the Delta to Byblos could be made in four days. The logs, after seasoning, were used for coffins, sacred boats, door lintels, and other objects that required good wood to be durable. Cedar of Lebanon thus brought Egypt into early contact with Byblos, which all through history appears to have been a sort of Egyptian outpost and the center of Egyptian culture in Asia.

THE END OF THE OLD KINGDOM

All dynasties come to an end, even in China. The Egyptian Sixth Dynasty had enjoyed a prosperous rule, yet weak kings had allowed the nobles to assume ever increasing power. The tombs of this and the preceding dynasty clearly indicate the wealth and powerful position that the nobles had assumed. Influence in government matters was being split, with one noble gaining power here and another there. While some strong kings reigned during these two dynasties, they were not powerful enough to halt the trend toward a feudal state in which nobles in effect become petty kings.

This uncentralized state of affairs left Egypt prey to foreign invaders whose coming marks the end of the Sixth Dynasty as well as the end of the Old Kingdom. Very little is known about

Courtesy The Oriental Institute of The University of Chicago

GOLDSMITHS WEIGHING GOLD IN A SCENE IN AN EARLY SIXTH DYNASTY
TOMB OF A NOBLE AT SAKKARAH

Courtesy The Oriental Institute of The University of Chicago

THE SAME TOMB SHOWING GOLDSMITHS AT WORK

these people except that they came from Asia, presumably from North Syria. They were probably Semites who entered in small but rapidly increasing numbers into the Delta, settled there, and learned the ways of the country. In time they themselves became strong enough to make the disruption of the government completely effective. A period of chaos followed, an era of almost total darkness as far as our knowledge is concerned. In this period of almost two centuries must be placed the Seventh, Eighth, Ninth, and Tenth Dynasties. The latter two of these covered periods of native Egyptian rule, but they were far from controlling the territory governed by the Old Kingdom Dynasties. Further excavation may do much to clear up the tremendous uncertainty of this period, but until then we must pass it by for the most part and pick up the threads of Egyptian history again with the advent of the Middle Kingdom, about 2100 B.C.

THE LAND OF THE TWO RIVERS IN THE THIRD MILLENNIUM B.C.

By 3000 B.C. Mesopotamia had gone through the laborious stages which lead to civilization. Cities had grown up, and communication with distant territories had been established. But most important, the country now possessed a system of writing which came into general use when the people who are called Sumerians assumed historic control of the country.

WEDGE-SHAPED WRITING

The system of writing used in Mesopotamia began with pictures, just as in Egypt, but the Babylonians developed their script in an altogether different way. The reason for this is that the clay tablet came into early use as the object on which writing was recorded. In Egypt there was plenty of stone and papyrus, whereas these materials were lacking along the Tigris and Euphrates. Furthermore, clay is not a particularly good material on which to paint or scratch pictures for permanent use. As a result the Babylonians developed the use of the stylus for impressing wedge-shaped characters on the soft clay tablet. In this way the original pictures were depicted in increasingly angular form until finally they became so conventionalized that the originals can be detected only with the greatest difficulty. This type of writing is called *cuneiform,* from the Latin *cuneus,* meaning "wedge".

We recall that Egyptian picture writing originally stood for ideas and not sounds. The same was true of Babylonian. But in time the necessary transition to sound recording was accomplished. In Mesopotamia, however, the signs came to stand for syllables such as *mar* or *duk,* but there was no possible way to represent the sounds *m* or *r, d* or *k,* or any of the other alphabetic sounds. Thus while the cuneiform system was phonetic it did not progress beyond the syllabic stage.

The Sumerians developed the cuneiform system to the point where it was convenient for recording their language. Then about 2550 B.C. their country was conquered by a group of Semitic

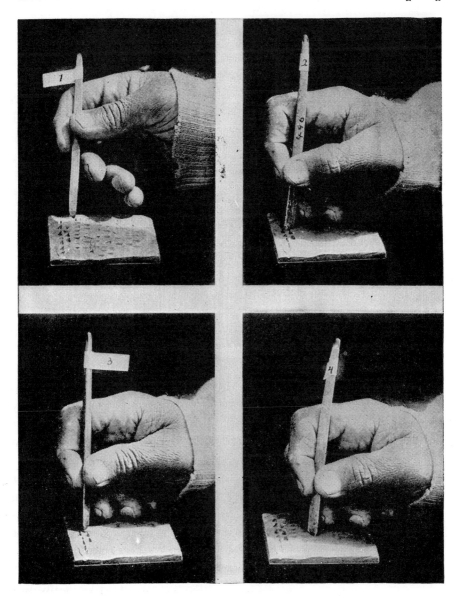

MODERN STYLUS
A demonstration of cuneiform writing. (After Langdon)

Courtesy Langdon *Excavations at Kish*

EXAMPLES OF EARLY PICTOGRAPHIC WRITING FROM KISH

nomads under the leadership of Sargon I. The nomads spoke a language different from that of the Sumerians, and in addition they did not know how to write. But under the influence of the civilization in which they now found themselves they adopted the Sumerian cuneiform system and began to write their Semitic language with the now established wedge system.

In later times cuneiform was borrowed by a number of different peoples speaking different languages, among them the Persians.

HOW CUNEIFORM WAS DECODED

A little over a hundred years ago cuneiform could not be read. In fact, it probably had not been read for almost two thousand years. But travelers to the Orient had brought back to Europe tablets and copies of inscriptions which aroused considerable curiosity and interest. Certain of these inscriptions, which had come from the walls of Persian palaces, were seen to contain a limited number of signs, far less than in some examples of cuneiform known from the Tigris and Euphrates area. It seemed there was a good chance that they could be deciphered. Slight progress had been made by 1800, but it remained for a German school-

	A	B	C	D	E
	Original pictograph	Pictograph in position of later cuneiform	Early Babylonian	Assyrian	Original or derived meaning
1					bird
2					fish
3					donkey
4					ox
5					sun / day
6					grain
7					orchard
8					to plow / to till
9					boomerang / to throw / to throw down
10					to stand / to go

Compiled and drawn by Professor Arno Poebel

DIAGRAM SHOWING PICTORIAL ORIGIN OF TEN CUNEIFORM
SIGNS

master named Grotefend actually to identify the names of Darius
and Xerxes. He made a couple of mistakes in the reading, but
was definitely on the right track.

A number of other scholars were also interested in the problem and made detailed contributions, but it was a young English
army officer stationed in Persia who made the first important
translation of a Persian text. At risk of his life Rawlinson copied
the cuneiform signs of the famous Behistun inscription in the
mountains northeast of Bagdad. The Persian king, Darius, had
selected a face of rock three hundred feet above the road as suitable for his monumental inscription in which he told of his tri-
umphs after becoming king. Rawlinson climbed daily up the
precipitous cliff, ignoring physical dangers that beset him at every
step, for the sole purpose of copying the characters on the wall.
He soon realized that there were actually three inscriptions. One
was in Old Persian, and he guessed shrewdly that the other two
were translations of the first. Here, then, was an Asiatic Rosetta
Stone. If one of the languages could be deciphered it might be
possible to understand the other two. And one of the others was
written in characters much like the many examples of cuneiform
that were by then pouring into the museums of Europe from the
Land of the Two Rivers. Here was a chance to unlock the mysteries that had long shrouded the history of Mesopotamia.

Rawlinson worked long and hard on the Persian inscription
since it alone seemed to be the key to the others, and in 1847 announced to the world that the Old Persian inscription had been
read. The results of his translation spurred a number of other
scholars to work on the Babylonian inscription which contained
many more characters, but it was Rawlinson again who finally
succeeded in reading the language. In 1850 he announced his
results, and from then on the curtain was lifted on the past
history of Mesopotamia. Through Rawlinson's genius it has been
possible to make use of the many thousands of written documents
that have been brought to the surface, and which give us detailed
information on the life and times of ancient Mesopotamia. Rawlinson's insight carries written history in that land to a point
almost five thousand years ago.

Courtesy University Museum, Philadelphia

HARP WITH GOLD BULL'S HEAD
AND BEARD OF LAPIS LAZULI
From one of the royal tombs at Ur.
Sumerian period.

Courtesy University Museum, Philadelphia

ENGRAVED SHELL PLAQUE FROM
THE HARP

THE SUMERIANS

The origin of the Sumerians is still clouded in mystery. It
may be that they were in the land before 3000 B.C., but not before that date do we get a full view of these people settled in their
cities on the lower stretches of the Tigris and Euphrates in the
land that they called Sumer.

Courtesy University Museum, Philadelphia

GOLD LAMP FILLER, TUMBLER, AND BOWL FROM THE TOMB OF QUEEN
SHUBAD AT UR. SUMERIAN PERIOD

Sumer never became a kingdom in the sense in which we understand that word. There were, on the other hand, a series of small city-states, all under the influence of a common culture, yet constantly at war with one another. Each city was ruled by a priest-king whose territory extended for some miles in all directions around the city. We might compare such a domain to a present day county with its county seat, but infinitely more powerful and independent. In those days Ur, which later became famous through association with Abraham, was among the stronger of these city-states; Lagash and Kish were others.

The Sumerians are important, less for the fact that they controlled a considerable portion of lower Mesopotamia for a number of centuries, than that their culture became the basis of later Babylonian civilization. They passed on their mode of life, their system of writing, their laws, their art, and a good part of their religious practice. Many hundred years later rituals were still being recited in Sumerian in exactly the same way that Latin is today. Sumerian became the classical language in Babylonia.

SARGON OF AKKAD AND HIS DYNASTY

It was about 2550 B.C. that a wave of Semitic people from the Syrian Desert swept into Babylonia and, under the leadership of Sargon, settled just north of the land of Sumer. They called their

A STATUE OF THE GOD OF
FERTILITY
Sumerian period. Now in the Bagdad
Museum.

STATUE OF MOTHER GODDESS FROM
TELL ASMAR
Sumerian period. Now in the Bagdad
Museum.

ARCHAIC COPPER FIGURES OF THREE
BEARDED MEN

ONE OF THE COPPER STATUETTES
FROM KHAFAJE AFTER CLEANING

Sumerian period at Khafaje. Upright figure now in Bagdad Museum.

CYLINDER SEAL IMPRESSION OF A DRINKING SCENE. SUMERIAN PERIOD
The seal was found at Khafaje, not far from Tell Asmar.

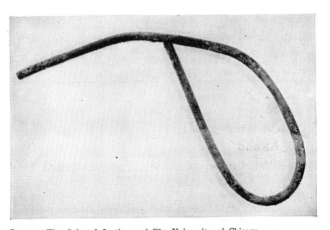

A BENT COPPER DRINKING STRAW FROM TELL ASMAR
Sumerian period. Its purpose was suggested by the scene depicted
in the figure above.

country Akkad, and from that time on Semites dominated the Babylonian scene. The Sumerians were soon conquered and one of their last priest-kings, Lugalzaggisi, was led through the city of Nippur in chains. He had carried his own conquests to the Mediterranean, and at his downfall his territories fell into the hands of Sargon. Semitic victories also took place to the east of Babylonia in the mountains and highlands bordering Persia, and before he died Sargon had welded together an empire of considerable extent.

Sargon became the hero of heroes to later Babylonians, and quite naturally incidents in his life became subject for folklore. The story was told that he had been born in secret and was placed in a basket of reeds upon the river. The current carried him down stream where he was found by a peasant who brought him up as his own son. He became a gardener, and finally, through the love of the goddess Ishtar, ruler of the kingdom. From basket on the waters to ruler of his people! But where have we heard a story very much like that? Shades of Moses, and the basket and pharaoh's daughter. The ancient east had many popular tales into which past heroes were placed. The story of Romulus and Remus, the foundling founders of Rome, is but a variation of the tale of the miraculous and wonderful early days of Sargon and Moses.

Sargon was followed by other great kings and warriors who were fairly successful in keeping together the gains that had already been made. There were revolts, of course, but these were halted, and new territories were added to the already considerable Kingdom of Akkad. Naram-Sin, one of the greatest of Sargon's successors, called himself "King of the Four Quarters of the World". Some time after his death, however, the land of Akkad was subjected to one of those periodic uprisings of the eastern mountaineers on the borders of Babylonia.

These people, called the Guti, left their homes in the Zagros Mountains and at length took possession of the fertile lands and busy cities along the Tigris and Euphrates. Their rule began about 2400 B.C. and lasted for a century or more, after which the Sumerians, who had been subdued by Sargon, again came to the fore and established themselves for a century. But conditions were far from settled. Sumerians and Semites continued to struggle, and Elamites from the edge of Persia descended into the plain. The time was ripe for the coming of a powerful people who could establish themselves as sole rulers. At length they came, a Semitic people from up the Euphrates, who first settled at Babylon and later conquered all of Babylonia. This was the First Dynasty of Babylon, destined to give to the world the famous king, Hammurabi. Before 2000 B.C. Babylon had been a very insignificant town. Thereafter it was to assume an importance as great as any city in ancient Asia.

Courtesy Bagdad Museum

A BRONZE HEAD OF THE AKKADIAN PERIOD FROM NINEVEH
About the 26th Century B. C.

Courtesy The Louvre

RELIEF OF NARAM-SIN FROM HIS VICTORY STELA

Courtesy The Oriental Institute of The University of Chicago

BABYLON

Showing the immense mound from southeast beneath which the city is buried.

Courtesy The Oriental Institute of The University of Chicago

A LINK BETWEEN INDIA AND MESOPOTAMIA
Cylinder seal and its impression from a house of the Akkadian period, 2500 B. C. The elephant and rhinoceros were animals unknown in Mesopotamia.

TRADE WITH INDIA

Many hundred miles lie between Mesopotamia and the Indus Valley in India. The land journey is difficult and the sea voyage is treacherous even today. Yet, almost five thousand years ago, trade relations between the two territories had been established. Merchants went back and forth with their goods and, as the world travelers of that day, brought back tales of the lands they had visited. A clear indication of this condition is seen in the design cut on a cylinder seal found in a house of the Akkadian period (about 2500 B.C.).

We may be perfectly sure that there was intimate knowledge of India in the western countries because this cylinder seal, which is Mesopotamian in form, was cut with a typically Indian design. The elephant and rhinoceros which form the essential part of the pattern were animals unknown in the Tigris-Euphrates region. Moreover they were depicted in a manner closely resembling Indian representations of the same animals. Consequently we are certain that people from the Land of the Two Rivers had actually gone as far afield as India. They had seen and been impressed by specimens of Indian art, perhaps they had viewed the strange animals as well, and had brought home these ideas with them. The same thing was happening in India, for her merchants who had gone to Mesopotamia brought products and ideas characteristic of the Tigris-Euphrates back to the valley of the Indus. Excavation in prehistoric sites in India has really just begun, and in time we may know much more about relations between eastern and western Asia during this early period. It is possible that such communications began much earlier than we now believe, for shipping by sea and by caravan is an old institution, almost as old as simple barter between neighboring tribes.

THE CANALS AND RIVERS OF BABYLONIA

We are accustomed to think of the Babylonians in terms of commerce, money lending, and astronomy, and in this we are right, for they had aptitude in all these matters, even in early days. But the Babylonian was essentially a farmer who earned his "daily bread" through the cultivation of wheat, barley, and millet. We have seen that Egyptian farmers were dependent on the yearly overflow of the Nile for water for their crops. In Babylonia the water of the rivers was just as important but had to be obtained in a different way. Because the rivers did not rise far enough out of their banks to flow over the surrounding country, it became necessary to install a vast irrigation system covering the entire land. The god Marduk was given credit for the discovery of irrigation, and its importance is shown in the royal inscriptions. From earliest times every king who has left us any mention of himself or his administration tells of constructing or repairing canals by which water might be brought from the two rivers to the fertile land. Trading may have been a strong mark of these people, but farming was the backbone of their life.

THE DYNASTY OF HAMMURABI

About the time that Egypt was recovering from the disorders that had taken place when a foreign people invaded their country, the First Dynasty of Babylon established itself in the fertile lower stretches of the Babylonian plain. These people who had come down the Euphrates to find themselves in the midst of civilization were related in language to the Semites who had entered the country with Sargon four hundred years earlier. They made the town of Babylon their capital and soon it became the greatest city of the land.

III—9

Courtesy British Museum

A BRICK OF HAMMURABI RECORDING THE BUILDING OF A TEMPLE TO
SHAMASH, THE SUN GOD

The most important name of the First Dynasty of Babylon
is that of Hammurabi, and frequently one speaks of the Dynasty
of Hammurabi. But he was not the founder of this line of kings,
for he came to the throne a hundred years after his ancestors had
swept into the land. The earlier kings made successful conquests
which tended more and more to make the country Semitic, but
not until late in Hammurabi's reign was the whole country unified. The Elamites and other natural enemies were conquered,
and Marduk, originally an insignificant local god of the town of

Babylon, became the patron god of the entire country. In later days Babylon was to be ruled by foreign dynasties, but never again did it lose its Semitic quality.

The First Dynasty of Babylon lasted for about three hundred years—until 1750 B.C.—but the peace of Hammurabi's later years was short lived. The country was rich and naturally became the object of envy of the surrounding peoples. After his death trouble rained on the head of the son who succeeded him. Cities revolted, and in the south along the Persian Gulf an independent dynasty, known as the "Sealand Dynasty", established itself so thoroughly that it outlived the Dynasty of Hammurabi. About 1760 B.C. a raiding band of Hittites from the northwest entered the city of Babylon and sacked it, and out of the ensuing period of disorder the Kassites emerged as the ruling people about 1750 B.C.

THE LAW CODE OF HAMMURABI

Long after Hammurabi's death, a monument on which he had inscribed the laws of his country was taken from Babylon by a conquering Elamite who set it up in Susa, his capital city in the mountains on the border of Persia. It was there that the French found it during their excavations. Hammurabi is pictured on the monument as receiving the laws from the sun god Shamash, and below the relief and on all sides of the monument were cut in cuneiform the laws that governed conduct in Babylonia about 2000 B.C.

Quite wrongly these laws have been attributed to Hammurabi, and while some of them were undoubtedly developed during his reign, it is certain that most of them went back to Sumerian times. It is a case, then, of the king having gathered together the existing laws, some of which had experienced a long and complex history, and putting them together in one volume. The stone monument on which they are inscribed may properly be called a volume on law.

The Code of Hammurabi was the basis for part of the later Biblical Code of the Covenant. Its provisions were extensive and

(Right) THE LAW CODE OF HAMMURABI
INSCRIBED ABOUT 2000 B. C.

Showing the Sun God, Shamash, giving the laws
to the King.

Courtesy The Louvre

DETAIL OF THE CUNEIFORM INSCRIPTION
ON THE STELA

in the main were extremely humane for the times. Through them we are given a view of the everyday life of Babylonia, and, in order to gain this feeling ourselves, we shall cite a few of the more interesting provisions.

The first law said that if a man accused another of murder, but could not prove it, he himself was to be put to death. Death was the penalty for many misdemeanors. If a man stole from the temple or the palace he was to die, and the receiver of the stolen goods was to meet the same fate. The penalty for kidnapping a minor son was the same. A man who aided a slave to escape paid the same penalty. The captured thief likewise paid with his life.

There was burglary insurance in Babylonia in those days. If the thief was not captured the man who had been robbed could go before the god and swear as to his loss, and the city and governor in whose land the robbery was committed gave him full value.

All business was conducted by written contract. Even the shepherd who grazed his sheep on another man's property had to come to an agreement as to the value of the grass eaten by the animals. If a man neglected to get a receipt for money or grain owed him there was no way in which he could force the payment. Today we often hear the statement, "Put it in writing". The Babylonians four thousand years ago were keenly aware of the dangers of oral agreements, and we may believe that few of them were careless more than once.

There were barmaids who, if they gave short measure, were to be thrown into the water. If the barmaid learned that a conspiracy was being hatched in the wineshop, she was to notify the authorities or else be put to death.

An eye for an eye and a tooth for a tooth was the law of the land as we see in the following provisions: If a man destroy the eye of another man, they shall destroy his eye; if a man knock out a tooth of a man of his own rank, they shall knock out his tooth. But if a man knocked out the tooth of a common man he merely paid a fine. A man striking his superior on the cheek received sixty lashes from an oxtail whip in public. But if this same man struck a man of his own rank he paid only a fine. We see that there were grades to society and penalties were judged accordingly. If a slave hit the son of a gentleman the offender paid with the loss of an ear. On the other hand if two men got into a quarrel and one of them was hurt, the incident was closed by the other swearing that it was not intentional and then paying the physician's fee.

The physician himself must always have felt a deep sense of responsibility when he took over a case. He seems not to have been free to charge according to his whim, but received a set sum for a certain type of work. Yet, if a wealthy patient died as a result of an operation or lost the use of an eye, the surgeon paid dearly by the loss of his hand. If a slave died after an operation the surgeon was forced to substitute a slave of equal value.

There were laws on debts, marriage, bankruptcy, partnership, inheritance, adoption, and even collision of ships. These and many others make up the inscription on the black rock that Hammurabi set up in the city of Babylon about 2000 B.C. and which was carried off to Susa as a trophy of war long after the great king had died. But the laws themselves could not be stolen and many centuries later we find the Hebrews, newly come to the "Promised Land", adopting those measures which best fitted their society at the time.

Here was a people with trade by great caravan routes and sea. To facilitate this, they had banking houses and a system of credit. A tablet inscribed in cuneiform and bearing the proper credentials might travel hundreds of miles and be good for a shipment of goods simply on presentation. There were libraries containing thousands of tablets on diverse subjects, and works of art for those who appreciated them. Indeed, it is difficult to overstress the qualities of the civilization of Hammurabi's time.

THE NO-MAN'S LAND OF PALESTINE AND SYRIA

Although there are scattered references to Palestine in the Egyptian and Babylonian records, the story of the country during the third pre-Christian millennium, that is between 3000 and 2000 B.C., must be told largely from debris turned up by the archaeologist. The people were apparently of the same Mediter-

ranean physical type that had inhabited the land during the preceding period, but important trends toward civilization are to
be seen among the excavated cities of the fertile plains.

THE POTTER'S WHEEL IS INTRODUCED

Before 3000 B.C. the potter had made his jars, jugs, and bowls
by hand, and had become very skillful. But it was slow work and
not always perfect. Then, about five thousand years ago, a type of
pottery wheel on which the plastic clay could more easily be
molded and handled found its way into the country. It is likely
that the idea for this device was transmitted from the north, by
way of Syria. The wheel, which allowed the potter to spin the
raw clay on a revolving plate and quickly work it into even shaped

Courtesy The Oriental Institute of The University of Chicago

A POSSIBLE POTTERY WHEEL

The stone disk set up on an experimental rigging was found in a deposit at Megiddo in
Palestine, dating about 3000 B. C. While one Egyptian turns the disk, the other fashions
a pot. Perhaps wheel-made pottery, which was introduced to Palestine about 3000 B. C.,
was made in some such fashion.

MODEL OF A POTTER AT
WORK FROM THE TOMB OF
NANUPKAU, OLD KINGDOM
EGYPT

Courtesy The Oriental Institute of The
University of Chicago

vessels, proved a great time saver and no doubt lowered the price of pots. Peasant folk have always been quick to save a penny, or grain and vegetables as it probably was in those days, and as a result the wheel became a fixture in this civilization. The form of the wheel is unknown except through its effect on the structure of pottery. But we know that it was of simple construction and had to be turned by hand. Yet, simple as it was, it was nevertheless part of the "machine age" which was being ushered in. It was a very modest machine age when thought of in terms of today, yet invention was by that time many thousands of years old.

At the same time that the pottery wheel was introduced, the furnaces in which the pottery was baked were tremendously improved. They gave a greater hardness to the clay than had the old furnaces, and burned the vessels more evenly so that all parts of a pot tended to be of about the same quality. This improvement may be difficult for us to understand, but the new techniques must have been much appreciated by the women who did the cooking and needed vessels on which they could depend. These inventions, of course, did not lead to the making of unbreakable pots, and for that we may be truly thankful, for, as we have seen, the broken pots of antiquity have become the fossils by which we tell the age of buried cities.

EGYPTIAN AND MESOPOTAMIAN FORAYS

At all times Palestine and Syria have been the corridor leading to Egyptian forays on the Asiatic powers. At the same time Syria had to be controlled by Mesopotamia to keep the population of the upper Euphrates country from breaking loose over the fertile plains of Babylonia. Palestine and Syria have thus in a sense always been pawns in the great political game of empire in the Near East. We know little of the first interplay involving Palestine and Syria except that as early as the time of Lugalzaggisi, who was later conquered by Sargon, Mesopotamian armies marched to the Mediterranean. All the country between the Euphrates and the mountain of Lebanon on the coast was apparently in Sumerian hands. When the Akkadians came into power about 2550 B.C. this vast foreign territory fell prey to Sargon, for he too marched to the

Courtesy Neilson C. Debevoise

WATER WHEEL ON THE ORONTES RIVER AT HAMA, SYRIA

Courtesy A. T. Olmstead, *History of Assyria*

SOME OF THE FEW SURVIVING CEDARS OF LEBANON

Mediterranean and even went as far north as Asia Minor. The details of these forays are lacking, and we can only guess as to their meaning and consequences. The bare facts, however, can be interpreted to mean that Syria was highly desirable in the eyes of Mesopotamian monarchs. If nothing else, her rich fields in the valley of the Orontes River and the cedar wooded slopes of the mountains would be most attractive.

By these incursions and the resulting settlement of some of the conquerors, the high civilization of the Tigris-Euphrates country was carried westward. Perhaps it is to these beginnings that we must trace the later cultural influence on the eastern Mediterranean states.

Egypt, too, was interested in the Levant, the coastal region of Palestine and Syria. We have seen that Byblos possessed an Egyptian temple as early as the Second Dynasty. Trade between Syria and the Nile was lucrative, and the merchants of Byblos seem always to have felt that becoming Egyptianized was well worth the price if their profits were large enough.

Thus it is not surprising to find that the Egyptian army and navy, as well as merchants, gained a knowledge of the country that lay between. Fragmentary and tantalizingly meager inscriptions tell of punitive expeditions to the region beyond Sinai. The earliest known of these occurred about 2400 B.C. when, during the reign of Pepi I, troop ships were sent to quell a revolt somewhere on the Levant coast. The troops landed and, according to the inscription, every insurgent was slain.

It is undoubtedly a fact that every powerful ruler in Egypt or Mesopotamia cast envious eyes on the narrow strip of Palestine and Syria. Perhaps more of them than we suspect played an active part in the history of this territory. The study of the history of the Near East is still young enough to cause little surprise at the discovery of long hidden documents. We have only to recall that a few years back almost nothing was known of the Hittites.

SYRIANS OVERRUN EGYPT

A number of times in her history Egypt fell prey to marauding foreigners from Asia. The first clear cut instance came at the end of the Old Kingdom, about 2270 B.C., when the country had already been weakened by the spread of power among the nobles. The evidence, however, lacks many of the details that we should like to possess. The foreigners have been traced to North Syria through a peculiar type of decorated seal which they brought with them to Egypt. These seals have their counterparts in numerous specimens that have been found in Syria. But one of the mysteries regarding their movement is that such seals have never been found in contemporary deposits in Palestine. If we grant that the foreigners came from Syria, we must ask how they got to Egypt if they did not cross Palestine. It is possible that they went by sea. On the other hand it may be that evidence of their passage through Palestine still lies buried in the ruins of cities along the coast.

The invasion of these people was in any case an event of extreme importance to the history of Egypt. The advance of civilization was momentarily halted and the whole country found

itself in turmoil. But out of this condition emerged the glories
of the Middle Kingdom which we shall soon have occasion to
view.

ON THE OTHER SIDE OF THE TAURUS

The Taurus Mountains which separate Anatolia from the
region south and east have always been an effective barrier to
progress of culture. Anatolia remained a cultural backwater until
about 2000 B.C. when we find the first instances of writing.

The Copper Age lasted for about six hundred years, ending
around 2400 B.C. There was again a distinction between east and
west. The second city at Troy was related to the first, but in central Anatolia there seems to have been an incursion of new people
from the northeast. Copper became plentiful, and bronze was
also known.

The distinction between east and west remained during the
Early Bronze period which followed. Troy's outlook was to the
sea and to Europe; Central Anatolia was purely Asiatic. It is likely
that another wave from the northeast entered the land during this
period. Perhaps some of them were Indo-Europeans. We now approach the time when Anatolia took an important part in the
political interplay of the Near East. The earliest known written
records come from about 2000 B.C., at a time when Egypt and
Mesopotamia could look back on a long and venerable written
record.

AN ASSYRIAN TRADING COLONY

Later we shall hear much more of the Assyrians. Before 2000
B.C. they had established themselves in upper Mesopotamia and
had formed a small kingdom on the Tigris River. But the great
days of Assyria lay centuries ahead, and the greatest did not come
until after the time of David and Solomon.

The excavations in Anatolia have revealed the existence of a
small group of these people who left their homes on the Tigris
during the twentieth century B.C. We know they were Assyrians

because most of their names left us on tablets are made up of the names of the Assyrian gods Ashur and Adad and the goddess Ishtar. This is excellent evidence that the people came from the territory in which these deities were supposed to reside. The people described on the tablets were independent and had their own judges. They lived in a foreign quarter of the towns they inhabited, probably in much the same way that Christians, Jews, and Arabs live today in separate parts of Jerusalem. The Assyrians in Anatolia were evidently transients, there for the purpose of trading with Assyria's neighbors to the northwest.

When the tablets were first discovered they created much excitement not only among those interested in history but also among the nearby natives. It was not long, therefore, before forgeries began to appear in the market of antiques. Fortunately they were so badly done that nobody was deceived. In recent years authentic tablets of the same general type have come to the surface, and these with the others give clear-cut evidence that there was a considerable group of Assyrians in the country in the twentieth century B.C.

THE OLD HITTITE KINGDOM

There were two Hittite kingdoms, called the old and the new by modern historians. A comparatively short time ago their existence was doubted by some, and nothing was known of the kings and events of the time. Now, however, we not only know for certain that there were Hittites, but much of the detail of past periods can be filled in.

The history of the Old Kingdom begins at the time of the Assyrian merchant tablets. The country had for some time existed as a series of small disunited city-states, each with its native prince. Such a situation we have seen before, and we are not surprised in the least to learn that one of these princes made plans to join some of the cities under his personal rule. He was successful to a certain extent, but much larger plums were in store for his son Anittas. Before the end of Anittas' reign a large part of central Anatolia succumbed to his might. But then darkness falls upon the scene, for there are no records for the next few decades.

At length we learn of a king named Labarnas who began a dynasty shortly before 1800 B.C., which was destined to have considerable influence on the history of the Near East. The land became a true kingdom under his rule, and was divided into provinces for tax and administrative purposes.

As far as we know it was during the reign of his successor, Hattusilis, that the Hittites first attacked North Syria and captured the city of Aleppo which at that time was one of the strongest city-states in the region.

The kingdom reached the peak of its power under Mursilis who came to the throne about 1775 B.C. He engaged in wars at home, but was also able to enter Syria as his father before him had done. And then, after subduing this region, he made his famous raid on Babylon some four hundred and fifty miles away. This happened about 1760 B.C. and proved to be the death blow to the dynasty of Hammurabi, for Babylon was sacked and plundered, and the population were made slaves. It is one of the unaccountable facts of history that the Hittites then turned homeward carrying their booty with them, leaving Babylonia to the Kassites.

A period of misfortune for the royal family and decline for the kingdom followed, and we may bring the Old Kingdom to a close about 1650 B.C. The two succeeding centuries are ones of darkness, but we are then allowed to resume the course of Hittite history with the interesting story of the New Kingdom.

THE LION OF MARASH SHOWING HITTITE PICTOGRAPHS

BASALT PANEL FROM A TEMPLE OF THE TIME OF THUTMOSE III AT BETH SHAN. EXCAVATED BY THE UNIVERSITY OF PENNSYLVANIA.

The dog is the guardian of the temple, while the lion represents the god of pestilence and death.

THE TIME OF THE PATRIARCHS AND THE JUDGES

THE Middle Kingdom of Egypt is usually regarded as including the XIth, XIIth, and XIIIth Dynasties which lasted from about 2100 to 1700 B.C. The XIth represents for us the reaction against disorder and the rebuilding of the country. The XIIth is certainly the climax of the movement and is, moreover, the classical period of Egyptian culture. This was one of the most prosperous periods in the history of Egypt. Buildings were erected in all towns of consequence, and literature and art flourished. The XIIIth, which is much less known, stands for political decline. It came to an end at a time when another foreign people, the Hyksos, found Egypt a favorable spot to end a long journey through Asia.

The origin of the XIth Dynasty is very obscure. We know that it arose in Thebes which before that time had been an insignificant Upper Egyptian village. Now kings by the name of Intef or Mentuhotep established a rule stronger than any since the Old Kingdom. The feudal system with local lords still prevailed, and the kings had to be extremely careful how they treated them. But neither were these kings weaklings. They had welded the various elements into an Egyptian state, and the national unity is illustrated by the revived expeditions to the mines in Egypt and Sinai, commercial ventures to the Levant, and an extensive building program at Thebes.

A MODEL OF A
MIDDLE KING-
DOM BAKERY

Courtesy The Oriental
Institute of The Uni-
versity of Chicago

Amenemhet I, the first king of the XIIth Dynasty, claimed to be related to the Intef family. He overthrew the last of the Mentuhoteps and established a strong line of kings whose names were either Amenemhet or Sesostris. Their pyramid tombs, which are smaller than the largest of the Old Kingdom, lie near the Fayum, south of Cairo. The last ruler of the dynasty which lasted from 2000 to 1788 B.C. was a woman who reigned but four years. The first Amenemhet had probably been vizier under the last king of the XIth Dynasty. He was a strong willed person and carried Egypt's conquests abroad, but even he in his resulting strength was unable to subdue the powerful landed families that made up Egypt and which traced their ancestry to the VIth Dynasty lords. In all probability it was through the aid of the strongest of these that Amenemhet became king. But all he could do with the insidious feudal system was tactfully to readjust the various provinces within their normal bounds and be content with ruling a feudal state. The extent of the king's political strength is clearly shown by the fact that some of the provinces had their own priestly and governmental organizations, and dated documents from the reign of the local prince.

Amenemhet appears to have been supported by most of the south, for he deliberately founded his capital in the north near

Both photos courtesy The Oriental Institute of
The University of Chicago

Above: METAL STATUETTE OF THE
        GOD OSIRIS

Right: METAL STATUETTE OF THE
       GOD AMON-RE

Memphis. From there, commerce developed to heights never before known in Egypt, for Egyptian ships traded with the Aegean
territory, Crete, the Levant, the Red Sea, and Nubia as far as the
second cataract. Military campaigns occupied a good deal of the
following kings' time, and it is likely that Egypt had much more
to say about conditions in Palestine and Syria than has been suspected in the past.

The vizier was a powerful individual, for he supervised all the
government offices. He thus handled the taxes which were paid in
kind, and had something to do with the standing army. The great
military power, however, still lay with the local princes, and we
see again how dependent the king was on the good will of his lords.

Courtesy The Oriental Institute of The University
of Chicago

Courtesy The Oriental Institute of The University
of Chicago

THE GODDESS ISIS WITH HER SON
HORUS UPON HER LAP

HORUS AS THE HAWK

The literature of the period was of a high order, and in it we
find the first works written for amusement although such had
probably existed earlier. A Sinbad the Sailor tale was frequently
told, as were numerous other stories of a popular nature. Much
of this material is preserved to us because for the first time the
schools were teaching a uniform system of writing.

In religion there was a great change and development. When
the VIth Dynasty ended the sun god Re was supreme, but now
the local god of Thebes who had guided the destinies of the Middle
Kingdom kings gained national status. He was Amon who in time,
through a peculiar oriental way of thinking, became merged with
the sun god Re. The result in the minds of Egyptians was Amon-
Re, supreme god of the country of the Nile. There were many
local gods as well, all related in the mythological genealogies.

Osiris rose suddenly in the religious thought of the people and became the universal judge after death. He was such a strong figure that his life, death, and resurrection were enacted by local theatrical groups in much the same way that the Passion Play is presented at Oberammergau in Bavaria. Even the powerful princes fell under the sway of this god and became models of benevolence. When the crops were bad they helped support the people and created work. One of these princes says in his tomb biography, "Then came great Niles, rich in grain and all things, but I did not collect the arrears of the field". This high ethical standard was due almost entirely to Osiris. There was a definite realization that the acts of this life determined one's position after death. Osiris, in his capacity as judge of the dead, determined where the deceased were to reside, sending them either to the crocodile or lion executioners, or proclaiming them "triumphant". The latter entered the Egyptian heaven, called Yaru, where fruit was plentiful and grain grew twelve feet high.

THE SHIPWRECKED SAILOR

One of the more popular tales told by singer and story-teller during the Middle Kingdom concerned a man who had set sail from a Red Sea port for the mines in Sinai. At sea a terrific storm broke loose. The ship and all on it perished save our friend the sailor. A mighty wave cast him upon an island and there he rested, eating fruits and cucumbers, fish and fowl. Then he fashioned a fire-drill and made a burnt-offering to the gods.

After that the sailor heard the sound of thunder; trees broke and the earth quaked. He uncovered his face to find that a serpent had drawn nigh, a serpent thirty cubits long with a beard of two cubits. His body was overlaid with gold and his eyebrows were of real lapis-lazuli, a blue stone much favored by the Egyptians. The serpent said to him, "Who brought you here, little one? Tell me or you will be turned into ashes". The sailor became all but speechless, whereupon the serpent picked him up in his mouth and took him to his lair. There the sailor told of his voyage by sea, the storm, and the wave that had tossed him upon the shore.

The serpent then told him there was nothing to fear. He was to stay there four months, after which time a ship would come from Egypt to take him to his wife and children. The sailor was most grateful and promised to tell the king of the serpent's greatness. Pure and precious perfume and incense would be sent to the island, and at home sacrifice of oxen and geese would be made for the safe deliverance of the king's servant.

But the serpent laughed at him and said, "I am the prince of Punt, and the incense and perfume of which you speak come from this very island. Besides, you need not trouble to send me anything, because this island will disappear when you have departed".

Then the ship arrived and on parting the serpent gave the sailor large quantities of precious perfume and incense, giraffe tails, elephant tusks, greyhounds, monkeys, apes, and all good things. These were placed on the ship, the sailor thanked and praised the serpent, and the northward voyage began.

After two months the sailor found himself in the presence of his sovereign to whom he presented all the treasure which he had brought from the island. The king was appreciative and thanked him in the presence of the officers of the entire land, and as a reward he was given a position of great prestige in the court of the king.

THE PHYSICIAN AND SURGEON IN EGYPT

It has long been known that there was a large medical literature in the Near East before the rise of Greek medicine. We have seen that the Code of Hammurabi recognized the rights and duties of the physician. There exist also a number of Egyptian works on medicine, which, although they contain much magic, were on the whole leading to true medical knowledge. Science too, had its beginnings in magic.

The earliest known surgical treatise, on the other hand, shows an amazing amount of real medical knowledge. It is the Edwin Smith Surgical Papyrus, named for the man who purchased it in Luxor during the American Civil War. The papyrus was copied about 1600 B.C. from earlier sources, some of them older than

Courtesy New York Historical Society and The Oriental Institute

A SECTION OF THE EDWIN SMITH SURGICAL PAPYRUS DEALING WITH
HEAD WOUNDS
The importance of this document was first revealed by James H. Breasted.

the Middle Kingdom. The inscription was never finished, for
what reason we do not know. It starts with the head and pro-
ceeds systematically downward like a modern textbook on anatomy. The lower part of the body is missing in the discussion of
cases. The document consists of 48 cases, each of them classi-
fied by one of the three following remarks: 1) favorable, 2) uncertain, or 3) unfavorable. The last, which was expressed by the
phrase "an ailment not to be treated", pertained to a group of
cases which were considered by the surgeon to be hopeless.

In view of the fact that the Egyptians all but discovered circulation of the blood and the function of the heart, and came close to realizing that special parts of the brain had definite functions, we may well pay our respects to them as keen medical observers. A few cases will clarify the method followed in the Edwin Smith Surgical Papyrus.

"If thou examinest a man having a gaping wound in his head, penetrating to the bone and perforating his skull, thou shouldst palpate his wound. Shouldst thou find him unable to look at his two shoulders and his breast, and suffering from stiffness in his neck, thou shouldst say regarding him: 'One having a gaping wound in his head, penetrating to the bone, and perforating his skull, while he suffers with stiffness in his neck, an ailment which I will treat'."

The treatment is then given: "Now after thou hast stitched it, thou shouldst lay fresh meat upon his wound the first day. Thou shouldst not bind it. Put him on his customary diet until the period of his injury passes by. Thou shouldst treat it afterward with grease, honey, and lint every day, until he recovers."

Another case which was considered fatal follows: "If thou examinest a man having a crushed vertebra in his neck and thou findest that one vertebra has fallen into the next one, while he is voiceless and cannot speak; his falling head downward has caused that one vertebra crush into the next one; and shouldst thou find that he is unconscious of his two arms and his two legs because of it, thou shouldst say concerning him: 'One having a crushed vertebra in his neck; he is unconscious of his two arms and his two legs and he is speechless. An ailment not to be treated'.'

EGYPTIANS KNEW MORE THAN THE TABLE OF 2'S

By the XIIth dynasty the Egyptians had established a system of mathematics of considerable complexity which served them in accounting, land measuring, and other practical matters. This knowledge had been built up through the centuries, for as early as the Ist Dynasty the system of numbers was well established. Land measures that were used later had already come into use by the IVth Dynasty, and by the end of the Old Kingdom simple fractions of the bushel were in common use. Egyptian fractions were very cumbersome, for with the exception of 2/3 and ¾, none had a numerator higher than 1. Thus, 63/64 was written ½ + ¼ + ⅛ + 1/16 + 1/32 + 1/64.

About the time of the XIIth dynasty, mathematics had progressed to the point where numbers could be squared, and an understanding of the square root existed. The cube and cube root are not indicated. But the area of a rectangle and triangle could be computed with little error. The circle was conceived to be a square with sides equal to 8/9 the diameter of the circle. To obtain the area the Egyptian mathematician then multiplied 8/9 D by 8/9 D, in doing which he made an error of only about ½ of 1 percent when compared with the true area of the circle. This formula was used to ascertain the contents of granaries which were cylindrical in form. The volume of such a granary was correctly seen to be equal to the area of the base multiplied by the height.

Egyptian mathematics grew out of practical needs such, for instance, as the laying out of the Great Pyramid, or measuring a pile of grain which lay upon the ground. Nowhere is there any indication that Egyptians were interested in theoretical problems.

THE COMING OF ARYAN SPEAKING PEOPLES

While Egypt was approaching and passing the heights of prosperity during the Middle Kingdom, a dark cloud appeared over the horizon in Asia. The XIIIth dynasty, which was mainly restricted to the south, perhaps sensed little of its meaning. But the XIVth dynasty, which had set itself up in the Delta soon after the end of the XIIth dynasty, must have seen the danger more clearly. A host of Aryan speaking peoples were leaving their homes north or northeast of Syria and Mesopotamia and were bound for the pleasant valleys and rich cities of civilization. But before telling of these people let us first inquire into the meaning of "Aryan".

The word "Aryan" is commonly misused in everyday speech, being incorrectly understood as a racial term. Aryan is actually a linguistic expression which includes the large group of Indo-European languages both ancient and modern. Those who speak English, German, French, Italian, Rumanian, Greek or Sanscrit, among many others, speak Aryan tongues. The only people who may rightly be called Aryan are those who spoke the original Aryan language, but since that early time there has been so much inter-racial mixture that Aryan has lost all meaning as an expression of race.

Aryan speaking people began drifting into Anatolia during the third millennium, and the language of the Hittites has proved to be Indo-European, whether written in cuneiform or hieroglyphic. This has been among the most astonishing discoveries made in the field of ancient history since the Great War. Those who know Latin recognize many familiar forms in Hittite.

The Aryans who first entered Anatolia probably came from the northeast. Some authorities believe that the plains of southern Russia were the original home of these people who soon were to rock the Semitic world and in time take it for its very own.

There are also indications of Aryan influence in Mesopotamia, for the Kassites, who took the throne of Babylon after the Dynasty of Hammurabi had collapsed, had worshipped Aryan gods before reaching the plains. They came from the northern Zagros Mountains, but as soon as they reached civilization they were quickly absorbed by the Semites.

About the same time a related people were moving on Egypt, the Hyksos or so-called Shepherd Kings. Their history is all too vague, yet we know that they established themselves in the Delta by about 1730 B.C. at the expense of the XIVth dynasty. There they conducted their government with considerable success for a century and a half, at times drawing heavy tribute from the south where native princes did their best to keep up a semblance of kingship. The Hyksos constitute the XVth and XVIth dynasties.

The native XVIIth, which arose at Thebes in the south long before Hyksos rule was completed, became strong enough in time to drive the Hyksos out of Middle Egypt. A few years later, about 1580 B.C., the first king of the XVIIIth dynasty succeeded in

Courtesy Muller,
Egyptological Researches

crushing the hated foreigners at their capital in the Delta and driving the remainder back into Palestine.

But who were the Hyksos? There are indications that some of them came from the steppes of southern Russia or Turkestan, and as such they may have spoken an Aryan tongue. The Hyksos brought the horse to Egypt, and its name can be traced to an Indo-European origin. But there are no known Hyksos names that can be similarly traced. We may only suppose that the Indo-Euro-peans among the Hyksos rapidly lost their native language when they came into contact with the peoples along the Mediterranean.

There were other elements among the Hyksos, Semitic being the most prominent. And the movement which culminated in the establishment of two dynasties in Egypt may also have picked up Hittites along the way. It is plain, also, that a people from eastern Anatolia called Hurrians, whose language was unrelated to any we have here mentioned, were among the composite group that came to be known as Hyksos. These are the newest people to make themselves known from the lost cities of the Near East, for it is but a matter of a few years since the Hurrians became known and were identified with the Horites of the Bible. Another of the lost peoples of antiquity have been found and take their place with the Hittites, Cretans, and others whose effect on the history of the world was long unsuspected.

The Hyksos, then, included Aryans, Semites, Hurrians, and quite possibly Hittites—a group of composite people who made a lasting impression on the minds of Egyptians for many centuries afterward. These were scattered through Syria and Palestine before destiny placed some of them on the throne of Egypt. Those who went to the land of the Nile became Egyptianized, and some of their kings took good Egyptian names. If Hyksos parents had given names in keeping with the original languages they or their ancestors had spoken, how much easier would be the problem of the Hyksos.

This is the period of Abraham and Isaac, Jacob and Joseph. Their history, as told in the Old Testament, can fit quite well into the Hyksos background. They were Semites, some of whom went down to Egypt, and the story of Joseph as vizier to the king of Egypt could hardly fit anywhere else. A Hyksos king might well have welcomed a man of Joseph's caliber, especially if he too were a Hyksos. And while there are other records of Semitic groups settling in Egypt, we can hardly fail to see that the Hyksos period would have been an exceedingly appropriate time for Jacob and his sons to migrate to the Delta. In general, then, the biblical account of the patriarchs merges into the historical background.

Bronze had been known long before this in Anatolia and Mesopotamia, but it was the Hyksos who brought the secret of the alloy to Syria, Palestine, and Egypt. Bronze is a mixture of copper and tin, and when properly smelted produces a metal which is harder than copper and which can be cast more easily. The new metal was rapidly adopted in the countries of the eastern Mediterranean, and the perfection attained by the metal-smith is ample testimony that culture had taken another long step forward. The Hyksos are often regarded as barbarians, but this is largely an echo of the Egyptian verdict. Actually they lived in a high type of civilization which recognized the benefits of organized living. They practiced commerce by land and sea. Accounts had to be kept, and the writing that the Hyksos in Palestine used was a progressive alphabet which had just been invented at the mines in Sinai. We recall that the Egyptians also called the Greek barbarians. The Hyksos may have been fighters, but they were not wholly barbarian.

SODOM AND GOMORRAH

The story of the destruction of Sodom and Gomorrah, the most famous of the cities of the Dead Sea plain, is known to all. The Lord promised Abraham that if ten just men could be found in the wicked city of Sodom it would be spared. But only Lot and his family qualified, and they were told to flee the city before Sodom and Gomorrah should be destroyed by brimstone and fire. They were warned, moreover, not to look back lest they be turned to salt. Lot and his wife with their two daughters then hastily left the city, but Lot's wife turned back in a moment of curiosity and was turned to salt. Many have been the stories that peculiar erosional salt formations around the Dead Sea, called the Sea of Lot by the Moslems, actually represent the remains of that venerable woman.

But what of the cities that perished? Troy and Mycenae of Greek legend have been found, as have other cities famous in legend and history. Archaeologists have thought at times that the cities lay at the north end of the Dead Sea, but now there is almost general agreement that they must have existed to the south. However, the search for the lost cities may never be successful, since it is altogether likely that they now lie beneath the rising salty waters in the shallow embayment at the lower end of the sea. Aviators claim to have seen ruins in the water, but this has never been verified. Yet we may be certain that any ancient settlements in this region were built, not upon rock, but on sinking bottom lands in a valley which still slips whenever there is an earthquake. Possibly that was the fate of Sodom and Gomorrah.

THE STORY OF THE ALPHABET

It was long believed that the Phoenicians, those famous merchants and sailors who lived in the busy seaports of the Syrian coast, had invented the alphabet. The fact is clear that the Greeks borrowed their alphabet from the Phoenicians, and after making certain modifications passed it on to the Romans. We in turn took our alphabet from the Latins. Now we know that the Phoenicians, too, at an earlier time, had borrowed this important mechanism of civilization from still another people, for, strange as it seems, the alphabet arose as a practical means of writing in the Sinai Peninsula about 1800 B.C.

Long before this the Egyptians had an alphabet of 25 signs, but in addition they used a large group of complicated hieroglyphs which stood for combinations of two or three of the simple alphabetic sounds. The Egyptians used their alphabet every day, yet never seem to have realized that they had an alphabet. Had they used it alone, their writing system would have been infinitely more simple.

During the XIIth Dynasty Egyptian kings sent numerous expeditions to the mines in Sinai. The natives who served the expeditions spoke a Semitic language quite different from Egyptian. One of them, perhaps a mine foreman, learned the principle of the Egyptian alphabet and applied it to his own language. He imitated Egyptian hieroglyphs but gave them a Semitic value in the same way that we might take Egyptian signs and give them arbitrary English values. Thus he regarded the head of an ox as

SINAITIC	CANAANITE-PHOENICIAN	GREEK				LATIN			HEBREW
ꝑ ꝗ	⪤ ⪦	A A ⅄ α				A A ⅄ ɑ ɑ			א
▢ ▢ ▢	ꝯ ꝯ	ⵀ B B β				β B B b			ב
L L	⌐	7 Γ Γ ∫ Υ				< C {C Gçğ			ג
⍙ ⍙	◿ ◹	Δ Δ ◿ δ				Ꭰ D δδ d			ד
ⵁ	Ɏ	⵵ E ϶ ε				ⵤ E ϶ e			ה
⟍o	Ɏ	ϥ ΥϜ ϝ				ⵤ F ϝ f			ו
= (?)	⊐⊏	‡ I Z Ꮓϛ				‡ Z z			ז
ⵁ 8	⊟ ⵂ	⊟ H H ʜ η				⊟ H ʜ h			ח
	⊗	⊕ ⊙ Ꮎ θ ϑ				⊗			ט
ⵝ ⵟ	ⵜ	ⵞ Ɩ Ɩ ι				Ɩ Ɩ i j			י
✝ ⵥ	Ɏ Ɏϖ	⵵ K Ⳗ Κ κ				K K k			כ
9Ϭⵦ	ⅽⅼ	ⵠ Λ λ λ				ⵥ L ⵑ l			ל
⵰⵰	ⵯ ⵰	ⵀ ⵀ ⵰ μ μ				ⵀ ⵀ ω m			מ
ⵑ	⵶ ⵨	⵴ N Ν ν ν				⵴ N n n			נ
⟺ ⟹	ⵤ ⵥ	‡ ⵣ ⵣ ⵥ				⊞ ✝ ✕ ✕			ס
◌ ◌	∘∘	∘ O O o o				O			ע
◻	ⵝⵝⵜ	ⵑ Γ ππ ϖ				P P p			פ
8 ∞	ⵟⵟⵟ	⵴ M ꝛ				⵴			צ
⵰	φφφ	φ ϙ				ϙ Q q q			ק
ⵀⵀⵀ	⵭	ⵕ P Ρ ϱϱ				ⵢ R ⵔr			ר
ⵓ	W	ⵦ ⵦ C ⵜ σ				ⵤ S ∫∫s			ש
✝	✕	Τ Τ Τ τ				Τ Τ ⵒ t			ת

Courtesy Martin Sprengling, modified after Butin

DIAGRAM SHOWING DEVELOPMENT OF THE ALPHABET

aleph, and the Egyptian hieroglyph that looked like the plan of a house he called *beth,* because *beth* in his language meant house. Our unknown native of Sinai continued this process until he had a sign for every consonant in his language. It did not occur to him to formulate signs for the vowels because the scribes with whom he talked wrote only consonants. That was the way in which Egyptian was constructed, and because of that the Canaanites, Phoenicians, Hebrews, Ethiopians and others who learned of the alphabet through Sinai, never used vowels.

It was probably in the eleventh century before our era that the Greeks borrowed the Phoenician alphabet. The shapes, names, and order of letters were taken over bodily. *Aleph* became *alpha,* and *beth* was pronounced *beta.* Semitic *gimel* was changed to *gamma* in Greek, and *daleth* became *delta.* In this manner arose the word "alphabet"—*aleph-beth* to *alpha-beta.* The original meaning was ox-house.

The Greeks improved the Semitic alphabet in a number of ways. They introduced vowels by appropriating signs for Semitic sounds that did not occur in Greek. The vowels *a, e, i,* and *o* were derived in this fashion. *Upsilon* was invented and placed at the end of the Phoenician alphabet. And since there were more *s* sounds in Phoenician than in Greek some of these letters were used for peculiarly Greek sounds. In addition to all this, the Greeks invented characters for the *phi, chi, psi,* and *xi* sounds.

In this manner the original alphabet was adopted by an Aryan speaking people and passed on to us. But credit for its invention must go to that unknown native of Sinai who about 1800 B.C. got his inspiration from Egyptian hieroglyphs.

THE EGYPTIAN EMPIRE—FROM 1580-1350 B.C.

About the year 1580 B.C. Ahmose drove the Hyksos from Egypt. Two hundred and twenty years later the royal family line of the XVIIIth dynasty died in the period of weakness following the reign of Tutankhamon. But the years between were rich in accomplishment for the group of kings most of whom were named Amenhotep and Thutmose. In this family we see such

Courtesy Gaddis and Seif

KARNAK
Sphinxes before the first pylon of the Temple of Amon, looking toward the Nile.

varied and interesting characters as the energetic warrior, Thutmose III, and the religious zealot, Amenhotep IV, who let the empire slip from between his fingers and changed his name to Akhenaton in honor of the god Aton whom he had chosen as his own.

The XVIIIth dynasty is the period of Egypt's first greatness as a world empire. Conquests in Nubia and Asia by the first kings provided wealth for a great building period at home, especially at Thebes, now the political and religious capital of Egypt. The great temple of the god Amon at Karnak had been started during the Middle Kingdom, but now it received new and monumental treatment. Huge gates, called pylons, arose, and behind them were erected buildings for worship of the god of Thebes. Pylons and buildings were covered with carved reliefs and inscriptions. Many of the latter consist of religious formulae, but on others are accounts of foreign campaigns and booty and prisoners taken for the glory of Amon. Obelisks similar to the one now standing in Central Park, New York, or on the embankment in London, were quarried in one piece and brought over a hundred miles down the Nile and set up in Karnak. The state of the treasury was excellent.

QUEEN HATSHEPSUT BUILDS A TEMPLE BELOW THE CLIFFS

Egypt's ruler at the beginning of the fifteenth century was a strong willed woman named Hatshepsut. No wars are recorded for her reign. Instead, she seems to have expended most of her efforts in a great building program and in keeping the young Thutmose III off the throne. In both of these matters she was extremely successful for a long time. Hatshepsut set up two obelisks at Karnak, and in other parts of Egypt she built temples. But the building triumph of her reign was the delightful temple of Deir el-Bahari set in a semi-circular area at the foot of the awe-inspiring cliffs across the river from Karnak. Behind a spur of this cliff lies the Valley of the Kings in which the great ones of the period were buried.

Few forget their first impression of Hatshepsut's architectural gem nestling at the base of the towering cliff. Built in terraces which lead successively toward the sanctuary cut deep into the rock at the rear, it has appealed to many Westerners as the perfect Egyptian structure. An avenue of sphinxes led to a lower court, which in turn gave way to the central court reached by means of an inclined ramp. At the back of both these courts is a series of colonnades on whose walls are depicted events of prime interest in the reign of Hatshepsut. The upper court is reached by another ramp, and at this level one arrives at the rock-cut sanctuary and a number of chapels on either side of the pillared court.

Among the reliefs on the walls we see ships bringing two obelisks from the quarries at Aswan. Another shows the process of their erection and dedication. The walls of one of the colonnades are devoted to scenes commemorating a trading expedition to the

MARBLE STATUE OF QUEEN HAT-
SHEPSUT FROM HER CHAPEL AT
DEIR EL-BAHARI

ONE OF THE OBELISKS ERECTED BY
QUEEN HATSHEPSUT AT KARNAK IN
THE FIFTEENTH CENTURY

land of Punt which was somewhere on the Red Sea coast. A village of this far-off land is depicted showing beehive huts built
over water in the midst of palm and incense trees. The natives
required ladders to reach their homes. We see the Egyptian fleet
arriving and being laden with a rich cargo of merchandise. The
queen's envoy is received by the prince of Punt who loads him
down with precious gifts. One learns here how the Puntites
looked, and then the fleet returns to Egypt with its spoil which
the queen dedicates to the god Amon.

Hatshepsut's temple was never completed. She was succeeded
by Thutmose III whom she had been so successful in keeping
away from the throne, and he in turn attempted to obliterate the
memory of the woman who had been so hateful to him. At Deir
el-Bahari he began to remove the name and figure of the queen
which appeared many times in the reliefs on the walls. But his

Courtesy James Henry Breasted, Jr. and The Oriental Institute

THE FAMOUS UNFINISHED OBELISK IN THE GRANITE QUARRIES AT ASSUAN, EGYPT

The obelisk was abandoned when a flaw developed near the end of the shaft. Had the shaft been completed it would have been the largest obelisk ever cut in Egypt.

Courtesy MacGillivray

HARD STONE BALLS USED IN QUARRYING AROUND THE UNFINISHED OBELISK

Courtesy Gaddis and Seif

DEIR EL-BAHARI, QUEEN HATSHEPSUT'S TEMPLE AT THE FOOT OF THE WESTERN THEBAN CLIFFS

workmen were careless at times and left tell-tale traces. In some cases Thutmose ordered that his own name and figure be inserted. The result was confusing indeed, and the unity of the inscriptions was further disturbed when late in the XVIIIth dynasty Amen-hotep IV, the devoted adherent of the Aton, destroyed all reference to Amon. The mutilated inscriptions and reliefs were left in this condition until Ramses II (1292-1225 B.C.) restored them, but with very poor workmanship. No changes were made on the temple until after the time of Alexander the Great when a few unimportant additions were made. After Christianity had been introduced to Egypt, a group of Coptic monks founded a monastery in the temple. The chambers that Hatshepsut had built were converted into chapels, and all representations on the walls which were considered heathen were crudely defaced.

Courtesy Gaddis & Seif

AN ATTEMPT TO OBLITERATE HATSHEPSUT'S FIGURE AND NAME FROM
A RELIEF IN HER TEMPLE

That is the story of the temple which Hatshepsut dedicated to the god Amon. In recent years the Metropolitan Museum of New York has done much to restore it to its original state without changing any of the writing or carving left on the walls.

THUTMOSE III, THE WARRIOR-KING

We know too little of the relationship between Thutmose and Hatshepsut. For a time they were joint rulers of the country, but the queen seems to have held the upper hand. Nevertheless, Thutmose considered that his reign began in 1501 B.C., the very year that Hatshepsut became queen. We must, however, believe that he did not become king in fact until the queen died in 1479 B.C. At the same time her adviser and architect, Senmut, disappeared most mysteriously.

Then, with the pent-up emotions of many years bursting their bounds, the new king set out on a series of devastating marches against the revolting countries of Asia which had not seen an Egyptian army for many years. The first expeditions by land across the Sinai Desert secured the territory nearest Egypt as well as the important seaports of the Syrian coast. With these well in hand, he was enabled to lead later expeditions by sea and thus save precious time for warfare with the more inland peoples. But each year his troops returned to Egypt before the heavy winter rains set in. The absence of the mass of Egyptian troops, and especially the dominating figure of the king, caused some of the more daring of the conquered to revolt, but they paid dearly when the king returned again. Thutmose made seventeen campaigns in all during the twenty-two years that he ruled alone, and at the end of that period Egypt could fairly claim sovereignty over Palestine and Syria. Neighboring kings sent gifts as tokens of their respect for the martial king of Egypt. Among these were the kings of Assyria, Babylonia, Anatolia, and the island of Cyprus. The land of Mitanni, which lay in the great bend of the Euphrates, was conquered and although it later revolted, its rise as a nation was delayed until after the death of Thutmose. From the countries that had been subdued there was collected a yearly tribute calcu-

Courtesy Cairo Museum

PORTRAIT OF THUTMOSE III WHO DEFEATED THE
ASIATIC COALITION AT MEGIDDO IN 1479 B. C.

lated to tax the offending nations that they might realize the benefits of peace with the great country on the Nile. Tribute after all
was better than appropriation by the soldiers of the king.

Thus the energetic Thutmose welded together an empire
which extended from well up the Nile in Nubia to the Euphrates
in Asia. Only in the reign of his son, Amenhotep II, did Egypt

possess greater holdings, but the basis for this slight expansion had
been provided by the tireless years of conflict during which Thutmose was the most respected and powerful man on earth.

THE BATTLE OF MEGIDDO

Thutmose ordered that the story of his wars be inscribed on
the walls of the temple at Karnak. The scribe who was probably
also a priest of Amon began very well and gave a tolerably full
record of the first campaign in the year 1479 B.C. But as he
progressed he lost interest in the details of warfare and devoted
himself mainly to recording where his majesty had gone and how
much had been brought back for the temple of Amon. Of the
later campaigns we learn in full measure of the horses and chariots, gold and silver vessels, and other valuables that the army had
taken from the enemy. It is really only the account of the first
campaign that can be said to give even the skeleton of any of
Thutmose's many battles.

The Battle of Megiddo was the first engagement of the first
campaign. Thutmose and his troops crossed the one hundred and

Courtesy The Oriental Institute of The University of Chicago

A MODERN CARAVAN EMERGING FROM THE PASS THROUGH WHICH
THUTMOSE III AND HIS ARMY MARCHED ON THEIR WAY TO SURPRISE
THE ENEMY AT MEGIDDO

sixty mile waste of the Sinai Desert in nine days and then proceeded up the coast until they reached a point opposite the pass
leading to the city of Megiddo in northern Palestine. Here Thutmose called a council and asked his officers what they had in mind
to do. The enemy included all the important states of northern
Palestine and Syria, and their army was collected at Megiddo prepared to fight the Egyptians. There were three roads which would
lead eventually to Megiddo, standing on the southwest side of the
Plain of Esdraelon. Two of these were indirect; the third was
narrow but led straight to Megiddo which guarded it at the other
end. Thutmose listened to his officers argue for the first two, but
the king characteristically said that they could do as they wished.
He was going to take the direct pass and would personally lead
any who wished to follow him.

Early in the morning Thutmose began the march and by about
one o'clock emerged from the pass to see Megiddo looming up
ahead. At this time his rear had not yet entered the heart of the
narrow defile and he therefore waited until all could assemble by
the brook south of the fortress. The Asiatics had lost a wonderful
opportunity to destroy their foes as the latter went single file
through the pass.

By the next morning Thutmose had swung a wing of his army
to the west of Megiddo, and this with the wing that had remained
south of the city then closed in on the Asiatic defenders, who by
this time had taken a position between the Egyptians and the city.
The first Egyptian charge was so effective that the enemy line
broke and ran headlong for the city leaving the horses and chariots
of gold and silver. The gates of the city had been closed and the
demoralized enemy had to be pulled over the wall by means of
clothing which was lowered for them. The ringleader, the king
of Kadesh, as well as the king of Megiddo, thus saved their lives
and presumably escaped through the northern gate, for we hear
nothing more of their whereabouts.

After the rout the Egyptian soldiers gave themselves up to
plunder. Horses and chariots, living prisoners, and hands cut
from the dead were at length brought into the presence of the
king. But he was grieved and seriously annoyed that his troops

AN AIRVIEW OF THE ANCIENT MOUND OF KADESH, SYRIA
Modern town on the mound and the Orontes river in the background.

had stopped for booty when they might have captured the city. In rebuke he said to them, "Had ye captured this city afterward, behold, I would have given many offerings to Re this day; because every chief of every country that has revolted is within it; and because it is the capture of a thousand cities, this capture of Megiddo".

Thutmose then ordered that the city be surrounded by an inclosure of earth and cut trees. He would besiege Megiddo until it surrendered. Sentinels stood continually on guard and no foe escaped after the inclosure had been finished. After about five months the besieged city opened its gates and surrendered, and the chiefs came forward bearing gifts with which to placate the great king Thutmose.

The spoil taken from the captured city gives an idea of the wealth of Palestine and Syria at this time. Included were nine hundred and twenty-four chariots, over two thousand horses, two hundred suits of armor, five hundred bows, the beautiful tent and rich household furnishings of the king of Kadesh, besides large quantities of gold and silver. Thousands of head of cattle, as well as the harvest of the nearby fields, also fell to the lot of the Egyptians.

Megiddo had been thoroughly tamed and never again during the reign of Thutmose did northern Palestine cause him any trouble. Future revolts were centered around Kadesh in Syria, but we have seen that in the end Thutmose was ruler over all of Palestine and Syria.

It is more than likely that battles had been fought before this on the plain of Megiddo, the Armageddon of later times and the proverbial battleground of the ages. There followed others of which we know. During the World War the same pass, by which Thutmose had surprised the Asiatics, became the means by which Lord Allenby's cavalry bottled up the fleeing Turks in the historic plain, and caused their commanding officer to dash hurriedly out of Nazareth in the middle of the night clad in his pajamas.

THE TALE OF THE CAPTURE OF JOPPA

A tale concerning Joppa probably has no historical foundation as far as its details are concerned, but it proved popular to the Egyptians who repeated it long after the death of Thutmose. For us it recalls the legendary story of the wooden horse of Troy.

Joppa is the present day Jaffa, seaport of Jerusalem, and during Thutmose's reign it was besieged by the Egyptians. The king was in Egypt, so all plans lay with the general who is the hero. He had been unable to take Joppa by storm and decided to see whether the same result might not be obtained by ruse. The prince of the city was asked to attend a conference and there, out of sight of his people, he was entertained in royal fashion. But while under the influence of drink, which the Egyptians had given him, he was struck on the head with a club and fell down senseless.

Then the general ordered that five hundred sacks be brought, into which were placed two hundred soldiers equipped with handcuffs and fetters. Five hundred others were commanded to carry the five hundred sacks and were told, "When ye be come into the city, let out your comrades, and lay hold on all the people that are in the city and put the fetters on them".

The charioteer of the prince of Joppa, who had been waiting for his lord, was then told to go to the wife of the prince and say that the Egyptians had surrendered, and here in the sacks was the booty which the prince had taken. The charioteer did as he was bid, the city gates were thrown open, and the soldiers carrying the sacks, and those released from them, fell on the unsuspecting city and captured it for the glory of Amon and the great king Thutmose.

Courtesy Gaddis and Seif

LUXOR TEMPLE

Note obelisk in front of pylon at left.

AMENHOTEP THE MAGNIFICENT

Amenhotep III was a great grandson of Thutmose III and grandson of Amenhotep II who had advanced the boundary of the empire to Mitanni. His father had married a Mitannian princess, perhaps because he saw the inherent weakness of Egyptian control in Asia. When his father died at the early age of thirty, Amenhotep III inherited a vast empire which extended from the Euphrates to the Third Cataract of the Nile. In his earlier years as king he showed some energy, penetrating Nubia farther than any king before him. But as time went on he settled down to the life of a glamorous and exotic oriental king.

Amenhotep was early dominated by the will of his remarkable wife, Tiy, a woman of unroyal and otherwise obscure background. It is true that the king had other wives as well, among them a

Courtesy Gaddis and Seif

LUXOR TEMPLE
Showing a curious combination of Egyptian Empire, early Christian,
and Moslem architecture.

daughter of the king of Mitanni, but Tiy remained throughout
her life a woman of tremendous will and apparently considerable
charm. It was unusual enough for a royal queen to be continuously
named in documents, but Tiy soon became used to such distinction.

During the early part of the reign the empire was secure, and
for once the troublesome states of Syria were quiet. Egyptian
officials collected the taxes there and elsewhere, and Egypt became
exceedingly wealthy. Under such conditions it is perhaps only
natural that a king of the temperament of Amenhotep should
build up a court which in its brilliance may well be compared with
that of Louis XV. The finest artists in the country were engaged
on a host of projects which extended far up the Nile as well as
across the desert into Syria. Colossal additions were made at
Karnak, and one of the finest temples in Egypt was placed in

Courtesy Gaddis and Seif

THE TEMPLE OF AMON AT KARNAK LOOKING ACROSS THE SACRED LAKE

construction to the south in the present city of Luxor. The intervening mile and a half was beautified by avenues of rams cut
from stone, and in addition, an artificial lake, horse-shoe in shape,
was dug in the precincts of Karnak. But this was just on the east
side of the river.

On the opposite side near the line where vegetation gives way
to desert, Amenhotep erected a large mortuary temple in front
of which were placed two obelisks and the two colossi, which to
the classical world of a later day, were among the wonders of the
earth. These immense statues of the king were originally, before
the crowns fell off, almost seventy feet high, and while today they
are not things of beauty they nevertheless excite our interest for
their connection with the fabulous king Amenhotep and the
traditions of classical times. During the Roman imperial epoch
they were thought to be statues of Memnon who had slain Anti-

LUXOR TEMPLE AND THE NILE

lochus during the Trojan war and who in turn had been killed by
Achilles. The northern colossus is the famous singing statue which
in Roman times was said to have given forth musical notes at sunrise.

Between the mortuary temple and the western cliffs Amenhotep built himself and his queen a luxurious palace in bright
colors. It was filled with the finest art of the empire. Tapestries
hung on the walls, and the floors were painted with scenes from
wild life. Wonderful vessels of gold and silver, bearing designs of
exquisite workmanship, graced the tables. The front of the palace
was decorated with flagstaves bearing pennants, and above the
entrance was a comfortable cushioned balcony surrounded by
nicely worked columns.

The riches, pouring into Egypt, also allowed Amenhotep to set
aside a quarter nearby for his queen. Here he excavated a lake a
mile long and over a thousand feet wide, the sluices of which he
opened on the occasion of the twelfth anniversary of his corona-
tion. It was a festive day when the king and queen sailed out together on the royal barge to the accompaniment of music from
the royal band on shore.

But trouble was brewing. While the king had been building
his beautiful capital, a work which he often left for the pleasures
of hunting wild cattle or lions, the Hittites had become organized

sufficiently to invade Mitanni. From this time on, until they disappeared about 1200 B.C., the Hittites were to be a constant thorn in the side of Egypt. This was the period of the New Hittite Kingdom which had emerged from the darkness of two centuries. And in the reign of Amenhotep began the long series of letters written in cuneiform, telling the king of the dangerous state of affairs in the Asiatic states controlled by Egypt. The Hittites also attacked northern Syria and thus challenged Egypt directly. The king sent troops but failed to go himself. The trouble was halted for the time being, but Egypt's day as empire was fading. The energy of former kings was needed in such circumstances, but a rapidly aging king sat upon the throne. To add to his troubles a new element of disorder was making itself felt in Syria. The Habiru, whose relationship to the Hebrews we shall presently see, had

Courtesy the Oriental Institute of The University of Chicago

THE COLOSSI OF MEMNON ERECTED BY AMENHOTEP III
Behind these once stood a magnificent temple, built by the same king.

A FOWLING SCENE FROM A TOMB IN THEBES
Dating to either the time of Thutmose IV or Amenhotep III. The cat is seen retrieving a bird.

joined in the attack on Egyptian rule in Asia, and, to cap the situation, the more powerful of the cities belonging to Egypt began fighting among themselves for increased territory.

Amenhotep's efforts to stem the tide were futile, and when he passed away in 1375 B.C. after a reign of almost thirty-six years he left a sadly disorganized situation to his son who on ascending the throne bore the name Amenhotep IV.

AKHENATON, THE HERETIC KING

Had the new king been a figure of the caliber of Thutmose III, we may say with little doubt that the course of Egyptian history would have been altogether different. Instead, he was a dreamer, completely impractical as far as statecraft was concerned. His intimate group was composed of Queen Mother Tiy, his own queen Nefretiti who may have been of Asiatic descent, and his favorite priest, the husband of his childhood nurse. Doubtless he had been strongly influenced by the life of his father's court in which the seeds of social rebellion were already to be observed. While revolt was rising he gave himself up to religious philosophy and contemplation. The search for truth was of infinitely greater importance than affairs of state.

The disc of the sun shining in the heavens became for him the essence of all that was worth while, and it was soon established that the Aton should be the sole official god. We may well imagine the effect that this proclamation had on the existing priesthoods, especially that of the powerful Amon. For generations the revenues of war and peace had supported the holdings of the great god of Thebes, and had moreover been kind to that large body of men who ministered to Amon. From highpriesthood down, there was immediate rebellion and deep feeling against the interloper who at a stroke had supplanted the religious structure of centuries, for we can easily see that the Aton would now have recourse to wealth that had formerly been used for the glorification of Amon.

Amenhotep built a temple to the Aton between Karnak and Luxor and, in the fury of the feud between Amon and Aton, ordered that the name of Amon be obliterated wherever it oc-

A RELIEF OF AKHENATON
showing him and his wife, Nefretiti, worshiping before the Aton disk and its life giving rays.

A PORTRAIT OF QUEEN NEFRETITI FOUND AT TELL EL-AMARNA

BIRDS AND ANIMALS FROM A PAINTED PAVEMENT FROM THE PALACE OF AKHENATON AT TELL EL-AMARNA

AIRVIEW OF TELL EL-AMARNA
Showing excavated portions. The Nile lies in the background.

curred. Amon had been the patron god of Egypt since the Middle
Kingdom, and his name appeared widespread through the temples.
Even the Amon element in the name of his father Amenhotep III
was expunged, and finally the king took action on his own name
which was the same. Thus Amenhotep IV became Akhenaton,
which means "Spirit of Aton".

But even this was not enough. The residence of Aton in Thebes
lay in the midst of buildings and gardens associated with Amon.
Akhenaton decided that the Aton should have a city of its own,
and in his sixth year we find him established three hundred miles
down the river at Akhetaton, meaning "Horizon of Aton". The
ruins of this city which have been excavated are known as Tell
el-Amarna. Akhetaton lay in a bay in the cliffs near the river
and rapidly took on the aspects of a national capital. The court
came here and worshipped the Aton for political reasons if nought
else.

The town and adjacent territory were deeded to Aton by
royal decree "forever and ever," and specific revenues were allotted for its upkeep. Three temples to the Aton were erected, one for

Queen Mother Tiy, one for the princess Beketaton which means "Maid-servant of Aton", and the third for the king himself, while around the temples arose the palace and the estates of the nobles who had deserted Thebes. The Aton breathed his spirit into all the functions and life of the city through the dominant will of the king.

The mysterious qualities of Aton that so thoroughly molded the life of the king may perhaps be summed up in the word "truth". The old religious philosophy of many gods was not satis-factory, and here in the fourteenth century, long before the He-brews had begun to worship one God, an Egyptian was doing that very thing. He had grasped the idea that a single power ruled not only the destinies of Egypt, but also those of Nubia and Syria and the rest of the world. The birds and beasts as well as man owed their lives to this god's beneficence; all nature revealed the existence of the Aton. The Hymn to the Aton, which shows many parallels with the one hundred and fourth Psalm, is filled with the deep-seated thought that life and death are subject to the goodness of the Aton.

The spirit of truth invaded all aspects of life in the capital. Artists depicted what they saw and forsook the traditions of the guild that had stamped the works of their predecessors. Realism became the rule and even the king, who was queer looking physi-cally, was depicted as he was. Convention was dropped, and in its place stood a healthy attitude toward nature. The king appeared frequently in public in the company of his wife, Nefretiti, and their daughters, and the population came to know them from personal observation. In this, another of the once treasured tradi-tions of royalty was shattered.

Meanwhile the storm that we saw gathering in Asia grew blacker, encouraged by Akhenaton's lack of interest in military affairs.

EGYPT LOSES PALESTINE AND SYRIA

During the reign of Akhenaton's father, trouble had begun in the Asiatic possessions of Egypt, and the lax attitude of the court of Aton merely made matters worse from the empire point of

A TELL EL–AMARNA LETTER

This clay tablet written in cuneiform was part of the personal correspondence between Tushratta, King of Mitanni, and Amenhotep III. In it Tushratta announced the dispatch of gifts and also requested gold in return for his daughter whom Amenhotep had married.

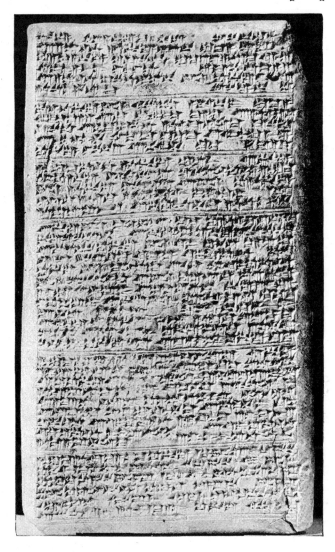

view. This we know from a large group of tablets written in cuneiform which were discovered in 1888 in the ruins of Akhenaton's city. These included the letters to Amenhotep III and Akhenaton written by the kings of Babylonia, Assyria, and Mitanni, and by Egyptian vassals in Palestine and Syria. These messages, giving as they do a detailed picture of events, constitute one of the most important bodies of ancient literature that has come to the attention of historians.

The first letters show the strongest Syrian chieftains striking out for more territory, turning a lax eye on Egypt and an intriguing eye on Anatolia where the Hittites had again come to life. Abdashirta, an Amorite chief in the valley of the Orontes, was one of these, and after a poor pretense at faith with Egypt, openly waged war with Ribaddi, the faithful vassal of Byblos. Abdashirta's principal allies were the Habiru, a roving people who came into Syria at the time of the first letters from Ribaddi. Meanwhile the Hittites had pushed down into Syria cutting off one of the larger cities. And toward the end of the period included in the letters we see Egypt's old ally, Mitanni, joining in the anti-Egyptian movement. One by one the Egyptian strongholds fell, and it was Byblos and Beirut which held out to the end. With the disappearance of Ribaddi the entire north country passed into the hands of the Amorites and Hittites.

The story of the faithful Ribaddi is one of the most interesting and touching episodes that has come down to us from the ancient world. Had he not been so staunch in the face of the inevitable overthrow of Egypt in Asia he might have saved his life. Message after message did he send to the court of Egypt, begging for troops and money with which to buy food for his starving people. The cities round about were falling rapidly before the onslaught of anti-Egyptian forces, and when they had all been captured how would it be possible for Byblos to hold out much longer? But no effective aid came from the Nile. Instead, court intrigues placed Ribaddi in a very unfavorable position in the eyes of the state department. Yet he did not desert the trust which had been placed in him, even when his family urged him to desert to the other side, or when attempts were made on his life by the people of his own city. At length the long series of complaining letters came to an end. Byblos fell, and Ribaddi probably met the same fate as other loyal vassals who had tried to preserve the name of Egypt in Asia.

In tracing the story of mass movements from the Amarna letters it is clear that the Hittites settled as far south as the Lebanons, while some of them may have continued on into Palestine. Letters from Palestinian cities complained about the Amorites and Habiru, and these cities too were soon in non-Egyptian hands. It is altogether likely that Joshua was a Habiru and that Jericho fell at this time.

The Egyptian empire in Asia had been squandered, but that seemed to cause Akhenaton little concern. The court at Akhetaton continued the life that it had chosen, and when the king died in 1358 B.C. a son-in-law stood ready to take his place, ruling from the city of the Aton.

Excavations at the Hittite capital have revealed what must surely have been a headline story in the year 1358 B.C. Akhenaton was dead and his queen, the beautiful Nefretiti, wishing to retain the throne for herself, wrote to the Hittite king, Shuppiluliuma, asking for one of his sons in marriage. The letter read, "My husband is dead, I have no son. You are said to have many sons. If you will give me one of your sons, he shall be my husband. I fear to take one of my slaves and make him my husband". The Hittite king suspected treachery, but, when at length he became convinced that Nefretiti spoke the truth and wished to have a Hittite as king of Egypt, he sent one of his sons. By this time, however, Akhenaton's son-in-law had become king and the Hittite prince was murdered on his way to Egypt.

Akhenaton's son-in-law was followed shortly by a youth who, on becoming king, bore the name Tutankhaton.

TUTANKHAMON, THE BOY KING

The new king had been born and reared in the atmosphere of the new religion, and when he came to the throne as a boy of about twelve probably knew little else. His short reign of six or seven years is noteworthy principally for the fact that before its completion he changed his name to Tutankhamon, thus eliminating the Aton element that was so distasteful to the old priesthood. The total eclipse of Atonism came in the next reign when King Eye moved the capital back to Thebes.

Tutankhamon apparently made one campaign into Syria in an effort to retrieve Egypt's lost possessions, but aside from that we know little about his short reign. Tutankhamon is probably the best known of pharaohs, yet his fame rests chiefly on the discovery of his richly furnished tomb which had the good fortune to survive serious plundering. It is likely that his tomb was poor in comparison with those of Thutmose III and Amenhotep III.

The glorious line of XVIIIth dynasty kings came to an end about 1350 B.C. with Eye who reigned for a very short time. For two hundred and thirty years a remarkable group of sovereigns had occupied the throne of Egypt and for almost two hundred years of that period Egypt had been supreme among the nations. The first world empire had risen to the heights and had been eclipsed. Egypt's greatest days ended with the religious revolution of Akhenaton which failed, but the world had been given a preview of things to come. And although Egypt's best days as empire were over, there were yet good days in store. A few years after Harmhab, one of Akhenaton's generals, had usurped the throne to begin the XIXth dynasty, kings named Ramses made their appearance on the Egyptian and foreign scenes.

THE EGYPTIAN EMPIRE—FROM 1350-1090 B.C.

When Harmhab began his career as king he restored Amon and all other Egyptian gods except the Aton to their former positions. Temples and inscriptions that had been despoiled by the heretic king were restored, while at the same time an effort was made to remove from the scene all that might recall the memory of the "criminal of Akhetaton". Akhenaton's temple in Thebes was demolished and the stones used to build a pylon for Harmhab, and his tomb and those of his nobles were wrecked. Revenues which had been allotted to the worship of Aton "forever and ever" were appropriated for Amon who was soon to become a force greater than the king himself.

Harmhab reigned for some thirty-five years during which time he spent most of his energy in reorganizing the country and purging it of its corrupt official element. Many laws were made in an effort to eliminate bribery of judges and executives, and honest and capable men found themselves in demand. For his efforts at reform Harmhab must be given a high place in history.

During his regime Egypt appears to have made no foreign conquests, all energies being applied to conditions at home. Harmhab was succeeded by the first Ramses who, however, was an old man when he became king. After two years his scepter was passed on to his son, Seti I, and again Egypt had a warrior king of the type that had made Egypt famous in earlier days.

SETI I PRESENT-
ING THE IMAGE
OF TRUTH TO
THE GOD OSIRIS
Relief from Seti's
Temple at Abydos.

Courtesy
Gaddis and Seif

Seti (1313-1292 B.C.) set out in his first year to reconquer Egypt's lost lands in Asia, and he was successful to the extent of subduing Palestine and certain ports on the Phoenician coast. He collected heavy tribute including cedar logs which were floated across the Mediterranean to the Delta. After quieting the always disturbing elements in Libya the next year, he again moved into Syria with the intention of giving battle to the Hittites. The two forces met, but this was not a contest between Egypt and a weak opponent. Two first class powers were on the field, and although we know nothing about the battle itself, it is clear that the Egyptains gained nothing. The Hittite boundary remained much as it had been during Amarna times, and perhaps because he saw that the Hittites could not be dislodged, Seti then or soon after concluded a treaty with the Hittite king. Egypt, however, had recovered a portion of her Asiatic empire and so matters remained until the next king, Ramses II, the most renowned of his name, came to the throne.

RAMSES THE GREAT

Ramses was not the eldest son of Seti. The rightful older brother had been brushed aside by the ambitious young Ramses who was to have one of the longest reigns in Egyptian history. Ramses ruled for sixty-seven years after his accession in 1292 B.C.

After he had consolidated public opinion, and especially the Amon priesthood, behind him, Ramses laid plans for his Asiatic campaigns. Like his predecessor Thutmose III he would gain control of several seaport towns in Syria before sending his army inland, since transportation by water was so much quicker and easier. The Hittites were still the power in northern Syria and they, being fully warned by Ramses' preparations, likewise laid their military plans. Everything pointed to a great and decisive battle between the Egyptians and Hittites. The latter brought together all the vassal kings of the now great Hittite Empire, while the Egyptians added mercenaries who were well paid for their services in the army. In the year 1288 B.C., Ramses advanced with

Courtesy Gaddis and Seif

STATUE OF RAMSES II AND HIS WIFE IN LUXOR TEMPLE

THE RAMESSEUM

The Temple of Ramses II on the west side of the river at Thebes. This view was taken during high Nile. At the right in the water stand the two colossi. Luxor Temple may be seen in the background at the edge of the regular course of the Nile.

his army of perhaps 20,000 toward Kadesh on the Orontes for what was to be the prelude to the last test between Hittite and Egyptian arms.

THE BATTLE OF KADESH

The Egyptian army approaching from the south consisted of four divisions, each named for one of the great Egyptian gods: Amon, Re, Ptah, and Sutekh. Ramses personally led the division of Amon and, anxious to get into action, pushed on faster than the other divisions could follow. When he was still some distance south of Kadesh, two Bedouins came to Ramses saying they were deserters from the Hittite army. They said that the Hittite king had retreated far to the north of Kadesh, and this Ramses believed because his own scouts had seen nothing of the enemy.

Courtesy The Oriental Institute of The University of Chicago

COLONNADED HALL OF THE TEMPLE OF AMON AT KARNAK

Dr. Breasted is shown viewing columns erected by Ramses II. It would be possible for 100 men to stand on top of one of these pillars.

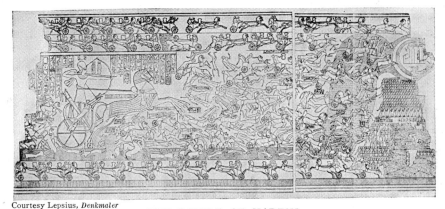

Courtesy Lepsius, *Denkmaler*

THE BATTLE OF KADESH
Ramses II charging the Hittites. From a relief in the Ramesseum.

With this information, Ramses and his household troops hurried ahead. In the meantime the crafty Hittite king had marshalled his troops on the opposite side of the high city of Kadesh, now an imposing tell, and, as Ramses approached, the Hittite at all times kept the city between himself and the unsuspecting Ramses. The two Bedouins had done their work well.

The division of Amon at length caught up with Ramses and pitched camp northwest of the city, and, while the horses were being fed and the troops were preparing their meal, a couple of Hittite spies were captured. After a merciless beating they confessed that the Hittite king and all his troops were at that very moment on the other side of the city. Ramses was alarmed and sent swift couriers to his straggling third division. Apparently the fourth division was so far behind it could not arrive on time; the second division, on the other hand, was seemingly close enough to be of assistance.

Ramses did not know that by then the Hittites had begun the battle having cut his second division in two. He first learned of this catastrophe when his routed troops dashed into his camp, followed by the Hittite chariotry. The fright of the second division was such that part of Ramses' own division also took to its heels, leaving Ramses with a mere handful of body troops, surrounded on all sides by enemy chariotry. The king was desperate and made an attempt to break through to the south in an effort to join his missing third and fourth divisions, but he soon saw that only to the east would he have any chance for success. Thus he and his chariots charged again and again with a power born of desperation, and succeeded in beating back their foe. But Ramses owed his life to a peculiar oriental trait that we have already seen at Megiddo. The Hittite chariotry at his rear, instead of closing in on the Pharaoh, found themselves in his deserted camp and gave themselves up to the rich plunder. Ramses had obtained a fortunate breathing spell and then, quite unexpectedly, a group of Egyptian troops from the west or north attacked the booty-maddened Hittites and slew them all.

The battle, however, had only begun. The Hittite king threw in strong reserves who engaged the remnants of the now collected first and second divisions, but although the Egyptian forces were far outnumbered they held their ground until late in the afternoon of that eventful day when the third division hurried into view from the south. The Hittites were thus suddenly placed in a most unfavorable position between the two Egyptian armies and after considerable loss retreated within the walls of Kadesh.

The battle was over, and although Ramses claimed a victory he returned to Egypt without laying siege to the city. His army had been seriously crippled, and the most one can say is that the engagement was a draw.

The loss of Egyptian prestige in Asia is clearly seen from the fact that most of Palestine revolted in the next few years, and Ramses was forced to begin exactly where his father had almost thirty years before. Ramses, however, possessed considerable military ability in addition to his firm desire to reconquer the empire of his XVIIIth dynasty predecessors. We see that in time he regained not only Palestine but also won battles in Syria, even north of Kadesh. And then, after fifteen years of campaigning, Ramses' wars with the Hittites suddenly ended.

It was in the year 1272 B.C. that Ramses and Hattusilis, then the Hittite king, agreed to their famous treaty which was witnessed by a thousand gods and goddesses of the Hittites and a similar number from the country of the Nile. Each ruler swore not to invade the territory of the other, the line probably being set some-

Courtesy The Oriental Institute of The University of Chicago

THE GREAT TEMPLE OF RAMSES III AT MEDINET HABU
The palace of the king lay to the left of the pylon.

what north of Palestine, and to come to the aid of the other should either need assistance. The treaty was apparently satisfactory to both parties since peace followed, and thirteen years later Hattusilis appeared personally in Egypt to give away his eldest daughter as the wife of Ramses.

We can readily understand one of the Hittite motives in terminating the long war. Mitanni had fallen and no longer proved a buffer to the states in Mesopotamia. In its place Assyria, the northern offspring of Babylonian culture, had risen to a threatening position. Assyria was still a youth among nations and her best days lay ahead, but power was being gathered and the Hittites were sensible of its threat.

During his long life Ramses built many edifices in Egypt, in Nubia, and in Palestine, and on their walls inscribed the valorous deeds of his wars. His personal triumph at Kadesh figured prominently as did the treaty, and both were considered by him as Egyptian victories. When he died as a very old man, he left a deep

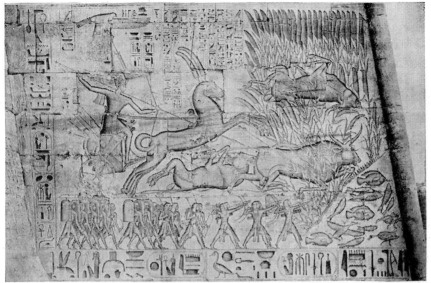

Courtesy The Oriental Institute of The University of Chicago

RAMSES III HUNTING WILD BULLS
Detail from the first pylon at Medinet Habu.

seated impression on his age, and during years to come Egyptian kings, most of them of far less ability, assumed the same name.

Ramses was succeeded by his son Merneptah, by this time also an old man, who after an ineffective reign of ten years was followed by three short-lived kings. The XIXth dynasty ended in 1205 B.C. when a usurper from Syria captured the throne, and held it for five years. It was at the end of this period that the XXth dynasty began.

RAMSES III VS. THE PHILISTINES

Ramses III was the second king of the XXth dynasty and was not related to the man for whom he had been named. He had inherited a badly disrupted kingdom, for not since the earlier days of Ramses II had Egypt been a threat to Asia. The intervening years had seen the approach of a new menace to peace in the Near East.

Immigrants and peoples driven out of Crete and Greece by barbarian pressure from the north had flooded the eastern Mediterranean. Some of the Hittite allies at the battle of Kadesh probably belonged to this strain, and during the reign of Merneptah the Sea Peoples, as they were called, raided the Delta as allies of the Libyans. Among these were a group of Acheans, related to the famous people of Mycenae and the besiegers of Troy.

Trade had first introduced these northerners to Egypt, Palestine and Syria, and, drawn by business, many of them came to settle away from home. Ras Shamra, on the north Syrian coast, received many of them, to judge from Mycenaean type burial vaults discovered in excavation, and many other trading centers must have known the early Aegean peoples in person. The Mediterra-

EGYPTIANS OF RAMSES III'S ARMY STORMING A SYRIAN FORTIFICATION
Detail from the temple at Medinet Habu.

Courtesy The Oriental Institute of The University of Chicago

FLEEING NEGROES SEEN ON A WALL AT MEDINET HABU

nean of that day was dotted with sailing vessels from numerous ports, bearing produce to the consumption markets.

The hope of capturing some of these markets was probably responsible for certain raids that occurred around 1200 B.C., but the principal urge came from the fact that northern tribes, who later became civilized Greeks, were driving the Aegean peoples out of their homeland. The whole northern sector of the then civilized world was menaced, and before the trouble subsided the Hittite empire had disappeared. Anatolia was invaded from the Balkans by an Indo-European group called Phrygians, and thereafter the Hittites lived principally in northern Syria. Troy was destroyed at about the same time and the Etruscans left their ancestral home to settle in Italy.

The same movement drove a group of people called Philistines to Syria and Palestine, women and children forming part of the group. The Philistines came by land and sea, probably from southern Greece, and shortly afterwards loomed as a threat to Egypt.

Ramses III in his eighth year (1191 B.C.) was faced with the necessity of giving battle to a coalition of Egypt-bound Philistines and related people, though Egypt was not as weak as they had supposed. The new king had gathered together a formidable army, composed in large part of mercenaries, and, somewhere along the Syrian coast, gave battle to the northern intruders. At the same time he dispatched his fleet to meet the enemy, and in both engagements he was victorious. Egypt was spared and Palestine and parts of Syria remained in her possession, but the Philistines were allowed to settle on the coast below the hills leading to Jerusalem. Here they formed a league of five strong cities—Gaza, Ascalon, Ashdod, Ekron, and Gath. The troubles that Saul and David experienced with the Philistines at a later time dated back to the period when Egypt allowed them to establish themselves on the fertile coastal plain. It is a curious fact that the Philistines who were so despised by the Hebrews are the very ones who gave Palestine its name.

Courtesy The Oriental Institute of The University of Chicago

SCENE FROM A SEA BATTLE BETWEEN AEGEANS AND THE FLEET OF RAMSES III AS DEPICTED AT MEDINET HABU
The Aegean ships have a goose-head prow, while the Egyptians are distinguished by a lions-head prow.

Courtesy The Oriental Institute of The University of Chicago

PHILISTINES WITH CRESTED HEADDRESS HELD PRISONERS BY AN
EGYPTIAN AS SEEN AT MEDINET HABU

Ramses III was the last great king of that name. Eight others of the same name followed him after his death (1167 B.C.), but they were inconsequential for the most part; no mining was carried on in Sinai after Ramses IV. The empire died with Ramses III who despite great energy and ability was faced with insurmountable handicaps. Thereafter Egypt slipped rapidly, a good share of the trouble lying in the increased power of the Amon priesthood. Ever since the Aton revolution had been quashed, Amon had risen steadily in power until most of the revenue of the state went for the upkeep of his buildings and officials. Matters grew rapidly worse after the death of Ramses III, foreign policy was forced to one side, corruption made headway, and in 1090 B.C. the last Ramses gave way to the high priest of Amon, who became the first king of the XXIst dynasty, one of the weakest native dynasties in all Egyptian history.

JOSHUA AND THE HEBREWS

The origin of the Hebrew people will continue to cause much discussion between those who read the Bible literally and others who try to fit historical evidence into the Biblical narrative. Complete agreement is not always possible where two sources offer differing statements concerning a single occurrence.

The difficulties probably arose from the fact that the Bible was written late in Hebrew history, long after many of the events which it chronicles. Abraham and Isaac, Jacob and Joseph, are hazy characters at best, but we have seen that the Patriarchal period fits well into the Hyksos background. When we come down to the story of Hebrew entry into Palestine the problem is greatly aggravated, principally because we have so much information on the period.

The Bible states that the Hebrews entered at the time of the Exodus from Egypt where they had been oppressed for many years. Moses was their leader, taking them through the Red Sea and the wilderness of Sinai. Before reaching Palestine, the Promised Land, Moses died and was succeeded by Joshua who took Jericho and other cities in Palestine. There followed the long period of the Judges during which no king ruled Israel.

Courtesy The Art Institute, Chicago

We can say that there is much truth in this narrative and if we had it alone there could be little to question. However, we have seen that a group of people called the Habiru were coming into Palestine in numbers around 1400 B.C. when the Aton in Egypt had diverted attention from Asia. These Habiru settled in the country and gradually took on the attributes of natives. But what does this have to do with the Bible story?

We know from the excavations at Jericho that the city was destroyed and deserted about 1400 B.C. This catastrophe apparently happened during the period when the Habiru were entering the country. But Joshua is so closely associated with the fall of Jericho in Hebrew tradition that it is therefore necessary to place his lifetime around 1400 B.C.

Moses on the other hand appears to be linked to a period about two hundred years later, for the Hebrews slaved in the cities of Ramses. The story, then, of Joshua following Moses seems to be a confused version of two originally different episodes. The Habiru who came from north of Palestine about 1400 B.C. bore a name Hebrew. Although there were before this time other elements in the country that contributed to the blood of the Hebrews, it was the movement of about 1400 B.C. that first began to settle Palestine with people we may call Hebrews. These were the northern tribes, first living in the hills and later taking Canaanite cities. The Moses group of Hebrews left Egypt about 1200 B.C. and probably came into Palestine from the south.

The period of the Judges thus began about 1400 B.C., which is not far from the date indicated in the Bible, and lasted for about 400 years during which time the Hebrews grew continually stronger. It was probably about the middle of the eleventh century that Barak defeated the Canaanite Sisera in the plain of Megiddo. This is also the period of Samson and Delilah and of many skirmishes between the Hebrews and their enemies in the land across the Jordan and on the Philistine plain. Toward the end of the period of the Judges we come to the prophet Samuel who in his later years anointed Saul king of Israel.

From the desert and the hills to civilization is the story of Hebrew origins. On entering the land as widely differing groups they adopted the "tongue of Canaan" as well as much of its culture. But there persisited that element in the Hebrew makeup that in the course of time gave Israel its God. It is this trait that principally distinguishes the Hebrews from all other ancient peoples, and to this source must we trace our own religions.

THE LAST THOUSAND YEARS BEFORE CHRIST

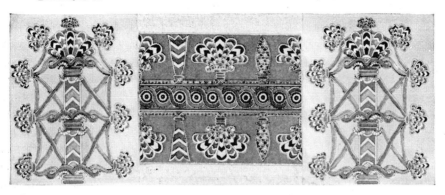

THESE WERE momentous years in the history of the world. The Egyptian empire had come to a lingering end, but three more Oriental empires were to bloom and pass, before Europe, through the Greeks, assumed the leading rôle. Assyrians, Babylonians, and Persians succeeded one another in turn, and the last was the greatest. Yet before any of them reached maturity a state was formed in the highlands of Palestine, a state which at the moment it was conceived might have risen to political heights. Instead it was destined to serve a much greater purpose through the religion it gave the world.

THE HEBREWS BECOME A NATION

Saul was last of the Judges and first of the Kings of Israel. He had been annointed by Samuel and later, at Mizpah, the people had gathered to choose him king, thus making his selection unanimous. The tribes, which heretofore had fought among themselves, were brought together and a united front was presented to the Philistines who had come up into the hill country around Jerusalem. But Jerusalem itself was still in foreign hands, and not until David was made king did it become Hebrew property.

Saul and his son Jonathan were effective military leaders and by the end of the reign the Hebrew kingdom included most of the Judean hill country except Jerusalem, and perhaps extended

as far north as the plain of Esdraelon on which stood the famous
stronghold of Megiddo. Saul also ruled over parts of Transjordan
and must be credited with forming the foundation of the kingdom of which David was later king.

David of Bethlehem became the armor-bearer of Saul and
gained renown in battle, so much so that the women of Israel began to sing, "Saul slew his thousands, but David his ten thousands". This resulted in David's banishment, for Saul wished no
rival for his newly won throne. At the same time Saul disagreed
with the priests of Yahweh, as God was called by the Hebrews,
and David soon found himself in their favor. But Saul hunted
him through Judah, and David at length was forced to seek protection from the Philistine lord of Gath. David wished for
Hebrew independence but valued his life as well.

Finally the Philistines gathered in the plain of Esdraelon at Mt.
Gilboa for one last attempt to destroy Saul and his kingdom, and
on that fateful day the Hebrews were routed and Saul and Jonathan killed. Their bodies were exposed on the walls of Beth Shan
and the Hebrews were momentarily without a leader.

David was still a Philistine vassal and had to proceed carefully,
but through his earlier marriage with Saul's daughter, and what
may have been several judiciously planned deaths, he became at
length the sole contender for the throne of the small state. Accordingly, the elders of Israel journeyed to Hebron, far in the
south of Judah, and annointed David "King of Israel and Judah".

DAVID, KING OF ISRAEL AND JUDAH

Soon after David became king, around 1000 B.C., he declared
his independence of the Philistines, and wars with these people
continued. Out of them grew one of the world's famous stories,
that of David and Goliath, a story that is as unhistorical as it is
fascinating. Far from being the hero of any such episode, David
appears to have been in danger of his life, but later Hebrew
romancers had no difficulty in placing Israel's hero in a more
favorable light. There appears to have been a Goliath of Gath,
but he was slain by Elhanan of Bethlehem.

Courtesy The Art Institute, Chicago

GENERAL VIEW OF DAMASCUS

In the course of time the Philistines admitted Hebrew independence, and David was allowed to look after other matters. It was then that Jerusalem ceased being a city of the Jebusites and became the capital of the kingdom. The capture of Jerusalem was of lasting importance, for from that time on it has remained the Holy City. Making Jerusalem capital of the country was strategic from several points of view, the principal one being that it lay between Israel and Judah but was part of neither. Friction always existed between north and south, therefore a neutral capital possessed many advantages.

David conquered almost all of Palestine and held Transjordan as far south as the Gulf of Akaba which leads out to the Red Sea. Damascus, which by now was inhabited by a closely related people called Arameans, was also controlled by David as was a good part of central Syria. The kingdom under David was the largest it had ever been or was to be.

The rise of the Hebrew kingdom may be attributed in large part to the tremendous energies that David exhibited in his early years and to his wise choice of generals, but at the same time the general situation in the Near East was favorable. Egypt was in eclipse and Assyria, soon to become the ranking oriental power, had not yet felt its strength. The Hebrew kingdom was short lived, and before David died there were signs of disintegration. His son Absalom revolted as did a number of the tribes, and harem intrigues created a situation well known in the east. The outcome was that Solomon, the son of Bath Sheba, became king at the death of David. We shall never know for certain what it was that David said on his death-bed. The only witnesses were Bath Sheba and the priest Nathan, and Bath Sheba was the ambitious mother of Solomon.

David was a man of great ability, an able general, and an astute politician who carried Israel to its heights among the nations. His reign is important too for its effect on Hebrew religion, for at that time Yahweh, or God, became the principal god among the many that the Hebrews worshipped. David was not a monotheist but he was leading the way to the later acceptance of God as the only true god. Succeeding generations glorified David in his relations with God far beyond the evidence and among other things claimed that he had written the Psalms. David was indeed a poet of considerable attainment, but it seems improbable that he wrote many of the Psalms or that he was the author of the twenty-third Psalm.

THE GLORIES OF SOLOMON

Solomon murdered all aspirants to the throne and thus began his "peaceful and wise" reign about 970 B.C. It was truly a reign of peace, for no military activity is recorded. But peace in the larger sense does not mean that there were no revolts. Some of these occurred early in his career as king, and soon his father's empire began to slip through his fingers.

While Solomon was not a military man he apparently knew a great deal about economics. He developed a large trade in horses, buying them from Egypt and selling them to the northern countries. During his reign the Hebrews carried on an extensive trade with the Red Sea countries. Ships went to Ophir and returned with monkeys, peacocks, and spices. Copper mines were discovered and worked in southern Palestine, and with Solomon's other activities added greatly to the balance in the treasury. These sources of wealth, to which must of course be added taxes levied on the people, resulted in the erection of a large number of royal buildings throughout the land.

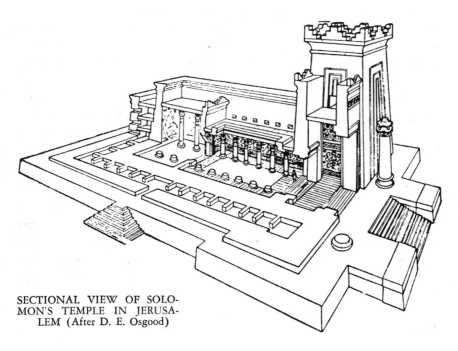

SECTIONAL VIEW OF SOLO-
MON'S TEMPLE IN JERUSA-
LEM (After D. E. Osgood)

The greatest of these was the temple which Solomon erected in Jerusalem and which stood until almost four hundred years later when it was destroyed by the Babylonians. Solomon also strengthened strategic points throughout the country, building horse and chariot stables in some of them. At Megiddo alone there were accommodations for almost five hundred horses, complete with stalls, tie posts, and stone troughs for food and drink.

Courtesy The Oriental Institute of The University of Chicago   Model made by O. E. Lind

MODEL OF THE STABLES OF SOLOMON AT MEGIDDO
Now in The Oriental Institute.

Solomon was remembered and glorified by later generations for his building of the temple to Yahweh, but he, like his father, worshipped more than one god. Nevertheless Yahweh had become the principal state god, and held a position in the minds of the people that may be compared to that of Amon in the Egyptian empire period. Yahweh was head of the Hebrew pantheon.

After a reign marked by great luxury for the upper classes, but untold hardship for those who made up the peasant and working groups, Solomon died. The kingdom that David amassed had largely disappeared, and, sadder yet, Solomon left to his young son Reheboam a country exceedingly close to revolt because of the heavy taxes and forced labor that had been customary for years.

THE DIVIDED KINGDOM

The sixteen year old Reheboam was accepted immediately as king of Judah, but the northern tribes assembled at Shechem, wishing first to have an understanding before accepting him as their king as well. Their spokesman said, "Your father made the yoke grievous upon us, and made grievous the securing of the food for his table; now therefore lighten it upon us, and we will serve you". Reheboam's young friends were indignant, and, urged by them, Reheboam replied, "My little finger is thicker than my father's loins; my father chastised you with whips, but I will chastise with scorpions".

Thus the promising kingdom, that Saul had brought together and David had enlarged, came to the turning of the ways. Judah and Israel had always been annoying to each other, and now the northern tribes cried out, "No portion have we in David, no heritage in Jesse's son! To your tents, Oh Israel! This man is no leader or prince". With that Reheboam fled back to Jerusalem to escape the fury of the mob.

The northern tribes then made Jereboam king of Israel. He had been an official under Solomon but had fallen into disfavor and fled to Egypt. Shishak, first king of the XXIInd dynasty, gave him his queen's sister as wife, and at the death of Solomon,

Courtesy The Oriental Institute of The University of Chicago

PART OF SOLOMON'S STABLES UNCOVERED AT MEGIDDO
BY THE ORIENTAL INSTITUTE
Note cribs standing by tie posts.

Jereboam hurried back to Palestine. Here he gathered together a force of men and when elected king of Israel he rebuilt Shechem as his capital.

Jereboam became king in 935 B.C., and from that time on there was continual friction between Judah and Israel. This situation was interrupted for a short time when in 930 B.C. Shishak invaded the country and momentarily revived the Egyptian empire. But Egypt lost power soon after his death, and, although she often in later years interfered with Palestine for political reasons, she never again as a native power attained a real footing in the country.

SAMARIA ON A HILL

A new line of kings, ushered in by Omri in 885 B.C., established its capital at Samaria. The hilltop site had not been occupied since prehistoric times, and any buildings that may then have existed had long since disappeared. The capital was thus a new and fresh city which alone would have distinguished it from other cities in the land. But other matters were to give Samaria its lasting name. Omri founded a dynasty that rose to real significance in the affairs of the time, and long afterwards Assyria referred to Israel as "The House of Omri".

Shortly before Omri became king, the dominant figure in Phoenicia was a young priest of the goddess Astarte, who had usurped power and called himself "King of the Sidonians". When Omri came to the throne of Israel, an alliance was formed between the two kings, similar to the one between Hiram and Solomon, and the pact was sealed when the Phoenician gave his daughter to Omri's son Ahab. This new member of the royal family of Israel was Jezebel, one of the most notorious women in the Bible, and destined to play an unwilling part in the development of Israel's religion.

Jezebel was strong willed in everything she did. If she wished for a temple to her native god, Baal Melkart, she got it, even though Ahab's principal god was Yahweh. If she desired to have a vineyard in which her husband might plant herbs, she acquired it by trickery when it could not be bought. Ahab had offered to buy Naboth's vineyard in Jezreel, a few miles south of Nazareth, or to replace it with another and better vineyard. When Naboth refused, Jezebel contrived to have him accused of insubordination to God and the king; Naboth was dragged from the city and stoned to death. Thereupon the prophet Elijah, already Jezebel's enemy because of their differing religious points of view, told Ahab that swine and dogs would lick his blood and dogs would feast on Jezebel. How true was this prophecy we shall presently see.

Meanwhile the Assyrian menace to the east had been crystal-izing, and in 854 B.C., twenty years after Ahab had become king, the army of Shalmaneser III marched into the west. But Ahab had not been idle. Temporary peace existed between Israel and Damascus, and a coalition of other Syrian powers, twelve in all, met Shalmaneser at Karkara in central Syria. Ahab was as impor-tant as any of the allies, and the ensuing battle resulted in a draw, if not a defeat for Shalmaneser. It was in any case a political vic-tory for Ahab who had been strongly opposed in his plans by the prophets of Yahweh. But the prophetic party eventually won the day in Israel, with the result that Judaism was allowed to develop. Hebrew history is significant chiefly because of Judaism and its offspring Christianity, but if not for Ahab, who in fighting with the prophets contributed his strength at the battle of Karkara, Israel might well have disappeared before it did. The Assyrians did not again prove a menace for over a century, and in that time religious views crystallized to the point where they could not be extinguished short of extinction of the whole people. Samaria and Israel succumbed in time, but Yahweh was a fixture in the land.

After the Assyrian threat had been repulsed, the coalition, which so successfully had met it, broke up. Israel and Damascus again came to blows, and in one of the battles in 852 B.C. Ahab was struck by a chance arrow which pierced his coat of mail. By evening he died, and with him went the last real opposition to the prophets. Ahab had worshipped Yahweh but he had also been a patriot for Israel.

ELISHA'S FOUNTAIN AT JERICHO

JEZEBEL AND JEHU

Ahab's son, who followed him, soon lost his foreign possessions and after a couple of years when he died he was succeeded by his brother Jehoram. Strife still existed between the royal house and the prophets, and, when Jehoram returned to Jezreel to recuperate from a wound received in battle with the Damascenes, the prophetic group plotted his downfall. Led by Elisha it decided that Israel's future lay best with a man sympathetic to Yahweh. It was thus that Jehu, senior general of the army, came to the throne of Israel.

Driving furiously toward Jezreel he was met by Jehoram and Ahaziah, king of Judah, who inquired whether all was well. Jehu directed his reply to Jehoram saying that things could hardly be well so long as Jezebel's influence remained unchecked. At this, Jehoram turned quickly to reach safety in the city but Jehu pierced him with an arrow and ordered one of his officers to throw the body onto the land that had been Naboth's vineyard. Ahaziah, too, was struck and after escaping he died in Megiddo.

Jezebel, who was in Jezreel at the time, soon learned of these events and knew that her time had also come. So quite calmly she fixed her hair and painted her eyes and then sat down at a window overlooking the gate of the city. When Jehu appeared she taunted him with the murder of his master and he in a fury responded with an order that two of her eunuchs throw her out of the window. Her blood splashed on the wall and her body was trampled by the horses where it was left for the dogs. In those days the zeal of Yahweh could bring about such atrocities.

Jehu, however, was not yet content. He slew all the relatives of the house of Omri and all who had been sympathetic with Jezebel and her sons. Moreover he alienated Judah which for a short time had fought side by side with Israel. And finally when, in 842 B.C., Shalmaneser of Assyria returned for a short foray into Syria and Palestine, Jehu bowed his head to the ground in token of fealty. Jehu may have been a champion of the people, but he had no thought of defeating Assyria's desire for empire.

THE NEW PROPHETS

Israel experienced another period of prosperity under Jereboam II (785-745 B.C.) as we learn from the prophet Amos, a Judean shepherd. But Amos predicted evil for Israel because of its unjust social abuses, and Assyria was to be the agent of destruction, the agent of the Lord. He saw in Yahweh a god opposed to the bloody reforms of Elijah's followers, and this message was so strong in his heart that he journeyed northward to Israel to denounce the evils of the day. He addressed the Israelites on the subject of their expensive clothing and homes, their corrupt lives and lack of feeling for the poor. He was the first great Hebrew social reformer and did much to point the way to a higher form of religion.

Courtesy The Oriental Institute of The University of Chicago

BALAWAT. SHEIKH'S TENT WITH MOUND IN RIGHT BACKGROUND
WHERE PALACE OF SHALMANESER III WAS LOCATED

Courtesy British Museum

BRONZE RELIEFS OF SHALMANESER III FROM BALAWAT

RELIEFS IN BRONZE FROM BALAWAT

A generation later there lived Hosea, an Israelite with much the same attitude toward social conditions, but he differed from Amos in believing that God still loved Israel even though it turned to other gods. Hosea also saw that Assyria would be the earthly means of Israel's downfall, and he, like Amos, protested violently against the religious setting that had been sponsored by Elijah and Elisha.

As predicted, Israel fell when the revived Assyrians returned in the latter part of the eighth century. Tiglath Pileser III (746-728 B.C.) raised Assyria from its temporary eclipse and swept westward, and soon his country was to reach its pinnacle, even taking Egypt. But before that happened the kingdom of Israel was to pass out of existence. Shalmaneser V of Assyria in 723 B.C. captured the capital at Samaria, and many of the people of Israel were carried off as captives. Thenceforth the Hebrew scene was shifted to Jerusalem.

Amos and Hosea were followed by the prophet Isaiah who lived at the time Sargon's son Sennacherib was slashing his way

A RELIEF FROM THE PALACE OF SENNACHERIB
Showing Assyrians scaling and capturing an Egyptian city.
Below Assyrians carry away prisoners and spoil.

through western Asia. Many of the Hebrews on looking at the wasted land of Palestine came to believe that Ashur, the principal god of the Assyrians, was a far greater god than Yahweh. But Isaiah addressed them on numerous occasions in the streets of Jerusalem, even as Sennacherib approached with his mighty battering rams in 701 B.C. Isaiah proclaimed that Yahweh ruled much more than simply Palestine. He ruled the entire world and Assyria was but the "rod" of Yahweh's anger for the wrongdoing of the Hebrews. In addition Isaiah predicted a great and glorious future for the Hebrews and disaster for Assyria.

His prophecy was fulfilled when Sennacherib's army, momentarily expected outside the walls of Jerusalem, was suddenly afflicted with a plague from the marshes of the Nile Delta. Jerusalem was spared and many Hebrews then came to believe in the beneficence of the world God, Yahweh.

Less than a century after Jerusalem's deliverance the Hebrews saw the collapse of Assyria (612 B.C.), but the downfall of Judah was likewise not far distant. The Chaldeans of Babylon became the next masters of Palestine and the unsubmitting Hebrews, having not yet learned their lesson from Samaria and the prophets, fell finally to Nebuchadnezzar in 586 B.C.

Thus ended the kingdom that Saul had founded. Short lived as a unified nation, it had split soon after the death of Solomon, and now, a little more than four hundred years after the annointing of Saul, Judah had gone the way of Israel. Its inhabitants were taken away as captives, but out of her new misery, the Exile, the Hebrews developed the spiritual concepts of Judaism that have been so enduring.

THE ASSYRIAN EMPIRE

For about two centuries the Assyrians played a leading rôle in the destiny of Palestine, but Assyrian interests were far wider than Palestine and included conquests in all directions from their homeland on the upper Tigris. Therefore let us retrace our steps and pick up the thread of history in the land of the god Ashur.

The earliest capital of Assyria was Ashur, named for the great god of a Semitic people who early in history settled in the northern part of Mesopotamia. To begin with, it was a small city-state subject to the great powers in the south. Sargon of Akkad in the twenty-sixth century and Hammurabi in the twentieth century had controlled it, but at the same time it had received the benefits of Babylonian culture. We have noticed the small but active Assyrian trading colonies that migrated to Anatolia about 2000 B.C., but in world affairs Assyria played a minor rôle until the fourteenth century when her kings pushed westward, sweeping back the Hittites. It was during the Amarna period in Egypt that Assyria first gave signs of emerging as a power. About 1100 B.C. the first Tiglath Pileser marched to the Mediterranean through the obstinate Aramean and Phoenician lands, but Assyria was not yet powerful enough to hold permanently these distant regions.

The Arameans, whose strongest city was Damascus, proved for several centuries to be a bulwark against Assyrian invasion, while at the same time their industrious merchants worked eastward, carrying with them their alphabet based on the one invented in

Sinai about 1800 B.C. The Aramaic alphabet in time displaced use of the more cumbersome cuneiform, and before its eastern march was completed it had penetrated beyond Mesopotamia and Persia into India and China.

The language spoken by the Aramaic merchants likewise gained extreme importance, finally becoming the principal language of the Near East. Many centuries later Jesus, like other Hebrews of the time, spoke Aramaic and not Hebrew, although the two are closely related.

We have seen that the strong Syrian-Hebrew coalition which included Ahab of Israel was able to stop Shalmaneser III at Karkara in 854 B.C. Nevertheless, Shalmaneser more than doubled Assyrian territory by incorporating former vassal states into the kingdom, and his grandson expanded it still farther. The former small city of Ashur was now surrounded on all sides by recently acquired territory. But Assyria's star was temporarily dimmed after the death of Shalmaneser's grandson, and for a few years the most important state in the world was Haldia whose capital lay far to the north near Lake Van. During this period the devotees of Yahweh in Israel were able to solidify their ideas of God.

It was Tiglath Pileser III (746-728 B.C.) who revived Assyria and launched it on its conquering way. The monarch laid hold of Babylon, the mother of Assyria's culture, and on the east he subdued a group of people including the Medes. Then, turning his attention to the Haldians, he met them first in northern Syria where their cities succumbed to the fury of the Assyrian king. Working southward he then invaded Palestine, and wherever he created new provinces he forestalled revolt by moving the population bodily from one part of the empire to another. Mountaineers were sent to the plains, and southerners left their homes for unfamiliar territory in the north. In each of the vacated places, others from far-off regions were sent to replace those who had been removed. Tiglath Pileser built temples in his new provinces and put in them statues of his god Ashur and himself. It is possible that the temple in Jerusalem possessed such images to the consternation of Yahweh's priests. Thus was the Assyrian empire controlled by its king and his governors.

Courtesy British Museum

WAR RELIEFS OF TIGLATH PILESER III FROM NIMRUD IN ASSYRIA
Royal scribes are seen taking notes on booty from a captured town.

Shalmaneser V (728-722 B.C.) continued the forceful policy of his father and, four years before he died, began the siege of Samaria that ended three years later in its surrender. The prophets had spoken the truth, and Samaria's inhabitants were forced to leave for distant parts of the empire. Shalmaneser himself died the year after Israel disappeared, and the Assyrian throne was taken by his brother who bore the famous name Sargon.

SARGON AND HIS SUCCESSORS

The second world empire was given a new royal city when Sargon (722-705 B.C.) was elevated from generalship to the kingship. Not content with the older capital he chose a fresh spot, the present Khorsabad, on which to build his city, and called it Sargonburg. It was larger and more magnificent than anything Asia had ever seen, and it truly reflected the grandeur and power of the king. The ruins of this mile-square city have been investigated by archeologists, most recently by the Oriental Institute of the University of Chicago, which has discovered vast numbers

Courtesy The Oriental Institute of The University of Chicago

WINGED BULLS IN A GATEWAY OF THE PALACE OF
SARGON II AT KHORSABAD

of reliefs depicting events in the reign of the king. But Sargon-burg was short lived. When the king was succeeded by his son Sennacherib in 705 B.C., Sargonburg was deserted and the capital moved to Nineveh. The famous city of Saragon had been built with the riches flowing into Assyria from her foreign possessions, but as a monument to its builder it has only in recent years come to the surface and become significant.

Sargon's conquests were followed up by Sennacherib whose name was feared far and wide. All of Mesopotamia, the border of Persia, the mountains north and northwest of Assyria, Anatolia, Syria, Palestine, and the frontier of Egypt, all knew his might from actual experience, and, although Jerusalem was momen-

Courtesy The Oriental Institute of The University of Chicago
WINGED BULL IN THE MUSEUM OF THE ORIENTAL INSTITUTE
It was transported from Khorsabad in a number of pieces. The weight
of this figure is about 40 tons.

tarily saved by a pestilence that destroyed the Assyrian army,
Hezekiah, Judah's king, realized his extreme good fortune.

Sennacherib (705-681 B.C.) had designs on Egypt and, while
he never succeeded in really entering Egypt, he defeated an Egyptian army in southern Palestine. Ever since the rise of Assyrian
power, Egyptian policy had been to stir up discontent among
those paying taxes or tribute to the state on the Tigris. It was of
the greatest necessity, therefore, that the Assyrians master this
source of trouble once for all.

Sennacherib had not been entirely successful in this respect,
and his son Esarhaddon (681-668 B.C.) therefore proceeded to
the Delta in 675 B.C. But there he was defeated in 673 B.C. in a
battle with Taharka, one of Egypt's Ethiopian kings of the

Courtesy The Oriental Institute of The University of Chicago   Drawn by Seton Lloyd

THE EARLIEST KNOWN AQUEDUCT

XXVth dynasty. Assyrian prestige in Asia suffered to the extent that after three years Esarhaddon's army was forced to return to the Delta. This time it could not be stopped, and the Delta, from Memphis northward, was incorporated into the Assyrian provincial system.

Egypt, however, was a long way from Assyria, and this made administration of the Delta difficult. The very year that Esarhaddon died, it became necessary for his son Ashurbanipal (668-626 B.C.) to march to the Delta to punish the Ethiopians, and seven years later, when the Ethopians made a serious effort to regain Egypt, Ashurbanipal's army drove them far up the Nile. This time the Assyrians sacked Thebes, and since then it has had no real importance.

Ashurbanipal set up an Egyptian named Psamtek as viceroy of Egypt, but, when Assyria's attention was diverted to more pressing matters near home, Egypt revolted and Psamtek became the first king of the XXVIth dynasty, ruling from 663 to 609 B.C. This was the last powerful native Egyptian dynasty, and before it fell to the Persians in 525 B.C. it had made a serious attempt

BY MEANS OF THIS AQUEDUCT WATER WAS BROUGHT FROM THE FAR OFF HILLS TO NINEVEH WHICH SENNACHERIB HAD RECONSTRUCTED

to revive Egyptian culture. This was a period of close contact with Greece. Greek settlers made their homes in the Delta and mercenaries from across the sea found service in the Egyptian army. At the same time Egyptian thought returned to Greece with the trading merchants, and early Greek art came under the influence of Egyptian sculpture.

Wherever Assyrian armies went, there they left a reign of terror; and ruins and desolation replaced busy cities and growing fields. But these depradations served the purpose of building the greatest empire the world had yet seen. At Nineveh we find that art was greatly stimulated, the reliefs of Ashurbanipal being the finest in all Assyria.

Ashurbanipal was rarely with his army, having been told by a goddess to stay at home. He was highly educated for the times and even knew Sumerian, although badly. He was a patron of letters and collected a great library, the largest of the earlier Near East, much of which is now in the British Museum. But other aspects of his character were most unattractive, especially his cruelty which was excessive even for those times.

SOURCE OF WATER FOR SENNACHERIB'S AQUEDUCT
At this point, the king left an important inscription on the rocks
giving an account of his great aqueduct.

Courtesy British Museum

RELIEF FROM ASHURBANIPAL'S PALACE AT NINEVEH
Showing the hunting of wild horses with hounds.

Courtesy British Museum

DETAIL OF THE LION HUNT FROM ASHURBANIPAL'S PALACE AT NINEVEH

III—15

Courtesy of Royal Air Force

AN AIRVIEW OF THE MOUND OF NINEVEH

The Assyrian star began setting long before his reign was over. Mercenaries, always a dangerous element, filled out the army and Aramean merchants controlled trade. These internal weaknesses were aggravated by the approach of two peoples soon destined to replace Assyria. Semitic desert tribes, known to us as the Chaldeans but not to be confused with a people north of Assyria, had for some time been establishing themselves at the head of the Persian gulf, south of Babylon. Eventually these people gained sufficient power to take Babylon itself, and it was their second king, Nebuchadnezzar, who forced the Hebrews into unhappy exile. The other movement was from the eastern mountains and consisted of Indo-European peoples led by the Medes and including the Persians. These had fought against Assyria before, but now, toward the end of the seventh century, they became an irresistible force, and in 612 B.C. through the cooperation of Medes and Babylonians, the famous city of Nineveh, symbol of world might, became a heap of rubbish.

Assyrian arms had been carried to distant parts of the Near East where its terrors were long remembered. Ruled from its various capitals, Assyria for a century and a quarter had been continuously master of western Asia. The next great empire, with its seat in Babylon, followed, to be cast aside in turn after a century by Cyrus the Great and his Persian forces.

NEBUCHADNEZZAR AND THE CHALDEANS

The Chaldeans began their dynasty when Nebuchadnezzar's father revolted on the death of Ashurbanipal in 626 B.C. Twenty-two years later the son came to the throne to begin a forty-three year reign that became one of the best known in history. Nebuchadnezzar's part in the story of the capture of Jerusalem, the destruction of the temple, and the exile of the Jews attained world fame through the spread of the Bible.

After Assyria fell, Egypt continued the same old policy of fostering discontent among the small states that lay between her and the Tigris-Euphrates. But Nebuchadnezzar defeated an Egyptian army in northern Syria, and as part of these military measures subdued the small state of Judah. The capture of Jerusalem and the deportation of Hebrews to Babylon figured less in the world news of the day than the fact that Egypt had been halted. Judah, after all, was an extremely small state.

Nebuchadnezzar was a busy warrior, bringing a large portion of the old Assyrian empire under his control. The revenues that thus poured into his treasury allowed him to rebuild Babylon on lines of splendor and beauty previously unknown. Temples were erected to the dieties that had long been at home in Babylonia, and the gateway of the city he dedicated to the goddess Ishtar, the patroness of love. His huge imperial palace and government offices lay beyond the gate, and overlooking it, on the roof of the palace, was a series of gardens filled with luxurious plants. These were the mysterious Hanging Gardens of Babylon which so intrigued the Greeks and caused them to include the gardens among the Seven Wonders of the World. Here among the palms and ferns on his roof the great king would chat with his inti-

Courtesy The Oriental Institute of The University of Chicago   Painting by J. Bardin, after E. Unger

CONCEPTION OF THE CITY OF BABYLON

Showing the tower of Babel. Dating from 604 to 562 B.C.

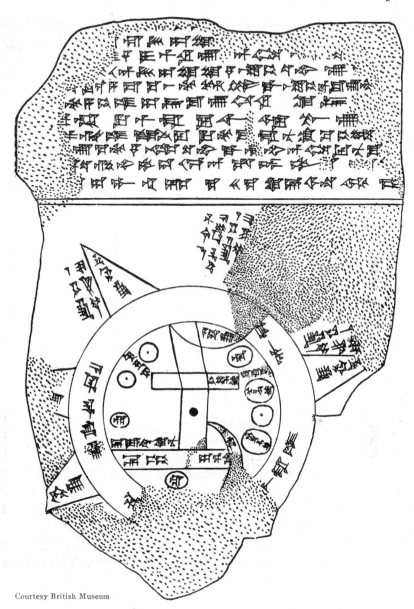

DRAWING OF A CUNEIFORM TABLET

Showing a Babylonian map of the world about the Sixth Century B.C. The seas surrounding the world are indicated by the large circles within which are noted various Babylonian cities. The two broken vertical lines represent the Tigris and Euphrates.

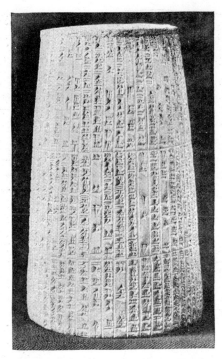

POTTERY BEARING AN INSCRIPTION OF NEBUCHADNEZZAR

mates, or in solitude consider matters nearest to his heart. Little remains of the glories of Babylon except heaps of tumbled mud-brick out of which the buildings were made, but the colorful Ishtar Gate and the tales of Hebrew and Greek have given us a very adequate picture of Nebuchadnezzar's Babylon. The old world was a colorful world and Babylon will always remain one of the greatest cities of that age.

The Chaldeans made great progress in the study of astronomy through an effort to discover the future in the stars. This art we call "astrology". Much information had been systematically collected by the Babylonians and from it we have here the beginning of astronomy. The groups of stars which now bear the name "Twelve Signs of the Zodiac" were mapped out for the first time, and the planets Mercury, Venus, Mars, Jupiter, and Saturn were known. Since these planets were thought to have special powers

Courtesy The Oriental Institute of The University of Chicago   Painting by J. Bardin, after E. Unger

PAINTING OF THE CITY OF BABYLON WITH THE ISHTAR
GATE IN THE FOREGROUND

REPRODUCTION OF THE ISHTAR GATE WITH LIONS FROM
PROCESSION STREET AT BABYLON
Doorway between halls in The Oriental Institute.

over the lives of men, they were named for the five leading gods
and goddesses. We refer to these planets by their Roman names,
but the Romans had adopted the Babylonian terms and simply
translated them into their equivalents in Rome. Thus the planet
of Ishtar, the goddess of love, became Venus, and that of the god
Marduk was changed to Jupiter.

Chaldean power and civilization reached their height during
the reign of Nebuchadnezzar, yet when he died in 562 B.C. Babylon's days were numbered. The exiled Jews of that city now looked
to the east for their deliverer, and in 539 B.C. he came. He was
Cyrus the Great.

THE PERSIAN WORLD EMPIRE

When Shalmaneser III of Assyria in 835 B.C. returned from
an expedition to the northeast he carried with him tribute from
the Medes and Persians. This is the first time that these Iranians

TOMB OF CYRUS THE GREAT AT PASARGADAE

PERSEPOLIS
Airview of the great terrace built by Darius the Great.

Courtesy The Oriental Institute of The University of Chicago

PERSEPOLIS

The grand double stairway leading to the audience hall of the emperor unearthed
by The Oriental Institute's Persian expedition.

appear in history and we see that they were far from their later
home. After a century and a half the Persians opposed Sennacherib at a point much farther south. When Cyrus took Babylon
the center of the Persian world was near Persepolis. Thus for
three hundred years those Indo-European speaking people had
moved steadily southward.

At the time of the downfall of Nineveh, the Medes had been
the leading group among the newcomers to Persia, and thereafter
expansion was made in the name of Media. But in 559 B.C. when
Cyrus became king of the Persians, then only vassals of the Medes,
he laid plans to take over the throne of Media as well. This he
succeeded in doing in 550 B.C., and thenceforth his great energies
laid the foundation of an empire that was to reach far east toward
China, and west to include Egypt, Babylonia, Assyria, Palestine,
Syria, and Asia Minor. Even Greece was included in the plans of
empire. Thus the last oriental empire was the greatest, exceeding

Courtesy The Oriental Institute of The University of Chicago

SCULPTURED WALL RELIEF ON THE MONUMENTAL STAIRWAY AT
PERSEPOLIS DEPICTING A LION ATTACKING A BULL
Reconstruction work is in progress.

by far even the large area encompassed by the Assyrians at their height.

When Cyrus made the Medes his vassals, he as king inherited a tremendous territory that included not only that occupied by the Aryans on the highlands of Persia, but also a large portion of Assyria and Asia Minor as far west as the Halys River. But across this river ruled a powerful king noted in legend for his extreme wealth. This was King Croesus of Lydia, a proud king, who refused to surrender to Cyrus' approaching army. Yet nothing could stop the king of the Persians, and Croesus' kingdom with its access to the Greek seas became part of the fast growing Aryan empire.

Cyrus then turned his attention to the east. Babylonia was still unconquered but her king was more intent on religion than on matters of state, and Cyrus could afford to ignore him for a few more years. Therefore he pushed on to far central Asia, sub-

Courtesy The Oriental Institute of The University of Chicago

RELIEF FROM THE GREAT STAIRWAY AT PERSEPOLIS

duing tribes as distant as the Jaxartes River which flows into the Aral Sea. Having in these operations enlarged the Persian empire to previously unknown proportions, the much feared conqueror returned to his native land, only to start out almost immediately for Babylon, the most famous city of the time.

With little effort Cyrus defeated Belshazzar, the crown prince, and captured Babylon in 539 B.C. Thus came into his possession not only Babylonia itself but also its foreign holdings including Syria and Palestine and the part of Assyria not already held.

It was in 550 B.C. that Cyrus had revolted from the Medes. A little more than a decade later this extraordinary man had, at the head of his peasant soldiery, created the greatest empire that the world had seen. Moreover, Cyrus was the first great Aryan conqueror of whom we know, and through his efforts the Semites, long the lords of western Asia, lost control until the coming of the Arabs a thousand years later.

CYRUS RELEASES THE HEBREWS FROM EXILE

Cyrus was very human to those he had subdued. King Croesus of Lydia lost his kingdom, but once pacified he was made an official in the old land of the Medes. Persian policy was to leave the conquered content, and it is therefore not surprising that Cyrus allowed the Jews wishing to return to Jerusalem to do so, there to rebuild the temple destroyed by Nebuchadnezzar.

Many, but not all, returned and took with them the religious conceptions which are included in Judaism, the religion of the Jews. During the exile Ezekiel and a great teacher whose name is unknown developed the view that Yahweh was the Creator and only God of the universe, and that hardship and affliction were necessary to make a people useful to the world. God had prepared those in exile for a greater service, and they would eventually be liberated and allowed to return to their land. But kingship was not revived, for Jewish thought now saw that kings were but the tools of God. It was then that the old Hebrew state became a Jewish religious organization. Instead of a King there was a High Priest in Jerusalem.

The Jewish leaders now set about restoring the city and the temple, and collecting the sayings and writings of the prophets and others whose history we now read in the Old Testament. As the service in the temple developed, there came into being the remarkable group of religious songs known as the Book of Psalms. Many of the Psalms were written during the Persian period, while some may be as early as the time of David. Thereafter Israel's greatness was to lie in her religion and in the fact that Christianity's great teacher was a Jew.

CAMBYSES MARCHES TO EGYPT

Cyrus was killed in 529 B.C. while in battle east of the Caspian Sea, and was succeeded by his son Cambyses. Why Cyrus had never tried to incorporate Egypt into his realm is not known for certain, although it is probable that he was much too busy in other sectors. At any rate Cambyses soon set out with that purpose in mind. Having marched his army across southwestern Asia he passed over the desert from Gaza and engaged the Egyptians near the mouth of the present day Suez Canal. The power of Egypt was gone, and Cambyses annexed the country of the XXVIth dynasty with ease in 525 B.C. Then with the ambition and madness of a world conqueror he decided on the capture of Carthage, even then a very important city on the north African coast. He planned to attack it by land and sea, but the Phoenician fleet from Tyre refused to fight against a city that had been founded by its ancestors and in which blood kin now dwelt. Cambyses was thus forced to concentrate on a land force which was to cross the treacherous desert west of Egypt. Fifty thousand men were selected and they reached several of the oases in safety, but after that nothing was ever heard of them again. It was as though they had been swallowed by some superhuman fury, and indeed it is probable that a great sandstorm was the means of keeping the conquering Persians away from Carthage. Nevertheless, Cambyses had taken Egypt and thereafter until Alexander came out of Greece the country remained under Persian control except for periods of revolt and independence.

THE PERSIANS INVADE GREECE

Cambyses died while returning from Egypt and after some typical oriental difficulty over title to the throne, it passed finally in 521 B.C. to Darius, a distant relative of the dead king. Darius was not only an excellent general but an able administrator, and after a few years the unwieldy empire attained a semblance of calm. It was then (512 B.C.) that further conquests were begun. Darius marched westward over his vast domain to cross the narrow waters of the Bosphorus that separate Asia from Europe. The principal result of this expedition was to take Thrace, in doing which he clearly threatened the rising Greek states. About the same time a Persian army entered the Indus valley in northwestern India.

Greece, however, was Darius' main objective because various Greek cities consistently aided the Ionian trouble makers on the Aegean coast of Persian Asia Minor. Matters came to a head in

Courtesy The Oriental Institute of The University of Chicago

THE TOMB OF DARIUS THE GREAT WITH EXCAVATION IN PROGRESS

MARATHON. MOUND RAISED OVER THE GRAVE OF THE
HEROIC ATHENIANS

492 B.C. when Darius led his army into Thrace, but the difficulties were great and in addition the fleet was wrecked while rounding a promontory. Accordingly the advance was abandoned in favor of a direct attack by water.

It was in 490 B.C. that the Persian army landed in the Bay of Marathon twenty-six miles northeast of Athens, intent on punishing that city for aid it had given the Ionian revolters. The Athenian forces were far outnumbered but through the strategy employed by their commander, Miltiades, the Persians were badly defeated, the survivors fleeing to their ships. News of the victory was carried to Athens by a despatch runner named Phidippedes who covered the twenty-six miles at his greatest speed and arrived crying, "Rejoice! We conquer!" only to fall dead. His feat was commemorated by the Greeks in their Olympic games and the marathon races of today measure twenty-six miles, the distance run by Phidippedes.

Darius realized that a stronger land and sea force was necessary and returned to his beautiful palace at Persepolis with plans for a return engagement. Three years later all was in readiness when the king, now well on in years, died, and left the fate of Greece as well that of Persia in the hands of his son Xerxes.

Athens became convinced after Marathon that its navy had to be strengthened if it was to ward off the Persians when they returned. The entire Phoenician coast with its well-trained sailors was subject to Persia and constituted an ominous threat, should its fleet be sent to Athens. This was actually part of Xerxes' plan, and in the summer of 480 B.C. the Persian army crossed the Hellespont into Thrace and followed the seacoast down into Greece, the fleet adopting a parallel course just offshore.

By this time Athens had induced Sparta to come to her aid, and with a small force the Spartan king, Leonidas, held the important pass of Thermopylae against the approaching Persians until a flank movement caught him in the rear. The Persians then proceeded unimpeded toward a deserted Athens which they promptly burned.

In the meantime the Persian fleet had skirmished with the Greek ships but the action was indecisive. Far more potent was

Courtesy The Art Institute, Chicago

MOUNT PENTELICON, NEAR ATHENS, SOURCE OF THE
FAMOUS PENTELIC MARBLE

Courtesy The Art Institute, Chicago

VALLEY BELOW DELPHI OVERLOOKING THE GYMNASIUM.
HOME OF THE DELPHIC ORACLE

the effect of a storm which destroyed two hundred Asiatic vessels. The Greek ships withdrew southward and came to anchor in the Bay of Salamis just west of Athens prepared to fight the approaching flotilla.

Xerxes was on the heights above the bay as the action began and before long he must have sensed its end. When the day was over, he had seen his ships, far outnumbering those of the Athenians, suffer almost complete annihilation. Salamis had been a brilliant Greek victory, and the worried Persian survivors and their king turned quickly for home.

An army of about fifty thousand was left to winter in Thessaly, and the following year the Persians advanced once more through Attica, but at Plataea they met their final defeat. Thus ended Persia's bid for supremacy in Europe. The Athenians hastened to occupy the northern side of the Hellespont and their fleet drove the remaining Phoenician ships from the Ionian coast. While there continued to be trouble on the Graeco-Persian frontier, never again did a Persian army set foot in Greece.

For another century and a half Persia remained mistress of Asia but many were the signs that foretold her doom. Revolts were continuous and palace intrigues weakened the kingship. At length a Darius, the third of his name and the last king of the Persian empire, came to the throne in 336 B.C. The same year a young warrior named Alexander became king in Macedonia several hundred miles north of Athens. The next part of our story is concerned with the young king's extraordinary will to conquer the world.

ALEXANDER AND HIS EMPIRE

Philip of Macedonia had been very successful in bringing the straggling Greek states under his control, and although there was a general revolt when his twenty year old son became king, all of Greece except Sparta soon looked on Alexander as its natural leader. To impress his power and the dangers of disloyalty upon the states, Alexander completely destroyed the city of Thebes in Boeotia which had revolted against him, and left standing only the house of Pindar the poet. Thus Alexander created not only an object lesson for those with a mind to revolt, but also demonstrated his deep sympathy for Greek culture. Throughout his life he, an outsider, considered Hellenic culture superior to all others.

Alexander now felt himself the champion of Greece against Persia. Being well versed in the classics, for no less a man than Aristotle had been his tutor in the Macedonian court, he compared the situation to that much earlier time when the Greek peoples united against their common enemy in Troy. Having gathered together his army he left Greece and marched into Asia Minor, pausing at the Temple of Athena in Troy to ask for success against the Persians. Continuing the march he met the Persians led by Darius III at the Gulf of Issus in 333 B.C. Here at the point where the Mediterranean shore turns sharply south toward Phoenicia a great victory was won by Alexander, and Darius fled, not stopping until he had crossed the Euphrates. From there he sent a message proposing that peace be made; Alexander could have all of Asia west of the Euphrates. But despite the counsel of his friends Alexander refused, and set off through Phoenicia taking each seaport as he came to it. This was a very necessary move, for had the Persian-Phoenician fleet been allowed to rove unmolested from its ports of supply it would have proved a serious menace to Greece. Tyre, then on an island, gave Alexander his greatest trouble, resisting for seven months, but when it fell with a great slaughter the fleet rapidly disappeared.

Alexander then passed down the Palestine coast and crossed the Sinai desert to Egypt, following the same route as his Assyrian and Persian predecessors. Egypt fell easily and then an incident occurred that was to have an important bearing on his later life. He journeyed out into the Sahara Desert to the oasis temple of the god Amon and entered the holy place alone. On emerging he was hailed by the high priest of the temple as Zeus-Amon. We shall presently learn of Alexander's efforts to have himself regarded as a god.

Having gained control of Asia Minor, Phoenicia and Egypt, the western outposts of the now crumbling Persian empire, Alexander left Egypt and the new city of Alexandria that he had founded, and directed his course for the upper Tigris River. Not far from Nineveh, Darius and Alexander again met in what has been called the Battle of Arbela. The Persians were crushed and shortly thereafter Darius was stabbed to death by some of his own people.

Alexander turned south from Arbela and in a few days was in the Persian winter palace in Babylon. The Persian empire was rapidly shrinking, indeed it was almost gone, for Arbela had decided the issue.

After resting his army at Babylon, Alexander crossed the plains to the mountain approaches to Persia and, coming to fabulous and magnificent Persepolis, capital of the Persian empire, visited the tomb of Cyrus. Then, quite contrary to custom, Alexander burned the palace of the Persian kings and in so doing avenged the burning of the Acropolis a century and a half before. The destruction of such wealth and grandeur may also have been

DEMOSTHENES, FAMOUS ATHENIAN ORATOR WHO DENOUNCED PHILIP
OF MACEDON FATHER OF ALEXANDER THE GREAT. AT THE VATICAN

Courtesy The Art Institute, Chicago

ALEXANDER THE GREAT. IN THE GLYPTOTHEK, MUNICH

THE GODDESS ATHENA, PATRONESS OF ATHENS, WORSHIPPED BY
ALEXANDER THE GREAT. IN THE VATICAN

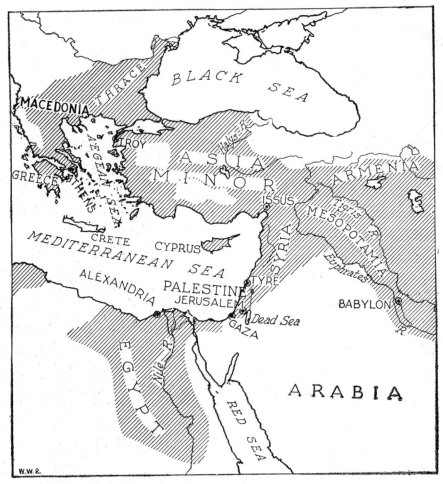

MAP OF THE EXTENSIVE EMPIRE OF ALEXANDER THE GREAT
(Indicated by shaded areas)

intended to symbolize the complete reduction of the empire that
had ruled the world for over two hundred years. Alexander could
hardly have realized that in this act of vandalism he was doing
posterity a tremendous favor, for the ashes have been the means
of preserving in all their original freshness walls with reliefs that
the Oriental Institute has recently uncovered at the capital of the
Persian kings.

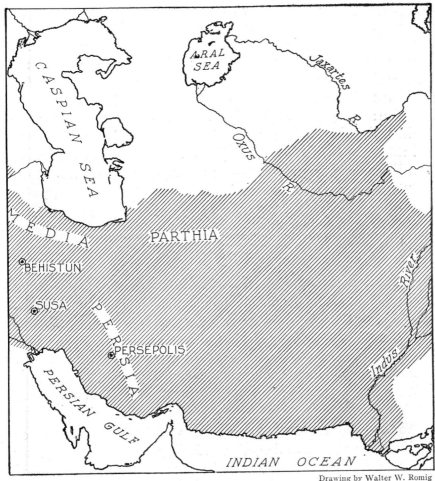

Drawing by Walter W. Romig

Turning northward, four years after leaving Greece, Alexander marched through Media and then began the conquest of the eastern portion of old Persia. By his march of many years, during which he was repeatedly wounded, he reached the Oxus and Jaxartes Rivers in the northeast, the Indus River in India, and the shores of the Indian Ocean. He founded cities bearing his name and carried Greek civilization to the heart of Asia.

But in India his men at last told him plainly that it was long since they had been in Greece, and Alexander turned west again. Reaching Babylon, seven years after he had left it, he prepared for further campaigns, first in the Arabian peninsula, and then in the western Mediterranean against Italy, Sicily, and Carthage. But fate was to intervene and shape the world far differently than he had planned. The man, who had set out to conquer the Persian world and had accomplished that purpose, fell sick with a fever and died. This was in the year 323 B.C. He had been king for less than thirteen years and was not yet thirty-three years old.

The tremendous problem of unifying Greece and Persia under one rule was recognized by Alexander and he went about it in several ways. He was determined to give Greek culture to the world, for in this way a better understanding would be accomplished. On the other hand he felt that he could not rule his empire as a Greek, and with that in mind he married Roxana, an Asiatic princess, and urged his high officials to enter the families of Asiatic nobles. Even the soldiers were requested to take Persian wives, but this created much dissatisfaction and many of them refused. Alexander adopted Persian raiment to some extent and his conciliatory measures extended to placing Persians in high office. In this way, peace and understanding were fostered, at least among the Persians.

For himself, he planned a greater magnitude. We have seen that he was proclaimed Zeus-Amon in Egypt. Several years later he demanded that all who approached him on state occasions bend down and kiss his feet. He was rapidly becoming oriental and before long notified the Greek cities which he had left behind years before that he was thenceforth to be considered among the gods of Greece. This was all part of a policy intended to give him lasting control of the Greek empire. But his attempts to assume a supernatural toga had grave consequences. His closest friends were forced out of his company by this and by his pro-Persian policy, and bitter enmity resulted. Alexander had adopted the course of oriental kings which decreed that if one is to rule as a divine being one must be elevated above man, and be lonely.

THE PARTITION OF ALEXANDER'S EMPIRE

When Alexander died the throne of Macedonia passed to a feeble-minded half brother Philip, for Roxana had not yet given birth to the baby Alexander. But the actual rulers of the empire were that remarkable group of Macedonian generals who had fought for Alexander and been his companions from boyhood. While Alexander lived they worked for a single purpose. When he lay dead in Babylon, leaving no leader strong enough to continue his labors, they quickly formed their personal plans. Ptolemy, one of the cleverest of these men, obtained the governorship of Egypt, and almost immediately took a calculated step toward the inevitable breakup. Alexander's body was bound overland for his royal city in Macedonia, or so it was thought, when Ptolemy suddenly turned up in Syria and took charge of the funeral train. In his high-handed manner he directed the cortège to Memphis, probably hoping thereby to increase the prestige of the man who dreamed of ruling Egypt. Later the body was removed to Alexandria. The great Alexander had truly been claimed by the Orient.

This incident opened a long series of wars between the Macedonian chieftains. It was a period of intense jealousy which nevertheless gave way to alliance when one of them appeared to gain unwarranted strength. During the course of events the fiction of a family successor to Alexander was completely wiped out by the murder of both Philip and the boy Alexander. In time the generals still surviving declared themselves kings of their respective territories, and eventually the former empire held by the will of one man was divided into three main parts, European, Asiatic, and African, ruled by three royal houses.

Successors of Antigonus, one of Alexander's ablest generals, gained control of Macedonia and attempted to weld together the Greek states, a task never successfully accomplished in ancient times. Seleucus came into possession of most of the Asiatic part of the empire and founded Antioch in Syria as his chief city. Ptolemy, the one who met Alexander's funeral train, became king of Egypt. Thus was dissipated the great empire. Of the generals who had traversed Asia with Alexander and who later fought among themselves for personal spoil, only one, the founder of the house of Ptolemy, avoided a violent death.

These Macedonians and their successors continued their feuds and wars for decades, trouble existing principally between the neighboring Ptolemies and Seleucids. The Macedonian empire soon had enough worries at home with the Greek states and foreign invaders.

The Ptolemies built up a strong navy and once more the eastern Mediterranean became an Egyptian sea. At times Palestine and parts of Syria and Asia Minor came within the orbit of Egyptian control, thus reviving the external aspect of political conditions a thousand years before. Alexandria became the busiest port on the Mediterranean and during the early part of the Ptolemaic period the famous light-house, some 370 feet high, was built on the island of Pharos which guarded the harbor.

Ptolemy I dated his reign from 305 B.C. There followed many eminent kings and queens of mixed, but non-Egyptian, descent. The last of the line was Cleopatra, actually Cleopatra VII, who by her enchanting ways captured the imagination of Caesar, Mark Antony and the world ever since. She was not an Egyptian as is so often said, but mostly Macedonian by blood with a sprinkling of Greek and Persian. Cleopatra was queen of Egypt until 30 B.C. when she allowed herself to be stung to death by asps rather than be exhibited in Octavian's triumphal procession.

The Ptolemies were rulers in an oriental country and were oriental kings to their subjects but remained Greek in their ways of living. Greek culture centered chiefly at Alexandria where a great library was formed and where philosophers and scientists assembled. Alexandria possessed the first scientific institution sponsored by a government, and many men famous for their scholarly contributions were attracted to this intellectual center. Greek artistic standards were maintained in this land across the sea, and Greek became the governmental language. This we see from many sources including the famous Rosetta Stone which was erected in 195 B.C. toward the middle of the Ptolemaic period.

A GREEK WARRIOR. IN THE BOBOLI GARDENS, FLORENCE

Courtesy The Art Institute, Chicago

THE DYING GAUL, IN BRONZE. IN THE MUSEO CAPITOLINO, ROME

The Seleucids never became quite as powerful as the Ptolemies though they had inherited the greater part of Alexander's empire. Indeed some of their troubles can be traced to the very magnitude of the territory they attempted to hold. From the Aegean to the borders of India they had nominal control but portions soon began falling away.

The early Seleucids founded many cities, even on the edge of India, and to these they gave home rule on the old Greek plan. Attempts were made to transplant people with Greek backgrounds to distant points of the empire in an effort to carry widespread the creed of Greece. To some extent this was successful, but gradually the territories farthest away from Antioch gained independence. A large part of western Asia Minor fell to the Galatians, a war-like group of Gauls who had invaded Greece in 280 B.C., and the eastern portion of the empire was lost to a group of small kingdoms which were to become significant in later times. The greatest of these was Parthia which came to dispute possession of Asia with Rome.

Courtesy The Art Institute, Chicago

HEAD OF A KING OF PERGAMUM, ASIA MINOR
Second Century B.C. Found at Eleusis near Athens.

Meanwhile Rome had long since gained control of Italy and had defeated the Carthaginians in two series of wars. The last had seen Hannibal banished from Carthage by Roman order and the western Mediterranean world safely placed in Roman hands (202 B.C.). Rome then turned to the Macedonian empire which had tried to aid Hannibal and in 197 B.C. disastrously defeated the Macedonian army. Alexander's homeland became a vassal state, while the Greek cities which had been allies of the Romans were granted freedom.

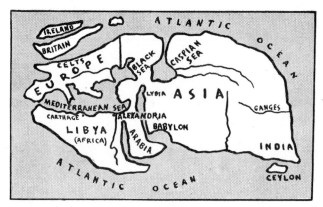

MAP OF THE WORLD ACCORDING TO ERATOSTHENES, 200 B.C.

The Seleucid king at this time was Antiochus the Great. Feeling a strength far beyond that which he and his army possessed, he attempted to seize some of the newly freed cities. Thereupon the Roman legions pushed farther east than they had ever been and in 190 B.C. the two forces met at Magnesia in Asia Minor. The Roman victory, which followed, placed under control another of the three empires which had been carved out of the empire of Alexander. Thenceforth the Seleucids were vassals of Rome.

Egypt, meantime, had been friendly toward Rome as well she might, since Rome was fighting her enemies the Seleucids, but herself became accountable to Rome in 168 B.C.

There were to be other Ptolemies and other Seleucids, but all were conscious of the new and great state in the western Mediterranean which in a few years had absorbed the world of Alexander's successors.

THE MACCABEE REVOLT

During the early part of the second century B.C. the Seleucids controlled Palestine, and King Antiochus Epiphanes (175-164 B.C.) made himself most objectionable to the Jews for a number of reasons but chiefly through his efforts to force them to worship Greek gods. An edict was issued ordering the erection of pagan altars throughout Palestine and officers were provided to see that the Jews obeyed. There followed the movement known as the

Maccabean revolt which began when Mattathias, a priest, slew a Jew who was willing to forsake Yahweh for pagan gods. Mattathias and his five sons then fled to the mountains to organize their followers for the fight against Syria. The old priest soon died and nominated his son Judas Maccabeus to carry on the fight for religious freedom.

The military genius of Judas defeated the Seleucid armies and the Jews regained their end. Temple practices were restored and guaranteed by Syria whereupon many of the Jews withdrew from the struggle. But Judas had visions of a politically free Palestine as well and the war continued. Judas was killed, yet his aim was accomplished by Simon, the last surviving son of Mattathias, who negotiated a treaty of independence in 142 B.C., a little over twenty years after his father had made his bold break.

For a short time Israel had her own kings, Simon becoming the first of the Hasmonean dynasty. During his administration the country prospered, but he and two of his sons were murdered by Ptolemy who wished to regain Palestine for Egypt. The third son, John Hyrcanus (135-105 B.C.), at length succeeded in establishing himself as head of the state and Palestine was enlarged to a size it had not enjoyed since before the Exile. However, internal troubles between the peaceful Pharisees and the warlike Sadducees, together with disturbing elements from outside, finally caused Rome to intervene and take matters in hand. Pompey besieged Jerusalem in 63 B.C. and reduced the Jews to vassalage.

HEROD THE GREAT TO THE FALL OF JERUSALEM

Then as always Palestine lay between contending nations, and it was in the interests of Rome that this small country remain peaceful and friendly if possible. Parthia had become the principal power east of the Euphrates, and Julius Caesar ere his death had planned a campaign against her. Thus it was that Herod, an Edomite from the southern end of the Dead Sea, became king of Judea with Roman sanction, but was forced to flee to Rome when the Parthians penetrated Palestine. Not until 37 B.C. did he return to Jerusalem, there to rebuild the temple and contend with the factions that split the Jewish people. Some were pro-Roman; others pro-Parthian. The Pharisees were content with any kind of rule as long as they could live as they wished.

In his thirty-third year as king Herod the Great died and it was in that year or earlier that Christ was born. The year of Herod's death was 4 B.C. It was not until the sixth century after Christ had lived his fruitful life that his birth was made a starting point in chronology. Soon afterwards it was adopted by the church in Rome and came into popular use in the tenth century.

Not long after Herod's death Judea became a Roman province administered by procurators sent from Rome. The best known of these is Pontius Pilate who presided at the trial of Jesus. Herod's descendants maintained a semblance of power in Palestine, but the Jews would not be reconciled to Roman rule. At length, through unwise and criminal actions on the part of the procurators, which thoroughly inflamed the already dissatisfied religious zealots, open rebellion took place in 66 A.D. and the death struggle with Rome began.

Murders and massacres by the infuriated and momentarily successful Jews finally brought Vespasian, one of Nero's ablest generals, to quell the rebellion. Approaching Jerusalem from the north Vespasian subdued one section of the country after another until he controlled all outlying fortresses except those at Masada and Herodium. At that point he was proclaimed emperor by his troops and yielded his former position to his son Titus who then advanced on Jerusalem.

Meanwhile the people of the city had been quarreling and annihilating themselves instead of conserving all strength and coming to a common purpose for the approaching siege. Various factions among the Jews continued to fight for control in a useless and hopeless strife that greatly reduced their numbers. And then, just before Passover in 70 A.D., Titus appeared.

For five months Titus attacked the city, breaking through one wall after another, meanwhile sending frequent messages to the inflamed Jews inside to surrender. Finally his engines of war proved too strong and the Roman soldiers poured through the last breach, and soon, despite all efforts of Titus, the temple, the

BUST OF
VESPASIAN. IN
THE VATICAN

Courtesy The Art Insti-
tute, Chicago

glory of Jerusalem and the Jews, was in flames. Yet at this intense
moment the Jews still quarreled in another part of the city.

With Jerusalem laid waste, the Romans had only to subdue the
remaining minor fortresses. The last to fall was Masada, far to
the south overlooking the Dead Sea. When its fanatic defenders
realized that it too must fall they decided that death with their
ideals was better than life under the Romans. Therefore according to plan the women and children were killed first, followed
by the men, until there remained one lone survivor in the midst of
almost a thousand bodies. True to the pact he likewise plunged
a sword through his own body after setting fire to the palace. The
Romans entered and learned of the desperate deed from two women who had hidden in a cave with five children.

The Jewish state was no more, but centuries of philosophy had
made Judaism impregnable. Nations were to come and go, but
Judaism survived wherever it went in its long travels.

Courtesy The Oriental Institute of The University of Chicago

LOADING LARGE PORTIONS OF THE WINGED BULL ONTO
A TIGRIS RIVER BOAT

We leave the Near East stage set for the parade of Byzantines, Arabs, Crusaders, Turks, French, English, and Italians. Often it is said that history repeats itself. No better example could be found than in the closing days of the World War when General Allenby (later Lord Allenby of Megiddo) sent his cavalry through the Megiddo pass in a surprise maneuver to capture the Turks. We recall that Thutmose III followed the same narrow route to take the stronghold of Egypt's enemies thirty-four centuries before.

EARLY CRETE, GREECE, AND ROME

THE REMOTE PAST OF CRETE

CIVILIZATION developed first in the Near East but its seat was transferred after many centuries to the northern Mediterranean where Greece and then Rome held sway. But before either of these northern territories gave the slightest indication of their genius, there developed on the Mediterranean island of Crete a state whose culture led directly to Greece of the days of Troy's fame.

It was natural that the people of Crete became sailors. They themselves were islanders and north of them lay hundreds of smaller isles that dotted the Aegean Sea. Beyond these were the delightfully indented coasts of Greece and Asia Minor which provided refuge for their ships and with whose towns they traded. In a southeastern direction stood Egypt, mother of a high civilization, only a few days away if the winds were right. Crete thus lay in the center of an active sea-world, and her sailing vessels came to be known in many ports. Products of the northern islands were carried southward, and bartered products returned in the holds of Cretan ships. Perhaps Egyptians themselves settled in Crete before the beginning of the First dynasty (about 3000 B.C.).

Because of its central position Crete became the cultural leader among the islands and coasts of the Aegean, rising from its Neolithic culture to heights that remained supreme until Acheans from the Greek mainland swept over the island about 1400 B.C.

Drawing by Walter W. Romig

MAP OF EARLY CRETE, GREECE, AND ROME

The people of Crete belonged to the white Mediterranean race and were not related by blood to the later Greeks. When copper was introduced to the island, civilization took a great step forward, leading gradually to the best days of Crete which began about 2000 B.C. when a palace was built at Knossus a few miles from the blue waters of the northern coast. Many influences had come from foreign shores, but the island developed its own sturdy culture on individual lines. Farmer, merchant, potter, shepherd, sailor and king spoke a language unknown to us. Their writing was influenced by Egyptian hieroglyphs, but the sounds which their signs represented are still a mystery in spite of much study. Gradually as trade increased and the daily needs of business grew greater the picture type of writing was replaced by a linear script which could be written with much greater ease and effect.

It is probable that Crete was ruled by a single king at Knossus, although this is not certain. In time the large collection of written materials which have been excavated and now repose in museums will probably be deciphered. Then facts of great interest and importance for the understanding of these island people will be released to pour forth like a newly opened oil seam. Then we may know the extent of territorial expansion and the part individuals played in the development of this kingdom which overlooked both the Aegean and the Mediterranean. But first must be found the key to their writing.

The Cretans were an artistic people from beginning to end, and although their art at length became somewhat flamboyant it always possesses more than ordinary interest. We often think of the potter as of a rather mechanical type of person with few ideas and a limited repertoire. The Cretan potter not only made vessels of exceptional grace but decorated them with designs rich in artistic sensibility. During the period of the first palace, pottery was decorated in several colors, the designs consisting mostly of pleasing curved lines and geometric forms. The quality of these

Courtesy The Art Institute, Chicago

KNOSSUS
View overlooking the queen's palace.

Above: KNOSSUS
A portion of the
second palace as re-
constructed by Sir
Arthur Evans.

Left: PORTION OF
AN ANCIENT
WALL AT PHAES-
TOS WITH SNOW
CAPPED MOUNT
IDA IN THE
BACKGROUND

KNOSSUS
Throne room showing throne and mural decoration.

RUINS AT PHAESTOS WITH THE THICKLY POPULATED VALLEY
IN THE BACKGROUND

Courtesy The Art Institute, Chicago
KNOSSUS
Passageway in the second palace showing large pottery vessels.

vessels was high, but during the period of the second palace the potter became an even better artist. At that time the earlier style passed out of use and was replaced by vessels covered with flowers, trees, and other delightful land and sea forms from nature which at their best seem to move with the impulse of life.

If potters showed such artistic breadth what may we expect of the sculptor, the frieze painter and the metal worker? To realize that here on the island of Crete were artisans superior to most that Egypt, Assyria, Babylonia or Persia ever produced, we have but to compare their works. The Cretan artist lived in an animated atmosphere free from the restraint that guided his oriental craft-brothers, and because of it he could express his full knowledge of nature. The best of Cretan goldwork can be likened with no apologies to the masterpieces of a Benvenuto Cellini, and frescoes found on the walls of Cretan palaces embody a feeling for breathing life and vibrant anatomy that would have done credit to many a painter of the Renaissance.

Frescoes and objects from the period of the second palace give a remarkable picture of the life of the times. Frequently the aristocracy gathered on the terraces of the palace for social purposes and to see boxing matches or bull fights planned for their entertainment. These sports were held in high favor by the Cretans as we may judge by their frequent occurrence in the art of the time. On such occasions women wore dresses that were exceedingly modern in form, much different from the garb worn by oriental ladies. Fashion of the period called for close-fit embroidered bodices and well-designed skirts which accentuated their small waists. Men, on the other hand, wore clothing which gave them the greatest freedom, being but an elaborate loin cloth. If the weather called for it they threw a cloak over their shoulders.

In many respects Cretan culture was far in advance of any civilization that existed at the time. During the island's most prosperous period it had widespread contacts and may have held even parts of southern Greece. Cretan art may well have influenced the naturalistic approach developed by the painters at the courts of Amenhotep III and Akhenaton, and the islands and mainland near Crete felt the full artistic impact of this astonishing culture.

Less than two generations ago practically nothing was known of Crete aside from Greek legends of fabulous King Minos. Now, due largely to the intelligent labors of Sir Arthur Evans, masses of information are available concerning the life of the island. We would gladly know more of this fascinating civilization which blossomed to its fullest during the Egyptian XVIIIth dynasty. The secrets held fast by the unread script of these people may eventually be released and then we may know the reasons for Cretan supremacy.

About 1400 B.C. all the palaces and principal cities on the island were destroyed and the royal residence at Knossus went up in flames. Cretan civilization did not die but it lost its virility in the presence of the conqueror. Thereafter the seat of power and culture in the island world was transferred to the south coast of Greece, to Mycenae—the home of Homeric heroes.

Courtesy The Art Institute, Chicago

AN ANCIENT FIREPLACE AT PHAESTOS

THE FAME OF GREECE came late in history, about halfway between the rise of the Egyptian and Mesopotamian dynasties and our own time, but at the beginning of history Greece was very backward indeed. The Neolithic peasant culture of the continent persisted for a long time and progress came slowly. With none too certain a step it advanced until around 1600 B.C. Cretan influences, then spreading in all directions, invaded southern Greece. Possibly the Cretan king regarded this territory as among his domains. At any rate Cretan culture gripped firmly the lives of the people who saw in it something superior to anything they had ever known before. Cretan merchants and perhaps artists first brought ideas of the advanced life that existed on the island, but in time local artisans carried on the tradition. Yet native thought also had its effect and at length there came into being that distinctive type of art and culture called Mycenaean.

The city of Mycenae, home of Agamemnon who led the Greek confederates against Troy about 1200 B.C., was ruled during the sixteenth century by the so-called Shaft Grave dynasty. Whether these kings whose magnificent burials have been discovered at Mycenae were Cretans is unknown, but their tombs give an idea of the riches for which kingship stood, while objects found show clearly the extent to which Cretan civilization had permeated Greece. Mycenae was at that time much smaller than during its greatest days a few centuries later, yet the structure of Mycenean power was being laid. During the fifteenth century kings were buried in beehive-shaped tombs and the culture which was grow-

Courtesy The Art Institute, Chicago

THE FAMOUS LION GATE AT MYCENAE

Courtesy J. Bradford Pengelly

THRESHING WHEAT ON AN ANCIENT THRESHING FLOOR AT MYCENAE

MYCENAE
Stairway beyond the Lion Gate.

ing up in Mycenae spread to the outlying regions. With the advent of the fourteenth century we find Mycenae the natural leader of a vast Aegean realm including Crete which had just fallen at the hand of northern invaders.

An unknown king consolidated the Mycenean world about 1400 B.C., and for two centuries he and his successors held the reins of power and leadership in the Greek and island spheres. No longer was Knossus the center of this universe. Instead, all Aegean eyes focused on Mycenae, now greatly enlarged and surrounded by a wall of huge stones whose main entrance was the famous Lion Gate. Sentinels, stationed high in the city or in the watch tower on the nearby peak of Hagios Elias, surveyed the many miles of approach, looking toward the passes to Corinth or far off over the plain of Argos to the gulf beyond. The kings of this dynasty built huge domed tombs, the most famous being

Courtesy The Art Institute, Chicago

MYCENAE
Entrance to the so-called Treasury of Atreus.

REPRODUCTION
OF ONE OF THE
WELL-KNOWN
GOLD CUPS
FROM VAPHIO,
NEAR SPARTA.
MYCENEAN
PERIOD

Showing Cretan
artistic influence.

Courtesy
J. Bradford Pengelly

SIDE VIEW OF
THE SAME CUP
SHOWING
DETAIL OF
MAN AND BULLS

Courtesy
J. Bradford Pengelly

the one known today as the Treasury of Atreus. Huge blocks of stone were used in its construction, and over the doorway is a slab which weighs more than a hundred tons.

Mycenaean merchant ships covered the Aegean and Mediterranean, carrying on a profitable commerce with Egypt and the Asiatic coast on the east, and Sicily on the west, as well as with all the territory near home. For two hundred years these people who included the Acheans became a major influence in all the civilized countries bordering the Mediterranean, and doubtless many of them migrated to foreign lands where they might better pursue the profession at which they were so adept.

The Near East learned to know well these people of the now greatly expanded Mycenaean world. Ramses II fought against some of them in the Hittite alliance at Kadesh in Syria, and his son warded off island raiders in the Delta. The Philistines themselves came from southern Greece, and pushing southward by land and sea were finally stopped, in the land to which they gave their name, by Ramses III soon after 1200 B.C.

It was about that time that the famous Achean advance on Troy took place. We read in Homer that the Trojan prince Paris, son of King Priam, visited Greece where he abducted Helen the wife of Menelaus and returned with his beautiful captive to Troy. Menelaus was the brother of Agamemnon, powerful king of Mycenae, who immediately gained support from most of the princes of Greece. Helen must be recovered and the wrong avenged. The Greeks gathered their fleets and with Agamemnon at their head sailed for Troy where they besieged the city for nine years. Included in the group were Achilles of the vulnerable heel and Odysseus, king of distant Ithaca, whose travels after the fall of Troy formed the substance of Homer's Odyssey.

Priam also had his allies and the war continued with no real result until the tenth year when the Greeks pretended to sail away. Then occurred the renowned incident of the wooden horse. The Trojans dragged it into the city and at night Greeks who had been hidden inside opened the gates of Troy to their returning comrades. Troy was demolished, the war was over, and Helen was restored to her husband.

It is a very pretty story and one which delighted many generations of Greeks before Homer. However, it cannot be regarded as purely historical. It is probable that Troy's position as a commercial city had as much to do with the war as anything else, even possession of the most beautiful woman in Greece, for Troy lay just across the Aegean near the mouth of the Hellespont and had risen rapidly as a dangerous rival of Mycenae. It is also probable that the royal families of Greece sought new territories for their colonial empire, and the nearby coast of Asia looked inviting. At any rate it was about that time that the Greeks began settling the western coast of Anatolia. Centuries later the cities they had founded lay on the borders of the rapidly expanding Persian empire, and it was because of their opposition to Persia and aid they received from Athens that Darius and Xerxes directed their arms against Greece.

THE ACROPOLIS
Showing reconstruction of a recently found wall older than the Parthenon.

Courtesy J. Bradford Pengelly

THE PARTHENON

The Achean Greeks were suppressed about 1100 B.C. by the Dorian Greeks, a northern tribe which settled in the city-states that had been ruled or at least influenced by the Acheans, and through them the seeds of later Greek civilization were planted. The Phoenician alphabet migrated across the sea at about this time and was modified ultimately to suit the demands of the Greek dialects. Other oriental traits also invaded Greece by way of Egypt, Syria and Asia Minor. It is likely that the splendid Ionic capital which later graced Greek buildings had its birth in the oriental background of Syria or Mesopotamia.

Greece was ruled by kings for several centuries, but there was a king in each of the city-states, for the temperament of the country was contrary to rule by any one man. Thus Athens, Sparta, Thebes and Argos became early centers of the superior civilization that in time spread not only over the Mediterranean world but deep into Asia as well. The nation of Athens consisted of the city and its surroundings to which were allied numerous smaller city-states, all on the peninsula of Attica. The other great centers were similarly organized.

Democracy came to be a distinctive trait of the Greeks, and gradually, as oppression became more and more unbearable, rule

Courtesy J. Bradford Pengelly

VIEW FROM THE ACROPOLIS OVER ATHENS
Showing the Temple of Zeus in right center and the new stadium in the center. The stadium is believed to be on the site of the original one.

by kings and nobles was largely replaced by truly democratic governments. Greek possessions in foreign lands expanded, reaching far up the coasts of the Black Sea and westward to southern Italy, Sicily and beyond. Naucratis in the Egyptian Delta was founded by Greeks with Egyptian permission and became the forerunner of the great seat of learning and trade at Alexandria. Greek culture was becoming a force in many parts of the ancient world.

Out of this background there sprang the Greek city-states of classical fame, and from this civilization came the stout warriors who turned back the Persians at Marathon, Salamis, and Plataea early in the fifth century. They rebuilt Athens and the Acropolis after these had been burned by Xerxes, and today the Parthenon with its Doric colonnades stands high against the sky, having suffered from man and time, but nevertheless a thing of stately beauty. Their descendants joined for a short period in the exploits that carried Alexander and Greek culture to central Asia and the borders of India. But the story of the Greek states, their struggles and accomplishments, their art and architecture,

SUNION
The southeast tip
of Attica.

Courtesy   J.   Bradford
Pengelly

literature and thought, their entire civilization which was guided from the heights of Olympus, must be told elsewhere.

Meanwhile another star was rising. The Greeks had subdued the east, but now the Romans were reaching the point where they in turn were to become conquerors of a world that included Greece. Let us therefore move westward across the Adriatic Sea to the land now called Italy to learn of her early career.

SUNION
The Temple of
Poseidon.

Courtesy J. Bradford
Pengelly

THE YOUTHFUL DAYS OF ROME

B Y THE time of Hammurabi of Babylon and the XIIth dynasty of Egypt, northern Italy had been settled by lake-dwellers from Switzerland. On reaching the warm and fertile lake and river lands they established pile-villages of the type in which they had lived on the Swiss lakes. Many of their settlements have been found, all of them built on piles over water or marshy ground as a means of protection.

About the same time another people were directing their steps toward the pleasant land of Italy. They were Indo-Europeans, closely related to the Aryan Greeks who gave Greece its distinctive and superior flavor, and more distantly linked to peoples who at that time were forcing themselves into the Near East from the north. Thus there was a broad frontier across which Indo-European speaking peoples were pressing southward. Into Italy they came in several migrations, the most important settlements being made by the Italic tribes in the central and southern parts of the peninsula.

Italy was then outside the pale of civilization, as far removed from the Aegean and the Near East in culture as in miles. The nature of the country probably had much to do with this condition, for the Apennine mountain ridge lies mainly in the eastern part of the peninsula thus creating a western outlook for most of its inhabitants. Then, too, the coast of Italy has fewer harbors and is not as sharply indented as the shore of Greece, for instance, and for that reason sailing and commerce by sea lagged far behind agriculture and pasturing which were bountifully provided for. Hence Italy remained outside the sphere of eastern culture until the East came to her.

Three distinct movements brought about a change in this situation. First came the Etruscans who perhaps left Asia Minor

Courtesy Field Museum of Natural History, Chicago   (After Charles R. Knight.)

DIARAMA OF AN ANCIENT SWISS LAKE VILLAGE ERECTED ON PILES

during the upheaval that resulted in the downfall of the Hittite Empire around 1200 B.C. Possibly some of these Etruscans had entered the Delta in the time of Merneptah, the son of Ramses II. At any rate, whatever the original home of the Etruscans, they were established in Italy by about 1000 B. C., having displaced the Italic tribes along the west coast and far inland in some places. Among the habits they brought from the Near East was the system of employing the arch in building. Thus was the arch, a very old invention, brought to Italy where it was later adopted by the Romans.

The next people to make their presence felt in the western Mediterranean world were the Phoenicians. Leaving their native harbors on the Syrian coast these Semitic merchants became world travelers and explorers. Utica, on the north African coast was settled first, while Carthage, which was to become the center of western Semitic influence, was not founded until about 825 B.C.

In time parts of Sicily, the islands of Malta, Sardinia, and Corsica, which later witnessed the birth of Napoleon, the Balearic Islands, and the coasts of Africa and Spain, all became part of the expanding Phoenician world. Even the western coasts of Africa and Portugal were visited, and at Cadiz the Phoenicians erected temples to their Syrian gods. From there they sailed still farther north to trade for tin with England.

In the century following the settlement of Carthage the third movement of eastern peoples made its appearance. These people were Greeks who established city-states in southern Italy and eastern Sicily, the most famous being Syracuse. They brought with them the vigorous culture which by then had developed in their homeland and soon theaters and stately temples to the Greek gods arose in the backward country, while other traits of their civilization became commonplace in these new communities.

By the eighth century Italy was thus beset by three powerful and ambitious peoples. Phoenicians and Greeks struggled for Sicily, while the Etruscans to the north lost no opportunity in extending their domains southward. The small Italic tribes were wedged between, at times fighting among themselves, at other times warding off their stronger neighbors as best they could. By the middle of the eighth century part of their group called Latins had settled as farmers and herders on the southern side of the Tiber River and had given the name Latium to the district. The Latins nearest the river were protected by a fortress on the Palatine Hill overlooking a bridge which crossed to Etruscan territory. There were also small villages on the neighboring hills, each of them looking to the Palatine stronghold in time of need. Near the river was an open market place where Etruscans, Latins, and others might meet to exchange their products. This was the Forum and the surrounding villages were Rome, founded according to legend by the twin brothers Romulus and Remus.

Their ancestor was said to be Aeneas, one of the Trojan defenders, who fled after Troy was destroyed, and finally after long wanderings had come to Italy. Soon after birth Romulus and Remus were set adrift on the Tiber as a result of a family quarrel. At the base of the Palatine Hill a friendly current set them ashore where a she-wolf nourished them until they could provide for themselves. In the course of time they returned to their home a few miles away to claim their heritage, and then founded Rome at the Tiber where they had been cast ashore. We are naturally reminded of the interesting river experiences that both Sargon of Akkad and Moses were reputed to have had as babes on the waters of Mesopotamia and Egypt.

The little city of Rome continued to grow, but in constant fear of the Etruscan menace. At length about 750 B.C. the Etruscans crossed the Tiber and converted the village settlements and the entire Latin plain into an Etruscan city-state. For two hundred and fifty years the Latins were ruled by their oppressors. But other influences also entered the little territory. Ships from the busy Greek mercantile centers sailed up the Tiber, and in time the Latins adopted and slightly modified the Greek alphabet for their own Latin speech. Thus was another step taken in the long travels of the alphabet that had originated at the mines in Sinai more than a thousand years before.

The Etruscans also left strong influences of their civilization, especially in art, architecture, religion, and the organization of tribes, but their tyranny proved their downfall. About 500 B.C. the last Etruscan king was forced to flee Rome, and thereafter for almost five hundred years Rome was a republic.

The greater Roman state had its beginnings in those years. Two *consuls* were elected from among the nobles to serve as heads of the state for one year, after which they were replaced by others elected by those bearing arms. In time, as oppression persisted, the people forced the consuls to provide other officers who would be more representative. Thus came into being the *tribunes* who had the right to veto any action taken by the consuls. As Rome grew and demands on the administration became greater new offices were added, while during the course of years the people came to have a greater voice in the acts of government. At length the consuls and senators who originally had been of the noble class began to admit qualified plebeians into their ranks, and gradually the Roman Senate became a body of representative minds chosen on the basis of merit and not birth alone.

THE LADY OF ELCHE
A Fifth Century B. C. sculpture found in Spain showing Phoenician influence.
(In the Louvre)

However, before this happened Rome struggled long for her very existence. Etruscans, Greeks and Carthaginians were forces to be feared and not all the Italic tribes were a unit by any means. The Etruscans might have proved a severe obstacle to Roman growth had not the Greeks of Syracuse destroyed their fleet early in the fifth century. Not long afterwards Etruscan territory was overrun by northern Gauls who reached Rome itself and threatened to destroy it, but Rome bought its way out of this predicament and ultimately gained a good share of the weakened Etruscan territory. By 338 B.C. Rome was head of the Italic states and although terrible wars followed, her position expanded until, less than half a century later, she controlled Italy from the Arnus River on the north where today stand Pisa and Florence, to the Greek states on the south.

These now united to ward off the growing power of Rome, but in a war which lasted for several years the Greeks were finally defeated, although Rome had been given a severe fright and several defeats. The Etruscans and Greeks were now (275 B.C.)

VIEW OF THE STADIUM AT SYRACUSE, SICILY

Courtesy The Art Institute, Chicago

SIXTH CENTURY B. C. GREEK TEMPLES AT PAESTUM, .ITALY

out of the way, leaving Rome and Carthage to dispute control of the western Mediterranean. The outcome of this natural conflict between two strong and ambitious powers was not to be decided for three quarters of a century.

The contest began in 264 B. C. over a dispute in Sicily, and soon the Romans saw the need of a fleet, funds for which the Senate collected. By the fifth year of the war the fleet was built and soon had two victories in Roman waters to its credit. The army was sent to Africa to close the war by striking at Carthage itself, but after considerable success the Senate interfered and withdrew troops, thus enabling the Carthaginian army to win a badly needed victory. The elements also conspired against Rome, and between disastrous storms and the Carthaginian fleet, Rome was driven from the seas.

Not until 241 B. C. did this, the First Punic war, reach a conclusion. By then Rome had built another and stronger fleet by contributions from the citizens, and this time the Carthaginian navy was thoroughly defeated. Since without ships aid could not be sent to her soldiers in Sicily, Carthage was forced to acknowledge defeat and accepted the hard terms of peace laid down by the Romans. Carthage gave up Sicily and paid heavy indemnity. The war had lasted for almost a quarter of a century.

Courtesy The Art Institute, Chicago

WOLF NURSING ROMULUS AND REMUS
An early Greek or Etruscan sculpture. The children are Italian Renaissance.

However, neither Rome nor Carthage remained quiet for long. Rome seized the Carthaginian islands of Sardinia and Corsica, and, defeating the Gauls in the north, added the Po valley to the Roman domain. For her part Carthage looked to her possessions in Spain for resources with which to carry on the war. Hamilcar Barca, the Carthaginian general, hoped to get silver from the mines and troops from the people. Although he died prematurely his young son Hannibal carried out his plans, and by the summer of 218 B.C. the Carthaginian army, greatly reinforced, left Spain to follow the northern Mediterranean coast to Italy. Hannibal hoped that by entering Italy from the north he would not only surprise Rome but would obtain aid from the newly conquered Gauls and others dissatisfied with Roman rule.

Coming to the Rhone River he quickly turned north to avoid meeting a Roman army marching toward Spain. By late autumn he reached the Alps and his troops, horses, and elephants began the dangerous and arduous climb over into Italy. The expedition might have stopped right there, for it was the worst season of the year in the mountains, had not Hannibal continuously stimulated and encouraged his tired troops. At length the army dropped down into the pleasant green of the upper Po valley. They were in Italy, destined to remain there for fifteen years. Thus began the second Punic war.

Hannibal saw that he must strike quickly. His force was small but the cavalry was far superior to that of the Romans. Swiftly he swept over the Po valley and crossed the Apennines, completely annihilating the Roman army at Lake Trasimene to the north of Rome. But Hannibal was not ready to attack Rome itself. Instead he crossed the mountains to the Adriatic, gathered horses and drilled his new Gallic recruits. The two armies met in 216 B.C. at Cannae across the peninsula from Naples, and before the battle was over the clever Carthaginian had maneuvered his troops until they completely surrounded the large Roman army. The rest of the day was devoted to slaughter of the trapped defenders of Rome, and when it was over Rome was desperate indeed.

Revolts against Rome followed, instigated by Hannibal, and the young statesman-general, who was still under thirty, even gained promise of support from the Macedonians. The Romans, however, learning of this, stirred up trouble in Greece and the Macedonian army never arrived. Meanwhile the Roman army had learned much about tactics in war and, strongly supplemented, it regained lost territories; even though Hannibal marched to the very gates of Rome he lacked the means of laying siege to the city.

When Carthaginian reinforcements from Spain were defeated in 207 B.C. the tide had turned. The Roman army under Scipio drove the Carthaginians from Spain and invaded Africa, and Hannibal after fifteen years in Italy crossed the Mediterranean to face the foe in his native land. Hannibal and Scipio met at Zama near Carthage in 202 B.C. and there these two marvelous leaders and tacticians manipulated their forces with the greatest skill. Hannibal was fighting now for the first time in the land in which he was born. Scipio on the other hand had a fine chance to remove once for all the Carthaginian threat to Rome. After a tense struggle the battle ended with Scipio and Rome completely victorious.

Courtesy The Art Institute, Chicago

BUST OF SCIPIO AFRICANUS. IN THE CAPITOLINE, ROME

The terms of peace were heavy. Carthage lost her independence and became a vassal state of Rome. In addition she surrendered practically her entire navy, and Hannibal, who had escaped after the battle, was exiled. He turned up later in Asia aiding the Seleucid king Antiochus III in his efforts against Rome.

With the fall of Hannibal and Carthage, Rome became undisputed mistress of the western Mediterranean and the strongest power in the world of the inland sea. Alexander's empire had been divided and was seriously weakened by futile struggles. Ptolemies, Seleucids, and Macedonians maintained a semblance of former strength, but they were soon to bow to the west. Into Macedonia marched Roman arms soon after the fall of Carthage to give the first warning of events to follow, events which were to create the great European, Asiatic and African domains of the Roman Republic and the Empire which followed Caesar. From a small republic three hundred years before, Rome had risen to a position as queen of the nations. Here we take leave of her, having viewed those youthful years in which she struggled for the chance to live.

Courtesy The Art Institute, Chicago

BUST OF JULIUS CAESAR. IN THE CAPITOLINE, ROME

Courtesy The Art Institute. Chicago

AUGUSTUS CAESAR, FIRST EMPEROR OF ROME, VATICAN

THE FORMATION OF THE COUNTRY has at all times been of the greatest importance in the history of India. To the north lie the highest mountains in the world, the Himalayas, always effective in preventing mass movements of people from that direction. South of this forbidding ridge lie the broad plains of the Indus and Ganges valleys. This, the territory called Hindustan, extends southward to the mountains feeding the Narbada River. To the south of these ranges is the plateau called the Deccan, bounded near the coast of the Arabian Sea by the mountains called Western Ghats and on the east by the lesser Eastern Ghats. The rivers of the Deccan flow eastward through valleys in the Eastern Ghats and drop down into the third great geographic division of India, the Carnatic, which stretches to the southernmost point of the great peninsula opposite Ceylon.

These three geographic divisions continually played a part in the settlement of races and peoples, but one feature of the land not yet mentioned was the most important. Often in the past had India been invaded by foreigners who entered by the one natural gateway, aside from the sea, which leads into the country. This was on the northwest where the Himalaya ranges tail off into the Hindu Kush, which, although extremely high themselves, nevertheless are deeply cut in certain places. Through these passes, the most famous of which is the Khyber Pass, and over the still lower territory between them and the sea, have poured many armies, peoples and influences, perhaps more than we shall ever know.

Recent excavation in the Indus Valley has revealed the nature of civilizations that lived there more than five thousand years ago.

The height to which these civilizations had risen, compared to Egypt and Mesopotamia then beginning their historic careers, is most astonishing, for it had long been considered that India was backward indeed before the coming of the Aryans. These impressions had been gained from the hymns of the Rigveda, the Hindu Bible, which indicated that the despised people the Aryans found on coming to India were far from being their equals. We may hardly doubt now that the Indus Valley, and probably other parts of India as well, had attained an excellence in many traits of civilization concerning which the Aryans knew nothing when they first became inhabitants of India. Perhaps the Aryans brought with them little more than their energy and a language which seems to have a tendency toward developing mentality.

In many respects the early civilization that has recently been discovered in northwestern India approximated those we have seen in Egypt and Mesopotamia. Grains were cultivated and numerous domesticated animals lived in the settlements. Among these animals were the humped zebu, buffalo, short horned bull, elephant, camel, sheep, pig, and dog. Oxen probably pulled the wheeled vehicles, for horses were apparently unknown.

MOUNT EVEREST SEEN FROM THE AIR

Courtesy The Art Institute of Chicago

GENERAL VIEW OF THE HIMALAYA MOUNTAINS,
NORTHERN BOUNDARY OF INDIA

The introduction of writing must always be regarded as among the major achievements of any civilization and we see that here, too, the Indus Valley was not behind Egypt and Mesopotamia. About 300 signs of the old Indus script have been found inscribed on seals and other objects dug up in the ruins of this pre-Aryan civilization. Unfortunately the writing cannot be read, but eventually scholars may find the solution. The point to be made at present is that phonetic writing had been developed in India some five thousand years ago.

There were among the Indus people clever metal smiths, sculptors, and jewelers, some of whose fine products have been fortunately preserved by the protective debris of ages. Cotton for textiles was used during this period, probably for the first time in the history of the world. The people themselves lived in commodious and comfortable houses, a strange contrast with most of the existing civilizations of that age; in addition there were ample provisions for bathing and for town drainage.

We know of the prehistoric peoples of India principally through excavations in and near the Indus valley, but there is good reason to believe that a related civilization extended widely in all directions. Already it is known that strong trade relations existed between the Indus and Tigris-Euphrates regions. It is likely that the more accessible parts of India came also within

A MOUND IN THE INDUS VALLEY
Below this mound was found a city which flourished over 5000 years ago.

Both photos courtesy Sir John Marshall, *Mohenjo-Daro*

"THIRD STREET" OF MOHENJO-DARO
The same site after excavation.

Courtesy Sir John Marshall, *Mohenjo-Daro*

SEALS OF THE INDUS VALLEY

Representations of the humped zebu, buffalo, and rhinoceros are found
with examples of the undeciphered inscriptions.

the sphere of influence of the high culture that has been disclosed on the Indus, but this we shall not know until proper investigation is made in the territory east of the Indus.

Perhaps eventually the earlier history of India may become known from its writings. Excavation is still young in that great sub-continent and many inscriptions may lie waiting for a fortunate discoverer. We recall that Egyptian and Mesopotamian writing, through which the vital history of the Near East has been recovered, was unread until a century or so ago.

THE COMING OF THE ARYANS

It was sometime after 1400 B.C. that the Aryans crossed the mountainous northwestern frontier of India and settled around the Indus. The early civilization of which we have spoken had by then disappeared and the people who confronted the Aryans were called Dravidians. The original home of the newcomers is not known for certain, perhaps it was on the plains of Southern Russia or Turkestan, but they formed part of the great Indo-European family several of whose members we have already noticed. In the west the Italic tribes that formed Rome and the Greeks of the classical period, in the east the Medes and Persians as well as others, all were descended in speech out of the same root from which sprouted the Aryan tongue of India. The new people lived many centuries in the country before writing down in Sanskrit the hymns and epics that tell of their entry and settlement of the land.

The Dravidians were forced southward where today their descendants may still be seen. Living first in the Indus Valley as simple farmers and shepherds, the Aryans gradually spread eastward into the valley of the Ganges and its tributaries. From early writings we learn that the people worshipped and sacrificed to forces of nature such as the sun, rain, and sky, and had gods and goddesses with the names Indra, Chandra, Varuna, Savita, and so on, some of them identical with Persian deities. The conception of transmigration, or future life in other forms, seems to have come in, if it had not already existed. The caste system was being

EXAMPLE OF
ANCIENT SCULP-
TURE OF THE
INDUS VALLEY

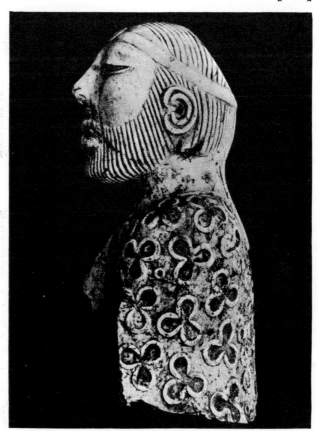

A TOY D O G
WITH MOVABLE
HEAD

Both photos courtesy Sir John Marshall, *Mohenjo-Daro*

Courtesy Sir John Marshall, *Mohenjo-Daro*

EXAMPLES OF EARLY INDIAN HANDICRAFT

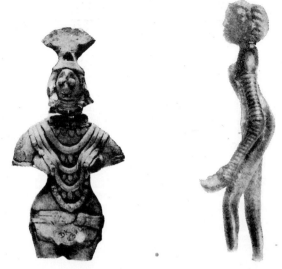

EARLY INDIAN FIGURINES

Both photos courtesy Sir John Marshall, *Mohenjo-Daro*

POTTERY OF THE INDUS VALLEY CULTURE

developed during this period, but in a much simpler form than at present. From two hereditary groups, the priestly and the noble, there developed three main castes, each of which excluded any of the conquered peoples who formed a fourth class.

The priests were the teachers and perpetuators of the Vedic tradition and came to be called Brahmans from the four-faced god Brahma. The noble class included warriors, while the commoners consisted of the large body of workers, herdsmen, farmers, and merchants. This social system developed until now we see a multitude of castes, each of them exclusive as regards marriage and way of living.

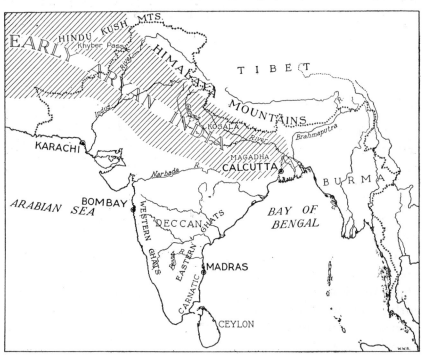

Drawing by Walter W. Romig

EARLY ARYAN INDIA

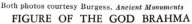

Both photos courtesy Burgess, *Ancient Monuments*

FIGURE OF THE GOD BRAHMA

FIGURE OF BUDDHA

BUDDHA IS BORN

During the middle of the sixth century B.C., at about the time that Cyrus the Great revolted from the Medes and launched Persia on the road to empire, a youth was born to noble parents near the foot of the jungle-covered Nepal Hills. In time this child came to be known as Gautama Buddha, founder of a religion that is still of tremendous world importance, although not in India itself.

Growing to manhood he was unable to find contentment in life and after a great deal of thought left his wife and new born child, to adopt the ways of a recluse in search of wisdom. Presently, still not finding the truths he was after, he became an ascetic, fasting, doing without sleep, and physically tormenting himself in a way common to many an Indian today. In his much weakened state he tried to pierce life's problems, his fame spreading meanwhile, but all to no avail. One day in his weakened

condition, still trying to discover a remedy for the ills of the
world, he fell unconscious from exhaustion. On recovering he
realized that his method of seeking the truth would never be
successful. To think well one had to have a healthy body, and he
accordingly demanded food of his companions. They were horri-
fied and deserted him in his heresy. Alone he wandered, wrestling
with his conflicting problem, when finally the religion he was to
preach dawned on him.

Buddha taught the extinction of desire and selfishness, and
kindness to all living creatures. He traced the troubles of life to
personal greed, envy and desire. If one wished to be truly happy
and serene one must forget one's self and live for others. Through
this ideal way of life one would finally obtain Nirvana, a state of
peaceful bliss. If not in this life, then in a succession of lives, the
perfect goal could be attained.

This of course was a direct blow to the caste system and in so
many words he made his point clear. As the four streams that
flow into the Ganges lose their names as soon as they mingle
their waters in the holy river, so all who believe in Buddha cease
to be Brahmans, nobles, commoners, and low caste.

Buddha gained disciples who spread his teachings, at times with
misunderstanding, until the new religion became a real force in
India and was adopted by royal families. As is natural with many
a religious founder, Buddha came in time to be given a supernatural birth and ultimately the distinction of being a god,
although at no time did Buddha claim divinity. Monasteries
were founded and the lower castes especially found pleasant the
new religion of equality. As Buddhism grew and kings embraced
the faith, missionaries were sent to surrounding countries, and
eventually it reached Turkestan, Manchuria, Tibet, China, Japan,
and the countries east of India, where still it is of the greatest
importance. Missions even visited the Near East. In India, however, the Brahmans had never ceased to preach the Hindu faith,
and growing stronger through the centuries they and the caste
system finally prevailed over Buddhism, although embodying
some of its better points. By the eleventh century A.D. Buddhism
was practically extinct in India, and the religion that had been

Courtesy Burgess, *Ancient Monuments*

A BUDDHIST TEMPLE BUILT IN A CAVE
This is one of the earliest Buddhist caves in India.

founded by an Aryan was thereafter practiced for the most part outside of India by Mongolian peoples. Thenceforth India's principal religion, except for a period under the Moghuls and Mohammedans, was Hinduism, with its many gods, sacred cows, holy rivers and pools, and supremacy of the Brahmans and the caste system.

It is not known exactly when Buddhism reached China, but many believe that it happened about the time of Christ. Buddhism spread east, west, north and south of the region of its birth, even penetrating the forests of Cambodia beyond Burma and Siam. At Angkor Thom one may still see the ruins of the old royal city of the Khmers whose civilization flourished from 900-1200 A.D., while less than a mile away stands the temple of Angkor Vat, that stately and exotic structure devoted to worship of Buddha, the god.

Courtesy Burgess, *Ancient Monuments*

THE INTERIOR OF A CAVE TEMPLE
The antiquity of this is certified by the absence of any image of Buddha.

In connection with Buddhism we should mention another religion with which it had points in common. Jainism can be traced to about 800 B.C. at which time its followers vowed not to injure life, not to steal, to be truthful, and to possess no property. The Jain sect gained influence during Buddha's lifetime through the efforts and reforms of a man named Jina, who in fact was Buddha's teacher for a time and whose name was ever after attached to this set of beliefs. The Jains are important for the part they played in history, for their sumptuous temples, and the fact that they still persist in India. Kindness was the chief virtue of Jainism as with Buddhism but it lacked the breadth of the latter.

Courtesy The Art Institute, Chicago

ANGKOR VAT

Courtesy Burgess, *Ancient Monuments*

A JAINIST TEMPLE

(The figures on the piers of this ninth century temple are distinctively Jainist.)

Courtesy Burgess, *Ancient Monuments*

A JAINIST CAVE TEMPLE

THE WESTERN EMPIRES INVADE INDIA

By the time Buddha was a young man various Aryan kingdoms had been formed in northern India, the most important
being Kosala and Magadha, while across the Hindu Kush Mountains dominant Persian armies marched over the eastern Iranian
plateau quickly enlarging the empire founded by Cyrus. It is
possible that Cyrus himself reached the Indus country, but
nothing is certain regarding the entry of Persian troops until the
time of his second successor, Darius the Great. It was probably
soon after 520 B.C. that the Persians gained a foothold in the
land of their blood- and speech-brothers in the northwestern part
of India. This became a province of the greatest importance to
the court at Perseepolis, about one-third of all Asiatic tribute coming from it alone. The Indus Valley remained under Persian con-

trol during the reign of Darius' son, Xerxes, who had Indian infantry and cavalry in the army which he led into Greece in 480 B.C. The evidence is extremely scant for the following period, but Darius III, the last king of his dynasty, called for Indian troops when he made his last stand at Arbela against the army of Alexander the Great.

With Alexander we reach firmer ground, for his conquests were fairly well recorded. After taking Persia and the immense territory that had formed the northern and eastern parts of the Persian empire he crossed the mountains into India. He was forced to spend ten months between the Hindu Kush and the Indus subjugating the mountain tribes, and did not arrive at the Indus until early in 326 B.C. Resting his army there for a month Alexander laid plans for conquests farther east. Resuming the march he had little trouble until he arrived at the Hydaspes River, now called the Jhelum, one of the eastern tributaries of the Indus. Here he met his most formidable foe, Poros, whose name is unknown except in its Greek form. The imposing six and a half foot Indian and his troops fought a brave fight, but at last succumbed to Alexander's luck and generalship. Poros himself was wounded but despite this he stayed in the battle to the end. His conduct so impressed Alexander that Poros was allowed to remain king in his territory as a vassal of Greece, and was even given additional lands.

Proceeding eastward the Greek army at last reached the Hyphasis River, now named the Bias. The troops were weary and had been away from home for years. Perceiving signs of unwillingness on the part of his men, Alexander addressed them on the glories of the conquests they had made since crossing the Hellespont and promised them the riches of Asia. His rousing speech brought not a cheer, the men facing their general and king in stubborn silence. At length one of his generals gained courage to reply. He recalled that of the thousands of Greeks and Macedonians, who had entered Asia eight years before, many had been sent home as invalids, others had been forced to remain in the numerous newly founded cities and garrisons, while the greater number lay dead in the bleak stretches of Asia. Those who re-

THE PLACE WHERE ALEXANDER CROSSED THE HYDASPES
(MODERN JHELUM) TO ATTACK KING POROS

mained were few, and they were tired and sick in body and mind. He urged moderation in the midst of victory, for, even though no mortal foe could withstand him, the will of the gods was unknown. At the conclusion of his impassioned speech the army cheered, and Alexander sulked in his tent for several days. On the third day he determined to retreat, and after erecting twelve large altars to the gods the now much happier army turned its steps toward home.

Alexander encamped on reaching the Hydaspes River again with plans for floating a fleet. All suitable river boats were commandeered, and those with knowledge of ship building were put to work constructing galleys. Phoenicians, Cyprians, Egyptians and natives of Asia Minor combined their abilities and soon there was a formidable fleet of about 2000 ships. These included eight galleys of thirty oars each and a large number of horse transports.

Then began the difficult passage downstream to the mouth of the Indus and the sea. Through hundreds of miles of unknown and hostile territory the fleet and marching army pushed ahead. Many towns were captured and in one of the skirmishes Alexander, through a needless bit of bravado and impetuosity, was seriously wounded. It was almost a year after leaving his most eastern point that Alexander at last reached the sea.

From there the ships set sail along the coast bound for the Persian Gulf. Alexander himself stayed with the army which battled its way back to Susa in Persia, arriving seven months after leaving India. It was spring of the year 324 B.C. when Alexander reached Susa, having swept a conquering path from the Hellespont over Asia Minor, Syria, Palestine, Egypt, Babylonia, Persia, the eastern Persian provinces and the Indus Valley. Little more than a year later Alexander lay dead in Babylon.

THE MAURYA DYNASTY

Greek rule in India was doomed the moment Alexander turned for the long march to Susa. Soon there was a general revolt against the garrisons he had left behind and within a year or so northern India had a new ruler. He was Chandragupta, the

SCULPTURE OF
THE SECOND
CENTURY, B. C.
The monument on
the left illustrates a
warrior of the sec-
ond century B. C.,
while that on the
right represents a
f e m a l e standard
bearer.
(After Ludwig
Bachhofer)

earliest great Indian conqueror of whom we know. The founder
of the Maurya Dynasty, named for his mother or grandmother,
gathered his forces, and perhaps after taking the territory over
which Alexander had so recently passed, proceeded to annex the
Ganges Valley as well which at that time was in the hands of the
Nanda Dynasty. Chandragupta had acted in the name of liberty
but he was soon better known for his tyranny. One district after
another bowed to his fierce power and eventually his realm extended from the Bay of Bengal to the Arabian Sea, and the Him-

alaya and Hindu Kush Mountains to the Narbada River at the edge of the Deccan. It is possible that he invaded the Deccan itself. The size of Chandragupta's kingdom was reflected by his army which is said to have numbered 30,000 cavalry, 9,000 elephants, 600,000 infantry, and a host of chariots.

Seleucus, the general who inherited most of the Asiatic portion of Alexander's empire, advanced hopefully with an army into the Indus country about 305 B.C. to meet Chandragupta, and although some are of the opinion that Seleucus met serious defeat, the essential facts of the case are unknown. The available details indicate that a peaceful solution may have been reached, for, while Chandragupta gained new territories to the northwest, Seleucus with 500 elephants marched away to the more important wars in Asia Minor. The fact, too, that Seleucus gave a daughter in marriage to Chandragupta suggests that enmity between the two kings was not at the breaking point. However, Greek political influence was thereafter a thing of the past.

From the accounts of writers, including Seleucus' ambassador to the Indian court, we learn much regarding the country, government, and life of the time. India possessed a high civilization, one which could meet the western cultures on terms of understanding and equality. Numerous foreigners traveled on peaceful missions to Chandragupta's capital, thus testifying to the intercourse that connected east and west. From these writers we hear of the royal palace which stood in a park, beautifully landscaped with fish ponds, trees, and shrubs. The gilded pillars were decked with golden vines and silver birds. All the luxuries of the age made Chandragupta's court a marvel of the day, as brilliant as that of a modern rajah. When the king traveled far from his capital he mounted an elephant covered with gold trappings. The court was often entertained by combat between bulls, rams, elephants, rhinoceroses, and even men. On other occasions the king and his intimate circle enjoyed the spectacle of a curious kind of race in which mixed teams of horses competed with speedy oxen drawing a vehicle. The course was over three miles long and provided much tension and anxiety for the observers who bet on the outcome.

Courtesy Burgess, *Ancient Monuments*

THE ASOKA PILLAR AT LAURIYA NAVANDGARH,
NEARLY 40 FEET IN HEIGHT

The government was efficiently organized, a war office and civil administration taking care of routine matters. Taxes were collected under close supervision and a bureau of vital statistics recorded births and deaths. Irrigation was closely watched so that all might get their share of water, and of course be taxed accordingly. Roads were much improved during Chandragupta's reign, the longest one connecting the capital with the northwest frontier. This was probably built for military reasons as much as for any other purpose.

The penal code of the times was very strict indeed and demanded death for crimes such as robbery. Third-degree methods for obtaining confessions were legal and freely used. The law recognized eighteen kinds of torture, including seven methods of whipping. In some cases it was legal to submit a prisoner to all eighteen varieties.

Chandragupta had been king for twenty-four years when he either abdicated or died in 298 B.C. The Jain sect has a tradition that he abdicated in order to become a Jain ascetic. In any case his son, Bindusara, succeeded him and although practically nothing is known of his twenty-five year reign it is probable that Bindusara extended the Maurya empire into the Deccan as far south as the Pennar River, a hundred miles or so north of Madras.

This was the empire that Chandragupta's grandson, Asoka, inherited when he came to the throne about 273 B.C. The following years were ones of vital significance to the history of India, and Asoka thereby takes his place among the distinctive monarchs of the world.

Asoka was king for forty years, but his deeds during the early part of the reign are unknown. In his thirteenth year he set out to add to his already large empire the kingdom of Kalinga on the coast of the Bay of Bengal. This war, possibly the only one in which Asoka participated, was bloody and ended in untold suffering for the people of Kalinga. Remorse for his actions set in almost immediately, and under the influence of Buddhism Asoka foreswore war and adopted the precepts of kindness that Buddha had preached several centuries before.

BULL-CROWNED CAPITAL OF AN ASOKA COLUMN, ABOUT 243 B. C. (after Ludwig Bachhofer)

The Buddhists were only one sect among many when Asoka became king, and in fact there were many sects within Buddhism itself. Therefore one of the first things Asoka did was to bring the elders together to decide on the official form of Buddhism. Long before he died it became the state religion and had traveled to other countries as well. Thus while Buddha had had the original revelation, it was Asoka who gave Buddhism the necessary vitality and prestige to place it among the world religions.

Asoka devoted his entire later life to propagation of the faith. Formerly a Brahmanical Hindu he now became a zealous Buddhist monk. He made a pilgrimage to the scenes of Buddha's birth, life and death, and endowed them liberally. The monk-emperor issued many edicts on ethical and moral behavior, some of which carved on stone have been found.

The Buddhism preached by Asoka insisted on the sanctity of all animal life. Belief in rebirth was the basis of this edict, for even an insect might once have been a god. Perhaps it was on

Courtesy Burgess, *Ancient Monuments*

A ROCK BEARING AN ASOKA INSCRIPTION

the way to being one again. All animal life was sacred, at times more hallowed than human life, for one could be put to death for killing an animal. On fifty six days of the year it was a crime attended by capital punishment to slay animals for food. As part of this attitude toward living things the royal hunt which had been an important function in the life of his grandfather was abolished. Instead, Asoka substituted acts of piety and dissemination of his faith.

Reverence, truthfulness, and toleration he preached with undying zeal. Toleration to other religions formed part of his creed, but in practice they were seriously impeded, for sacrifice was definitely restricted, even though regarded as essential by some of the sects.

While much attention was directed to animals it must not be understood that the Buddhism of Asoka neglected man. It was the human misery he had caused in Kalinga that proved the turning point in his life, and numerous acts prove his deep feeling and sympathy for the sufferings of men. Medical treatment of the sick was provided not only in his empire but in the neighboring independent kingdoms.

We see that Asoka had growing plans and ambitions for
Buddhism, and before the middle of his reign he organized a
large system of foreign missions. Ministers of the faith were dispatched to the surrounding countries and even reached the Mediterranean and Aegean. Egypt, Syria, Asia Minor and Greece were
visited by these holy deputies in an effort to spread the benefits of
what Asoka believed to be the only right and true religion. Whatever their adventures may have been, for that information may
be lost forever, they left the seeds of their faith in widespread
places, and some writers have suspected that Buddha's views contributed to the more orthodox forms of Christianity.

From his throne, but as a man of human feelings, Asoka
taught reverence, truth and sympathy. At the same time through
a long reign he successfully administered a vast empire. For these

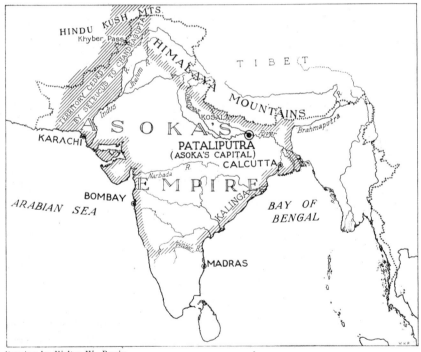

Drawing by Walter W. Romig

ASOKA'S EMPIRE

reasons and the fact that through him Buddhism became a world force Asoka must be counted among the immortals of history.

After his death about 232 B.C. Asoka was followed by several ephemeral kings who lacked the ability of their gifted predecessors. Perhaps, too, the Brahmans whose privileges had been seriously curtailed by Asoka now threw their weight into an attempt to overthrow the Mauryas. In any case the dynasty ended about 185 B.C. and the history of the country for several centuries thereafter was one of struggle between local dynasts and eastern Asiatic invaders from the northwest.

Of these the most important were the Kushanas who established a large empire in the first and second centuries A.D. which consisted of northwestern India, Afghanistan and Turkestan. Of the Kushan rulers the most famous was Kanishka, about 120 A.D., who as a vigorous patron of Buddhism ranks second to Asoka alone. Following the Kushan period, the country broke up into small states reunited for a brief period by the Gupta Dynasty in the fourth and fifth centuries, and again by Harsha, the last important native ruler, in the seventh century.

Mohammedans from the west, and Tartars and Moghuls from Turkestan, all played their part before European aggressors again made their appearance on the Indian scene. Then by sea came Portuguese Vasco da Gama in 1502 to bombard Calicut on the southwest coast. Europe had just emerged from the dark ages and once more trade with India assumed importance. For a century the Portuguese controlled the trade of the east, and then came the Dutch, French and English, the last eventually winning India through formation of the East India Company.

BRONZE DAGGER-AXES OF THE SHANG PERIOD

THE NAME OF CHINA

WE CANNOT be sure of the origin of the name China. It is usually believed, however, that the name was derived from the Kingdom of Ch'in (pronounced Chin) which in the days of the Ch'in dynasty (255-206 B.C.) brought the loosely knit Chinese states together as an empire. It is said that Malay sea-traders made the name, in the form Tchina, known to India and the west.

In the medieval period China became known to Europeans as Cathay. It was thus that Marco Polo, the Venetian traveler, referred to it. Russians still do calling it Kitai. The term Cathay owes its origin to the Khitans, a formidable group of Tatars from eastern Asia who were well known to eastern Europe in medieval times.

HE WHO EATS RICE AND HE WHO DOES NOT

The Chinese of today think of their country in terms of north and south. This is not a political division but rather one based on different ways of living. The principal difference between the two is that the north lives on millet, maize and wheat, while the south lives on rice. Of course, other foods are eaten as well.

By concrete geographical distinction China is further divided into groups of provinces in the same way that we set off New England or the Pacific Coast with their various states from the rest of the country. The Chinese groups of provinces are located as follows:

1) On the Upper Yellow River (Hwang Ho)
2) On the Lower Yellow River
3) On the Upper Yangtze River
4) On the Middle Yangtze River
5) On the Lower Yangtze River
6) On the South Coast

In the first of these groups, in the north, we find the Chinese at the dawn of history. The province of *Kansu*, a highland with great variety in scenery, has always been associated with adventure, and has been called the "Wild West of China". *Shensi* is made up largely of rich, rolling plains and is famous for its opium smoking population. *Shansi*, still another province of the Upper Yellow River district, is rugged for the most part and is noted, even far inland in Asia, for ability of its merchants.

The second group includes *Honan*, in the northern part of which evidence of early Chinese culture has been found. The people of *Honan* are strong of body and character but generally slow of mind. Peiping, the capital of China until 1928, lies in the province of *Hopei* which is called the "Metropolitan Province" by foreigners. *Shantung*, in this same group, extends to the coast and is noted as the birthplace of the great sages, Lao Tzu, Confucius and Mencius. To the present day the scholarly tradition persists in *Shantung*. The people of this province are regarded as being the finest physical specimens of North China, and it is of interest to recall that during the World War *Shantung* coolies were in great demand in the war area of France.

To reach the third group of provinces we travel south and west to the headwaters of the great Yangtze River, to the borders of Tibet and China. The land is extremely rugged for the most part and as a result we meet one magnificent scene after another. Due to the nature of the country some of the agriculture is done by terracing. Desirable mineral resources will some day make this area of extreme importance. Influences from India in the past have entered China by way of the Upper Yangtze valley.

Proceeding down the river we enter the fourth group of provinces which constitute the lake region of China. Here tea and rice are grown, but the territory is rapidly gaining greater importance for its commercial enterprises. At the junction of the Han and Yangtze Rivers three large cities have developed in recent years. They are Hankow, Wuchang and Hanyang, and many believe they will someday become the world's largest metropolis.

The Lower Yangtze group, our fifth, brings us at length to the sea, many hundreds of miles from the headwaters of the river. Tea and rice are important products of this area, but it is more significant for its industries. Shanghai, symbol of the coming of the industrial west to China, is situated on a small tributary near the mouth of the great river. It is not an old city, dating only from the middle of the nineteenth century.

The sixth group of provinces, on the south coast, is cut off from the rest of China by high mountain ranges and it is not surprising that noticeable differences of language and physique characterize the area. The south coast has excellent harbors, and the people have always looked to the sea. It is in this area that we find Canton, from which about ninety-five per cent of the Chinese in America have come. Hong Kong lies a little over fifty miles to the east of Canton. It was an uninhabited island until the British transformed it into one of the world's greatest ports.

The population of China is pretty much an unknown quantity and has been the subject of considerable guesswork. Recent estimates range between 270,000,000 and 500,000,000. The true figure is probably something less than 400,000,000, or approximately one-fifth of the total population of the world.

This, then, is the China whose earlier history we are about to investigate. When did Chinese civilization begin and when did it take on the form in which it is known to us today?

A ROYAL SHANG TOMB

The tomb consisted of an inverted pyramid dug into the ground. On the north, east and
west it was approached by steps of pounded earth, and on the south by a long,
smooth incline.

THE ERA OF MYTHOLOGY AND LEGEND

A T THE present time China's known history goes back no farther than about 1500 B. C. but in view of recent progress in the field of archaeology it is quite probable that this figure will in time be increased. In the past few years archaeology has produced a very respectable outline of the Shang dynasty (1766-1122 B.C.) which before that had been shrouded in the mists of legend. Preceding the Shang dynasty we learn from Chinese annals of an extremely long history. It is called history, but mythology is surely a more appropriate term. All peoples on earth have their creation stories.

According to the Chinese Genesis the first man had an unknown beginning. He simply came into being and immediately understood the wonders of Heaven and Earth. When he came into the world, order was made out of chaos. He is pictured working with chisel and mallet on huge pieces of granite floating in space. From this mass the sun, the moon, and stars emerged, and heaven and earth took their present form under the guidance of his knowing hand. And then, when his work was done, he died.

But the earth continued to develop. The original man's head was changed to mountains, his breath became wind and clouds,

The symbol YANG and YIN appearing at the top of this page represents the balance of forces in nature—negative and positive, male and female, dark and light. Later, the dragon and phoenix became associated with this dualism, the dragon with YANG and the phoenix with YIN, and hence came to be symbolic of the emperor and empress, respectively.

and his voice turned into thunder. His veins became the rivers and his sinews hill and dale. The fields were fashioned from his flesh. His beard became stars, and his skin and hair were turned into herbs and trees. His teeth, bones and marrow became metals, rocks and precious stones, and his sweat was turned to rain. Finally, the insects that had been attracted to his body became the Chinese people.

There follows a long period treated in much the same mythological manner with one culture hero following another. Among these are Huang-ti, Yao and Shun, names which play a significant part in the classical writings. About 2205 B.C., according to the chroniclers, there began the Hsia dynasty which immediately precedes the dynasty of Shang with which we may begin to view Chinese history with some degree of assurance.

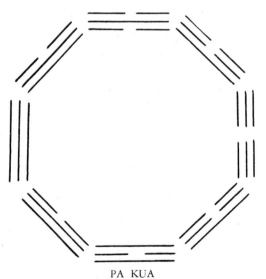

PA KUA

This eight sided diagram composed of opposite pairs of broken and full lines was used in divination. Traditionally it was invented by Wen, father of Wu Wang, the founder of the Chou Dynasty. At present the design is used both for decorative and protective purposes.

ARCHAEOLOGY RESURRECTS THE SHANG WORLD

INSCRIBED ORACLE BONES OF THE SHANG PERIOD, ILLUSTRATING THE
EARLIEST KNOWN FORM OF CHINESE WRITING

IN MUCH the same way that the Hittites have been brought to
life in recent years by the labors of the archaeologist, the Shang
dynasty today stands for a reality it did not possess a few years
ago. By handling the objects that they made and used with hands
as alive as our own we can in a sense transport ourselves back to
the time when Chinese history, as it is known to us, began.

THE ORACLE BONES OF SHANG

From time to time in the past ancient bones have been dug
up by ploughing in the fields of northern *Honan* province, not
far from the Yellow River. Not looking like the bones of animals
known to the farmers, they were taken to be dragon bones, and
thus the source of much medicinal benefit. They found their way
into the shops of Chinese pharmacists from where they were dis-
pensed to the needy and no doubt were considered to have done
much good. But the pharmacists were not fooled. They didn't
know that these were bones of the Shang period, but, when they
came across bones with queer looking figures inscribed upon them,
they realized for certain that they were not dealing with dragon
bones. The solution was simple. There was a market for the
bones and in order to arouse nobody's suspicion the ancient Shang
writing was scraped off. The Chinese people must not be deprived
of the benefits of ancient Chinese dragons.

[325]

Finally a Chinese antiquarian who knew the forms of ancient writing saw some of the bones and realized that the queer figures lying before him were related to the oldest forms known to him. We now know that the inscriptions on these bones are part of the royal records of the latter part of the Shang dynasty which according to tradition extended from 1766 to 1122 B.C. These writings are the oldest records known from far eastern Asia.

SHANG FORTUNE-TELLERS

We possess these inscribed bones with their wealth of information for the reason that the royal court employed fortune-tellers, or diviners, to question the ancestors and gods whether certain actions should be taken or not. Even the smallest matters called for consultation with the spirits, as they had tremendous powers of good and evil and had to be catered to. If not treated properly the spirits might cause an enemy to approach suddenly, or bring on dreaded disease. On the other hand they were endowed with powers to do good, if they were consulted correctly.

It seems likely that the divination took place in a temple devoted to the worship of ancestors. The ritual can be visualized only in general. The fortune-teller, or diviner, asked a question, one of importance to the well-being of the state or the people. Then he heated the bone which was usually the shoulder blade or leg bone of a cow, or might in other cases be the shell of a turtle. The heat developed a T shaped crack, and it was from the details of this crack that the diviner decided what answer was being given by the spirits. Fortunately for us the question was sometimes written next to the crack. We may guess that this was done mainly when following events proved that the diviner had been correct.

These inscriptions are not completely understood, but the study of the writing has progressed to such a point that the main idea of most inscriptions can be grasped. As in the Near East, the forger has come into the field and is doing a lively business, but experts can tell a faked inscription from an authentic one.

Photo Illustrated London News

BURIAL CHAMBER IN A SHANG TOMB
The body was placed in a pit in the center of the cross-shaped bottom.

A SHANG PIT DWELLING FOUND AT ANYANG

THE ARCHAEOLOGIST GOES TO WORK

Many difficulties have been placed in the way of organized scientific excavation in China. In the first place the Chinese have a strong respect for the dead and don't want them disturbed, no matter how many thousands of years have elapsed. Then, too, there are numerous more or less recent burials scattered all over the countryside. There are regular cemeteries as well, but the foreigner will be surprised at the number of mounds appearing in the most unexpected places. In China a person is buried in the spot regarded as being the most beneficial from a magical point of view, and as a result burials are most commonly found outside of cemeteries. To disregard the wishes of the spirits is a serious matter in China. A good burial site will probably bring good luck to the relatives of the deceased. Thus graves dot the countryside. The farmer will plough up to the edge of a mound but not over it. Whether the occupant of the grave is a relative of his or not makes no difference. It would be bad luck to disagree with the wishes of any of the spirits.

This same attitude, of course, creates an immediate difficulty for the archaeologist who in the course of his work comes across many tombs. It is his job to get information on the development of early civilization in any way that he can. An equally important part of his job in China has been gently to persuade the opponents of organized archaeology that such work is worth while.

Other difficulties facing the archaeologists are variations of the seasons. The winters are too cold for excavation. Summer presents the other extreme. Thus it is only during the spring and autumn that the work can be carried on, however handicapped by wind and dust.

Another problem that faces the person interested in piecing together the story of ancient China is the matter of illicit digging. When there are people interested in antiquities a market is created for the old objects of art. Thus certain groups of Chinese have organized themselves as grave robbers, doing their work under cover of darkness. The result is that while archaeologists may eventually have an opportunity to buy antiquities in the Peiping market, all the evidence of finding which is so important to correct evaluation of ancient materials has disappeared. One last difficulty besetting the scientific investigator in China is the bandit. The territory of the old Shang capital is full of bandits and it has been necessary to carry on excavation under the protection of armed guards.

THE BEGINNINGS OF CHINESE CIVILIZATION

According to the Chinese their civilization began with the great sages of very early times. An altogether different view is held by certain European scholars who claim that the really worthwhile matters in Chinese civilization came from the west. We need hardly develop the point that these are partisan views which in fact are not supported by the evidence. China appears to have developed as independently as any country can from very early times, but at the same time we observe that the Chinese are racially complex. Undoubtedly many foreign elements have contributed to the forging of the thing we recognize as Chinese civilization. No country on earth has existed without the benefits and drawbacks of contact with its neighbors. A fact that leads us to believe that the Chinese racial type has existed for many thousands of years on Chinese soil is that *Sinanthropus,* one of the earliest human inhabitants of the earth, had some Mongoloid characteristics.

By the time we reach the period of the Shang dynasty (about 1766 B.C.) we may be sure that we are in the midst of Chinese surroundings, primitive it is true, but Chinese nevertheless. And that brings up the question regarding the origins of the Shang people. One fact alone might appear to go a long way toward solving this problem. Bronze was introduced into China from the outside during the Shang period, and one might suppose that a foreign group had been responsible and had in fact set itself up as the Shang dynasty. But we observe a most interesting state of affairs in the nature of certain Shang bronzes. These include sacrificial vessels which, detail for detail, copy the form of earlier pottery vessels. One supposes that we have here a case of the immutability or conservatism of religion, since we are dealing with religious vessels. Still other elements in Shang culture appear to go back to an earlier beginning and argue for a connection between the peoples of the two periods. But perhaps a more important point to be made just now is that the question is not settled. Clearer evidence is needed.

Other elements are clearly foreign to the territory in which the Shangs lived; for instance, bronze, an alloy of copper and tin, which is far superior in many ways to pure copper. The idea probably came from the west, perhaps carried slowly over the central reaches of Asia from the Near East where it had been known as early as 3000 B.C. Rice, too, appears to have been brought into North China from the outside, this time from the south. It is clear that no cultural progress is possible without knowledge of the outside world.

A HUMBLE SHANG HOUSE

With a roof of mud-covered timber, these inhospitable pits probably served as homes for common Shang people.

HOW THE SHANGS LIVED

With continued digging in China we shall someday know much more than at present regarding the lives and occupations of the Shang people. But we know a great deal about these things already. We know, for instance, that the poor and probably the slaves lived in underground mud hovels. But others lived in complicated houses very much like Chinese houses of the present day. They were built on a platform of beaten earth. Today this platform is faced with brick. Excavation has shown that the ground plans of Shang houses have their counterpart in present Chinese architecture. Remains of wooden pillars have been found. One of the pictographs on the oracle bones represents a large building and seems to show us the type of roof that was used. Even then the gable seems to have been the favored style.

Among occupations of the people we may be sure that farming was the most prominent. The rich soil and level land of the Yellow River valley must then have yielded bountiful harvests. We know that in Shang times wheat and millet were grown extensively. In the Neolithic period only millet seems to have been cultivated. It is still the important food of North China, rice being eaten only by the wealthier people.

The Shang people also raised domesticated animals, or hunted and trapped for meat and skins for clothing. One of the methods of hunting was to set the grass on fire in order to get the animals into the open. From the rubbish heaps that have been dug and from the oracle bones we learn a great deal about the animals known to the Shang people. The rubbish contains a great many things of interest, among them animal bones tossed out by the housewives of long ago. When these are collected and studied by experts we shall have another valuable instrument for the understanding of Shang life.

A number of animals had become domesticated by this time. Very important among this group were the horse, two types of dog, cattle, sheep and goats. The horse became a natural draft animal, but for this purpose it is quite likely that cattle, oxen, and water buffalo were also used. Other animals that had probably yielded to domestication by Shang times are the pig and possibly one kind of deer. Once in a while elephant bones are found and it has been suggested that elephants were sometimes tamed. This is based on the form of one of the pictographs on the oracle bones which seems to show a hand leading an elephant by its trunk. The rubbish piles of Shang have even yielded monkey bones.

Animals which seem clearly not to have been tamed include the bear, tiger and panther, and the badger, tapir and hare. These are surely trophies of the hunt which on certain occasions became state affairs and seem always to have called for conference with the gods. Of birds which were known to the people of Shang and which have been identified in the remains we may mention the pheasant and the chicken. The latter seems to have been introduced to North China about the time of the Shang dynasty.

The dog and pig had been the most important meat animals in the Neolithic Age, and in the following period both continued to be important foods. The pig, however, appears to have had a more important position in the menus of the time. We know that the dog was sacrificed as well as eaten.

It is quite certain that the early Chinese did not use milk or other dairy products, for nowhere in the literature is there a hint that conditions as regards this aspect of things were any different than they are today. Nobody seems to know the answer, but the Chinese, Koreans, Japanese, Indo-Chinese and Malayans use no dairy products. On the other hand Mongols, Turks, and Tibetans seem always to have used them.

There are many things we cannot be sure of as regards Shang civilization. For instance, was irrigation practiced? Silk may have been made in Shang times. There is no doubt that the silk industry began in China. To this all traditions are agreed, the only question being, when? Certain traditions place it before the Shang dynasty. It is known that royal and noble families were keenly interested in the development of silk, but the secret was closely guarded. However, Japan finally gained knowledge of the process around 300 A.D. India received its knowledge of the silk process, it is said, through a Chinese princess who illicitly carried silk moth eggs and the seed of a mulberry tree hidden in her head-dress.

The money of the period consisted of a type of shell called the cowry. The qualities which made this shell useful as a monetary unit were its durability, its lightness, and the fact that it was by no means numerous. Metal coins did not make their appearance in China until the period following Shang.

The arts and crafts of the period were of a high order. One has only to view a typical group of Shang bronzes to realize that the metal-smith of the day had standards hard to approach at the present time. Chinese scholars interested in such matters have compared Shang work with some of the best of the European Renaissance. It is certain that the Shang craftsmen had at their command an ability that can only create wonder in our eyes. Sculpture was done in stone as well as bronze, and wood and bone

A SHANG RITUAL DRINKING VESSEL CAST IN BRONZE

were mediums for carving. The pottery of the period was either wheel or hand made, but in both cases presents an interesting product. The beginnings of glazing must be traced back to the Shang period. Painting, too, had made a start, for polychrome designs have been found on remnants of walls.

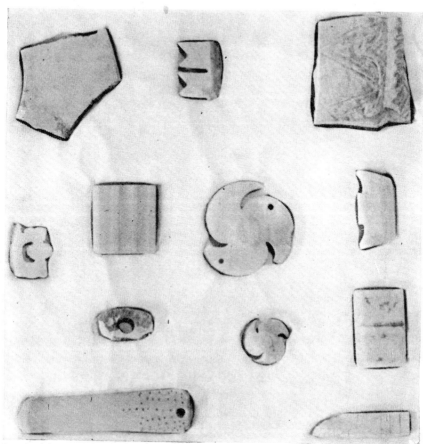

Photo by Raeburn Rohrbach

EXAMPLES OF SHANG HANDICRAFT

Showing a pot sherd and decorative objects carved in bone, stone and mother of pearl.

SHANG SCRIBES

It is most unlikely that there was widespread knowledge of reading and writing in Shang times. As in Egypt and Mesopotamia it was the scribe who carried on the serious business of transmitting messages. And because of this we are able to look at Chinese writing at a time when it still looked much like pictographic writing. As with the other great systems of early

EARLY SHANG SCULPTURE, A LIME-
STONE REPRESENTATION
OF AN OWL

REPRESENTATION OF A MYSTICAL
CREATURE CUT IN LIMESTONE

writing, that of the Chinese grew out of primitive pictures representing well-known objects of the time. But we have seen the
difficulties the people of the Near East had with this type of expression. Actions and ideas were at times impossible to express by
picture and so the written language began to develop and accom-
modate itself to the needs of easy written expression. Shang writing employed pictures but it was a long step beyond simple
picture writing. The basis of later Chinese characters had already
been established in Shang times. We see this from the inscriptions
on the oracle bones. Of course, many characters have since been
added. There are around 2500 Shang characters. Modern dic-
tionaries have something like 50,000, or twenty times as many.
Grammar and style have also changed considerably since Shang
times but by then the foundation for later development had been
laid.

Contrary to general belief, writing by brush came into use
during the Shang period as can be seen from the oracle bones. Prior
to this discovery it was held that the brush had been invented
in Ch'in times, late in the third century B.C.

SHANG RELIGION

The three great religions of present China were not known in Shang times. These are Confucianism, Taoism, and Buddhism. But it is an interesting fact that ancestor-worship, something that was very characteristic of Shang religion, is connected with each of these. The ancestor became a force to be seriously considered the moment he died. One's measure of success depended on offerings and sacrifices to the spirits of the dead. It is for this reason that objects of many kinds were placed at the graves.

But we get our best idea of Shang thoughts on supernatural beings from the written records of divination. The ancient Chinese appealed to the spirits for information on all manner of things. We may read the record on the oracle bones. For instance, questions were asked regarding sacrifices. To what spirits were they to be made? Sometimes the sacrifice involved a captured enemy. If the event called for an animal sacrifice it was necessary to find out what animal would be best suited to the purpose and, just as important, the color of the animal. At times the spirits were told of wars that were going on, or of serious illness in the group. Probably the spirits knew what to do under the circumstances. If a person were to undertake a journey it would be well for him to find out what day would be most propitious, or whether it might not be advisable to break the journey and spend some time at an intermediate point. Advice was sought with regard to hunting and fishing. What was the appropriate time and where was the best place? At the bend of the river? The spirits knew all of the answers.

War was of course a serious thing and the spirits were freely consulted. First of all, was it advisable to go to war? And if so, how many men should be taken? Or would it be better to remain on the defensive?

The weather was of as great interest then as now. Questions were asked about rain, snow, wind, and fog. Would there be good weather for a special occasion planned for the future? The farmer wished to know whether the coming year would be good for millet.

Illness and recovery were naturally matters of almost daily interest to the people of Shang, and their gods no doubt found much of their time occupied in considering the answers. A particularly common request to the gods was whether the coming week would be lucky or not. All these questions and more were forwarded to the spirits by the diviners who read the answers in the details of the T-shaped crack that developed on bones that had been plunged into fire.

In time to come we will undoubtedly be much better informed as to the history of the Shang dynasty, but the curtain has already been lifted. We have seen on the Shang stage the beginnings of that quality called Chinese civilization.

Courtesy Museum of Fine Arts, Boston

THE Chou (pronounced Jo) dynasty was the longest in China's long history. It is traditionally dated from 1122 to 249 B.C. To comprehend fully the meaning of these figures we should realize that about the same length of time is represented by the interval between the conquest of England by William and our own time. Much happens over such a period, and China of Chou times was no exception. It was a period of tremendous changes and within its limits falls the Chinese classical period. The great literary works and the names best known to the western world fall within this period. Confucius, Mencius, and Lao Tzu all lived and made their contributions to Chinese thought during the Chou period. The area of the empire was greatly extended during this era, and in its early years there occurred the first of a number of attempts at state socialism. Metal coins apparently came into use early in Chou times, and the plough, according to tradition, was introduced late in the period.

The origins of the Chou line are rather misty but it seems that a confederacy of western Chinese, led by the Chous, defeated the Shangs and captured their lands about 1122 B.C. The Chous themselves appear to have sprung from the same general Neolithic stock of North China which had produced the Shangs. But they were barbarians when they left their homes about 350 miles south-

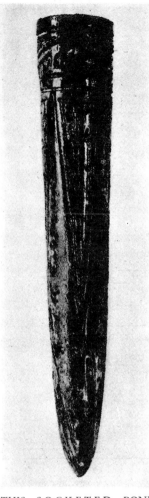

THIS SOCKETED BONE
SPEAR HEAD ILLUSTRATES
THE EXCELLENCE OF
SHANG ENGRAVING

west of the Shang capital and came into Shang territory on the Yellow River. There it was that they learned to write and painstakingly assume other phases of Shang culture that were superior to their own. The Chous borrowed divination, the system of writing, certain phrases, dating, architecture and some religious elements. Even some king's names were the same as those of the Shang dynasty. And like many other barbaric people in other parts of the world, the Chous required a genealogy when they came to power. The solution was found in short order, for it was soon being told that the Chous were descended from one of the earliest rulers of ancient China. The genealogy of Rome was manufactured in the same way, and with as little basis. But in both cases self-respect was satisfied.

We have mentioned cultural elements that the Chous borrowed. We are not to believe as a result that the Chous were dependent for everything. They developed these traits along very original lines, and before the dynasty came to a lingering end the culture of China had been greatly enriched.

THE MARTIAL KING—CONQUEROR OF SHANG

According to tradition the war between Shang and Chou went back to the time of the grandfather of the Martial King, the first Chou ruler. The Chou objective for at least two generations was thus the subjugation of Shang. Essential details are lacking and those we have may be regarded to some extent as myth. But we may accept as fact the defeat of Shang. The Martial King (Wu Wang) is said to have assembled a large army and decisively defeated the defending armies of Shang. The last of the Shang kings is said to have fled to his favorite resting place, a pleasure pavilion, where in his despair he dressed himself in all his finery and set fire to the building and was consumed with it. Shortly thereafter the Martial King made his way to the burned building and discovered the corpse, whereupon he shot three arrows into it. The final act of this scene which symbolizes the transfer of power from Shang to Chou was the cutting off of the head and setting it upon the new king's banner as a trophy. The Martial King had at last achieved an aim treasured by his grandfather.

Just how much territory had been conquered by the new people is unknown. It seems unlikely that it extended down the Yellow River to the sea. But the area was undoubtedly large and presented a real problem in government. The solution adopted was to parcel out different territories to relatives and allies. Thus the new governing system grew into a full fledged feudal order, as much so as that of medieval Europe. The local lords gave revenue (taxes), troops, and allegiance to the Martial King, but aside from these obligations they were kings themselves in their own territories. But this was too ideal a state of affairs; trouble always brews in such circumstances. In a feudal state personal ambition has ever been the cornerstone of unrest and war.

THE DUKE OF CHOU—BROTHER AND
UNCLE OF KINGS

On the death of the Martial King the throne passed to a son who was still very young. The solution then, as in many a similar circumstance in European history, was to set up a regency until the young king attained maturity. The Duke of Chou, younger brother of the old king and uncle of the new one, kept this office for seven years. He was such an unusual man that it will be worth while to look closely at his character and accomplishments. Indeed it is likely that without him Chinese thought and institutions would not be what they are. He was a great humanist and had vast influence in standardizing custom. He is regarded by some as the most remarkable man in Chinese history. He was possessed of an intellect, energy and force of character unique in any one person. Some Chinese have considered him greater than Confucius as a molder of thought, and Confucius himself regarded him as the inspirational source of his philosophy.

The duke held the empire together when it seemed on the verge of falling apart. At a time when many forces were working against the unity for which he stood, his will and strength of purpose served the country well. Two of his own brothers attempted to resurrect the old Shang dynasty, but the duke put one to death and exiled the other. Ultimately the young king reached maturity and assumed control, but the duke remained as aid and adviser. At this time the capital was moved eastward near the modern city of Loyang which is about 150 miles southwest of the old Shang capital. Other cities were also built and the duke had a large share of responsibility in their erection.

Interesting and no doubt characteristic stories have been told about this remarkable man. It is said, for instance, that the duke was so zealous in the accomplishment of his duties that he would see interviewers while taking his bath. No time should be wasted. Another tale relates that when his brother, the Martial King, was ill on a certain occasion the duke beseeched the spirits of his ancestors to take his life instead. The recovery of the king naturally proved the powers of the duke's prayers, and the fact that the spirits were on the side of the duke.

THE KINGS AND THE NOBLES

Early in the history of the Chou dynasty it appears to have been relatively easy to keep the various nobles under control, although we have seen that at the death of the Martial King certain factions schemed for power. First of all, many of the Chou subjects were newly conquered and would readily have revolted against the nobles had they broken faith with the king. Then, too, the king could play off one or more nobles against another. For instance if one of his vassals attempted to break away, the king could readily get aid from others by promising them any

A CHOU BRONZE
BELL

conquered territory. Thus in the early days of the dynasty the people and the king were able to keep the nobles under control.

But many factors enter into such a situation and it was not long before the Chou kings had their hands full. A few generations served to establish the nobles in their own territories and their subjects came to regard them as rightful rulers. With the spirit of independence thus growing and armies and wealth increasing it is little wonder that the king soon ceased receiving his accustomed revenues. Trouble naturally followed, and for many years the ambitions of local nobles directed the course of Chinese history.

BIT AND BRIDLE
EQUIPMENT OF
THE CHOU
PERIOD

Reproduced by permission of a private collector
Photo by Raeburn Rohrbach

The test of kingship in a state such as we see here lies in the character of the king. In a feudal system revolt will surely follow on the accession of a king unmindful of his duties to his people. Such a man was King Li who ascended the throne about 878 B.C. about the time that Samaria was being built in Israel. Li became a cruel tyrant and oppressor, and refused to listen to the wise counsel of his minister. Inevitable revolt took place and the king ended his days in exile. The prestige of the House of Chou was at low ebb, and although its passing was still some time in the future the end was in sight. In Chinese annals the Chou dynasty lasted until 249 B.C. but its real end as a dynastic power came with the death of Yu in 771. An interesting story is told of that event.

A CHINESE AESOP'S FABLE

King Yu became infatuated with a woman named Pao Szu and did everything possible to please her. But she was amused with great difficulty and that seriously disturbed Yu. However hard he tried he could not make her laugh. At length he thought of lighting the smoke signals which were used to summon his nobles and their armies when the country was in danger of attack. The nobles and their men came on the run but found everything serene except for Pao Szu's joyous laughter. The king, too, was extremely happy as a result of the woman's pleasure and had the beacons lit again and again. Recalling Aesop, you have already guessed that the nobles came finally to disregard the signals and that an occasion arose in which the king really needed aid. Lacking all support he was killed and the woman captured. Thus the House of Chou came to an end as a ruler of empire.

After that the Chou line became as one of its former vassals, a small state struggling for a place in the sun. None of the states was powerful enough to make a lasting union of the scattered dukedoms, but it was in this setting that there developed much of China's philosophical thought. In this latter part of the disrupted Chou period there lived a man whose effect on later China was to be of the greatest magnitude. That man was Confucius.

CHINA'S GREAT SAGES—LAO TZU, CONFUCIUS AND MENCIUS

To comprehend fully the significance of Confucius it will be well to look first at another great philosopher, Lao Tzu, who was born about fifty years before Confucius.

Lao Tzu, whose name was later Latinized as Laocius by the Jesuits, was the first great religious teacher of China. He was born about 604 B.C. a few years after the fall of Nineveh. Lao Tzu is very much a legendary figure and some believe him to be entirely mythical. However, he may have been a person of flesh and blood notwithstanding the fact that he enters Chinese history mysteriously and passes out in the same way. He is supposed to have been keeper of the archives of the city of Loyang, but did not take his duties very seriously. For some unknown reason he decided to leave China. Coming to the gateway at the western pass he was asked by the gatekeeper for a writing. Lao Tzu complied,

LAO-TZU

Courtesy Field Museum of
Natural History, Chicago

according to the story, and left with the keeper the famous *Classic of the Way.*

The religion advocated by Lao Tzu is called Taoism, that is the Way-ism. It is in most ways quite opposed to the teachings of Confucius. In general it may be said to advocate a harmony with Nature, and this is to be done by linking life to the Tao, or the Way. A definition of Taoism is very difficult to give since even Chinese scholars are disagreed as to the real meaning of the Way. Regarding a definition Lao Tzu himself said, "Those who know do not tell; those who tell do not know." In a later generation Confucius studied the Tao, for twenty years in fact, but was unable to comprehend it.

One of Lao Tzu's principles was that good should be returned for evil, but this, interestingly enough, was not supported by the practical Confucius who said that evil and wrong doing should be punished.

Lao Tzu had disciples, the foremost being Chuang Tzu. That he had learned well his lesson from the master may be seen in the following story. One day Chuang Tzu was fishing in the river when two officials went out to ask him to take charge of the administration of the Ch'u state. Chuang continued fishing and did not even turn his head, but said, "I have heard that in Ch'u there is a sacred tortoise which has been dead now some three thousand years, and that the Prince keeps this tortoise carefully enclosed in a chest on the altar of his ancestral temple. Now, would this tortoise rather be dead, and have its remains venerated, or be alive and wagging its tail in the mud?" "It would rather be alive," answered the two officials, "and wagging its tail in the mud." At that Chuang cried, "Begone! I too will wag my tail in the mud."

Taoism has had three major periods of development. In the time of Lao Tzu and his disciples it was sincere philosophy. During the Ch'in dynasty, that following Chou, it became for a short while the state religion. After that it deteriorated and became little more than the practice of magic under the influence of the Taoist priests. At present the cult is devoted largely to a search for the secrets of the "Philosopher's Stone" and the "Elixir of Life".

K'UNG TZU WHO WAS CALLED CONFUCIUS

Confucius, whose Chinese name was K'ung Tzu, was born in 551 B.C. about fifty years after the birth of Lao Tzu. Confucius represents the characteristic Chinese philosophy and today, over two thousand years after his time, a large portion of the people of the earth continue to be profoundly influenced by the workings of his mind.

Confucius lived during a very confused period in China's history and tried to save society by returning to the ways of old. He emphasized ethics, moral education and ceremonies, and preached the return to the virtue of the Golden Age of Yao and Shun. He said that the educated people, by their example, should lead China to new glories. This, of course, was not a new idea, and in fact Confucius never claimed to be the founder of a set of religious views. He was rather a coordinator of older teachings.

He was a very democratic man and is perhaps best remembered by the Christian West as the author of the familiar sounding Golden Rule: "What you do not like when done to yourself, do not do to others."

Confucius appears to have been a very stern and righteous man. As a father he was the same, apparently always acting with great reserve. A story, hard to credit, is told of his son who was asked by a disciple of the sage, "Have you learned any lessons from your father different from those received by us?" The reply was that Confucius had asked him only two questions, "Have you read the *Odes?*" and "Have you studied the Rules of Propriety?"

Confucius had strong moral characteristics and was a great teacher of righteousness. Early in his career, at a time when he had a government position as minister of crime, he was influential in bringing about certain reforms. For instance, he brought to justice those who watered their sheep to make them heavier before bringing them to market. It is said that during his time the spirit of honesty was so prevalent that lost jewels were left untouched on the highway.

The teachings of Confucius which have so profoundly affected China and its neighbors are included in the so-called *Confucian Classics.* This series comprises several works and is sometimes called the Old and New Testament of Confucianism. The sage had many followers who created a greater interest in his teachings after he was dead than they had enjoyed during his life. There was a brief period of persecution under the short lived Ch'in dynasty, but with the coming of the Hans (206 B.C.) the Confucian principle that government is for the good of the people and should always be based on justice was finally victorious.

Confucianism owes much to the sage Meng Tzu whose latinized name was Mencius. He lived several centuries after Confucius but was nevertheless one of his principal disciples. Much of his thought was original but he is best known as the interpreter and popularizer of the teachings of Confucius. He taught that in matters of government the people came first, then the gods, and finally the emperor. As a result he believed that the people had a right to rebel when the government consistently disregard-

CONFUCIUS

論語卷之一　　　　　朱熹集註

學而第一

此爲書之首篇、故所紀多務本之意、乃入道之門、積德之基、學者之先務也。凡十六章。

子曰、學而時習之、不亦說乎。

說悅同。○學之爲言效也。人性皆善、而覺有先後、後覺者必效先覺之所爲、乃可以明善而復其初也。習、鳥數飛也。學之不已、如鳥數飛也。說、喜意也。既學而又時時習之、則所學者熟、而中心喜說、其進自不能已矣。程子曰、習、重習也。時復思繹、浹洽於中、則說也。又曰、學者將以行之也。時習之、則所學者在我、故說。謝氏曰、時習者、無時而不習。坐如尸、坐時習也。立如齊、立時習也。

有朋自遠方來、不亦樂乎。

樂、音洛。○朋、同類也。自遠方來、則近者可知。程子曰、以善及人、而信從者衆、故可樂。又曰、說在心、樂主發散在外。

人不知而不慍、不亦君子乎。

慍、紆問反。○慍、含怒意。君子、成德之名。尹氏曰、學在己、知不知在人、何慍之有。程子曰、雖樂於及人、不見是而無悶、乃所謂君子。愚謂、及人而樂者順而易、不知而不慍者逆而難、故惟成德者能之。然德之所以成、亦曰學之正、習之熟、說之深、而不已焉耳。

○有子曰、其爲人也孝弟、而好犯上者鮮矣。不好犯上、而好作亂者、未之有也。

弟好、皆去聲。鮮、上聲、下同。○有子、孔子弟子、名若。善事父母爲孝、善事兄長爲弟。犯上、謂干犯在上之人。鮮、少也。作亂、則爲悖逆爭鬪之事矣。此言人能孝弟、則其心和順、少好犯上、必不好作亂也。

君子務本、本

A PAGE OF THE ANALECTS OF CONFUCIUS

The original text is printed in large characters with a running commentary composed by Chu Hsi of the Sung Dynasty.

ed their best interests. The democracy of Confucianism is here most apparent.

After about 350 B.C. it must have been clear to most Chinese that little headway could be made against the growing power of the state of Ch'in, and it was actually less than a century later that this state took over the destinies of China for a short but very significant period.

Courtesy The Art Institute of Chicago

A SECTION OF THE GREAT WALL

No geographical obstacle was sufficiently great to hinder the construction of the wall.
Watch towers were scattered at frequent intervals.

Courtesy American Museum of Natural History

SLOWLY BUT CERTAINLY THE "SHIP OF THE DESERT" CROSSES THE
DREADED DUNE LAND

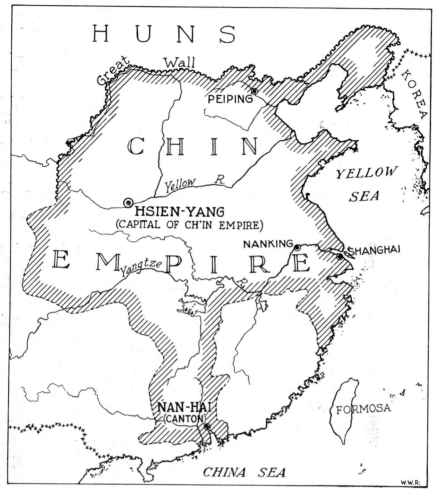

Drawing by Walter W. Romig

THE CH'IN dynasty lasted from 249 to 206 B.C., a very short period as important Chinese dynasties go. We recall that the Ch'in state was growing steadily in power during the last century of the Chou dynasty. When Chou finally collapsed it was Ch'in, of all the Chinese states, that was recognized as the rightful leader of the country. However, it was not to be that the chief of the Ch'ins was to enjoy for long the power he had earned. He had already ruled his own Ch'in state for fifty years when he found himself sole ruler of China. The old man died shortly and was followed by his son who reigned only three days.

The most important ruler of this dynasty was the fourth who, after gaining complete control, assumed the splendid sounding title of "First Emperor of the Ch'in Dynasty". He was an extremely forceful person and merits the further distinction of probably being China's greatest general and political genius. The Emperor's name and state were held in high regard and it is perhaps from the name of his dynasty, Ch'in, that the name "China" was derived, for we are assured that the First Emperor was the man who really brought all the states together. By 221 B. C., after a series of very deliberate campaigns, there was but one master of China.

There can be no doubt that the emperor was a despot since even his son protested and was banished for his pains, and the Chinese today show no particular reverence to the grave or the memory of the Chinese Napoleon.

It is easily understood that Confucianism, with its democratic principles, was hardly to the liking of the First Emperor. As a result he decreed that except for works on agriculture, medicine and divination, all the Confucian books were to be destroyed. The First Emperor was so successful in his attempt to remove Confucianism from the scene that when the Han dynasty came into power several years later it was with the greatest difficulty that the classics were gathered together again. It is said that a descendant of Confucius, a member of the ninth generation, had hidden copies of the works of his ancestor in the walls of his house.

At the time that the books were burned an attempt was also made to stamp out the followers of the sage. On one occasion it is said that four hundred and sixty of them were put to death in such a cruel manner that the son of the Emperor again protested.

At the same time the Emperor was heartily devoted to the teachings of Taoism. Perhaps its magic qualities, which embodied the hope of knowing the secret of life, had made a strong appeal to the monarch. He was personally fearful of death and sent expeditions in search of the "Elixir of Life". One of these expeditions is said by tradition to have reached Japan. It has also been suggested that his Taoist leaning was a natural course to take in view of his strong feeling against the dominant Confucian philosophy. It is a fact at any rate that Taoism flourished during the Ch'in period. One of the most interesting stories of the time was a forerunner of our Rip van Winkle tale.

A TAOIST RIP VAN WINKLE

An old man had been wandering through the mountains gathering fire wood when he chanced upon a group of men playing chess, whereupon he dropped his ax and stood watching the game. At length one of the players handed the old man a thing about the size and shape of a date stone and told him to put it in his mouth. Immediately the old man lost all sense of hunger and thirst. Some time had elapsed when one of the players told him that he had been there a long while and ought to be thinking of going home. The old man stooped to pick up his ax but found that its handle had turned to dust, while the blade was imbedded in a tree which had since grown around it. When he reached home he discovered that he had been gone for centuries and that none of his friends or relatives remained.

THE GREAT WALL OF CHINA

There had been earlier ramparts and sectional walls along the long northern frontier of China, but credit must be given to the First Emperor for building the mighty wall as it is known today. About 214 B. C. he united into one mighty rampart the sections that then existed in order to keep out the northern hordes who from time immemorial had regarded China as choice prey. The Great Wall winds in and out, over mountain and stream, for about 1500 miles. It starts at the sea opposite Peiping at Shan-hai-kuan and travels inland almost to the Gobi Desert. It is faced with either brick or granite and is filled with earth. The wall has an average height of twenty feet and the roadway which runs on

Courtesy The Art Institute of Chicago

ANOTHER VIEW OF THE GREAT WALL
It is said that over one million men perished in the task of building this wall
and that every stone cost a human life.

top is fifteen feet wide. As a means of additional protection there
are fortified towers at every hundred yards.

The Great Wall which remains as one of the more spectacular
monuments of the Ch'in age is truly a great engineering feat. But
it will be remembered also as a monument to the unremitting
power behind the name of the First Emperor, for the lower classes,
criminals, merchants, and even Confucian scholars, were driven
into the ranks of the corvèe.

FIFTY YEARS AND CH'IN PASSES

The First Emperor had raised a mighty empire, the greatest
that the Far East (or the Near West as some think it should be
called) had yet seen. The feudal system had been largely dis-
solved and government was centralized. But in this case the gov-

ernment was no stronger than the man and when the Emperor died, Ch'in's days were numbered. A son became the Second Emperor but the title was an empty one. The new king reigned but three years before he was murdered, and during that time the magnificent tomb of his father, in which several hundred maidens had been interred alive, had been sacked by one of the generals of the army. Thus Ch'in passed, giving way to strife between several of the army factions.

Courtesy The Art Institute of Chicago

A SCHOLAR COLLATING CLASSICAL TEXTS

A detailed study taken from a large painting showing a great number of such men at work.

Courtesy Chavannes, *Mission Archeologique*

GIANT BUDDHA OF WU CHOU SHAN
A fifty foot rock sculpture of Buddha.

HAN, THE FIRST GREAT NATIONAL DYNASTY

THE HAN dynasty (206 B.C.-220 A.D.) made such a lasting impression on those of later times that to this day the Chinese sometimes call themselves "Sons of Han". But the establishment of the house was not easy. There were several years of intense struggle after the breakdown of the Ch'in line. At length, however, Liu Pang emerged the victor and became the founder of the first great national dynasty. This was in 202 B.C. but he dated his reign to 206, thus including the period of internal disorder. For a while feudalism with all its dangers to government seemed on the verge of returning, but after about a century the hereditary nobles were removed from office. In their stead were placed officials who had proved their worth by examination. This was a true civil service, and although its origin probably went back to Chou times, it was the Hans who really adopted and developed the system. The basis on which the officials were selected was by examination in the Confucian classics which by this time had been revived from their short lived banishment during the Ch'in dynasty. In later Chinese history we see that the civil service was greatly enlarged.

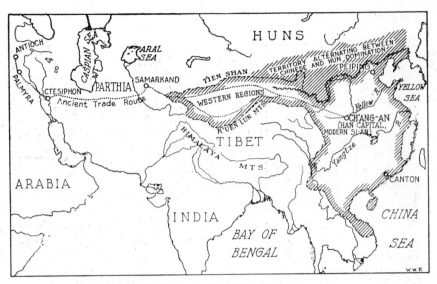

EXTENT OF THE HAN EMPIRE

During the Han dynasty China's interests expanded west-ward. The most famous of Han sovereigns was Wu Ti who reigned for fifty-four years (140-87 B.C.). He successfully fought the Huns and his troops penetrated deep into central Asia. Among the more notable figures of this period was Chang Ch'ien who explored extensively and brought back valuable information regarding the countries west of China. At the time of its greatest expansion the Han empire extended to the Aral and Caspian Seas.

After a territory had been subdued it followed naturally that trade would flow more easily than before. Soon Chinese products were finding their way over the thousands of miles of midland Asia into the Hellenistic world, and Mediterranean goods were being sent in return. Trade between China and Rome is claimed to have begun at the time Marc Antony was governor of Egypt. Soon Roman writers—Horace, Virgil, Pliny the elder and others —were telling about this trade with the Far East. The products which were brought from China included silks, furs, and iron. The long overland route lay through Turkestan to Ctesiphon whose arch still stands by the Tigris. From there the caravans might either go across country to Palmyra and Syria, or turn southward to the Persian Gulf to meet ships which would take

A CARAVAN PASSING NEAR THE JEWELLED PAGODA, CHINA

the goods around the Arabian Peninsula to Egypt. Still another route from China to the west lay over the passes of the Hindu Kush Mountains to the mouth of the Indus River, at which point the transfer was made to ships.

BUDDHISM REACHES CHINA

It was through such contacts with foreign countries that Buddhism found its way into China. No one knows for sure exactly when it was introduced except that it came during Han times. Many, however, believe that the Indian faith reached China about the time of Christ, and several stories are told of the event. From these it may be gathered that it was not pure Buddhism, but rather a modified Central Asiatic form, that came into the region protected by the Great Wall. And once in China it was changed still further to accord with the family traditions of the Chinese. Thus a third religion joined the two other great ones.

Chinese Buddhism today has traveled a long way in both time and manner from the Buddhism founded by Gautama in India.

The best of the mysticism of the Taoists was added to the Buddhist foundation and created a new article of faith. The influence of Buddhism on China has been extremely important in many respects. Art and architecture were enriched. The pagoda may be traced to such influence, and for simplification in such fundamental matters as speech and writing the Chinese owe a great debt to the Sanskrit world.

PAPER WAS INVENTED IN CHINA

The manufacture of real paper can be traced to 105 A. D. when Ts'ai Lun, a studious official, made the discovery. Before his time documents had been written on bamboo boards or on a near-paper made of silk. The latter appeared in the third century before our era. But silk was expensive and bamboo was heavy. Ts'ai Lun devoted himself to the problem and presently conceived the idea of using the inner part of bark, pieces of hemp, old rags and fishing nets. He announced his invention to the emperor in the year 105 from which time paper has been in general use in China.

It should not be understood that all the substances with which Ts'ai Lun experimented were mixed together. Each was kept separate and pounded into pulp to form hemp paper, bark paper, rag paper, and so on.

The use of paper remained exclusively eastern Asiatic until about the middle of the eighth century when, it is said, that the Arabs at Samarkand were attacked by the Chinese. The attack was a failure and during the flight certain Chinese experts in the art of paper making were captured. From these the Arabs learned the process, and developed it, and ultimately passed their information on to Europe.

Brush and ink, contrary to general belief, were invented long before paper, in Shang times in fact. This is an archaeological fact which contradicts one of the basic traditions of Chinese invention.

HAN AND HUN

We have seen that the rulers of the early part of the Han dynasty were successful in beating back the forays of the Hun marauders on the northwest frontier. But about the middle of the four hundred year period the Huns came on with added fury, so much so that it was considered necessary to move the Han capital eastward. As a result one speaks of the western Han and eastern Han dynasties. In the latter part of the period even the Great Wall proved to have little effect on the determined attacks of the barbarians who were related to the Huns who later made such a lasting impression by their forays into Europe.

Perhaps part of China's inability to cope with the foreigners lay in the fact that there was constant civil strife between weak emperors and upstart generals. It is true that to have been called general in those days was greater than being called emperor. Certainly the generals had more power. It was one of these who about the beginning of the third century A.D. captured the capital and ended the dynasty by disposing of the Emperor.

A GENERAL VIEW OF MONGOLIAN PLATEAU.
THE ORIGINAL HABITAT OF THE HUNS

漫画融秋風
蓬時壁不齲
鄱荊候溪等屋
家黄山滿河越
和山地人同
志伴同川艦
義莖表對月
運兎健
辛丑季真月
尚起

明王紱秋江泛艇

北平古詞陳列所珍蘊

Courtesy The Art Institute of Chicago

A MING LANDSCAPE PAINTING

A STELE OF THE WEI DYNASTY

*The following paragraphs carry us beyond the limits of this volume but are introduced as a means of connecting earlier Chinese history with the present.

AFTER THE FALL of the Han dynasty there were approximately three and a half centuries during which no state was able to hold power for any length of time. The first part is known as the Age of Romance, immortalized by the *Story of the Three Kingdoms.* There followed a period when invaders from the north beat their way into the country. The Chinese in the south organized to some extent in an effort to thrust back the barbarians, and as a result the period has been called the age of the northern and southern dynasties.

During these centuries civilization was greatly modified. The invaders brought with them non-Chinese traits, while at the same time they absorbed much that was thoroughly Chinese in nature.

[365]

Courtesy Chavannes, *Mission Archeologique*
THE NESTORIAN MONUMENT AT SI-AN DATING FROM
THE T'ANG DYNASTY

Buddhism became very popular and Chinese pilgrims visited the sacred shrines in India. The real growth of Buddhism in China can be traced to the last years of this intermediate period. It was during those years and the century or two following that Buddhism reached its peak as an influence in the life of China.

Due to the numerous military ventures that took place during the intermediate period a complicated code of chivalry sprang up. It was this age also that supplied later China with many of the romantic figures that we know from fiction and drama.

Courtesy Chavannes, *Mission Archeologique*

A PRESENT DAY MOSQUE AT SI-AN, WHICH, AS
CH'ANG-AN, WAS THE CAPITOL OF THE T'ANG EMPIRE
This mosque and the Nestorian monument bear evidence of the
religious tolerance of the T'ang court.

THE SUI AND THE T'ANG

The country was brought under control again by the Sui who
ruled for about thirty years (589-618 A.D.). The T'ang (618-
907 A.D.) followed and for a while China was the greatest and
largest empire on earth. T'ang armies marched to Korea, Turkistan, Tibet and northwest India. China attained its peak in cultural achievement during the period of what was perhaps the

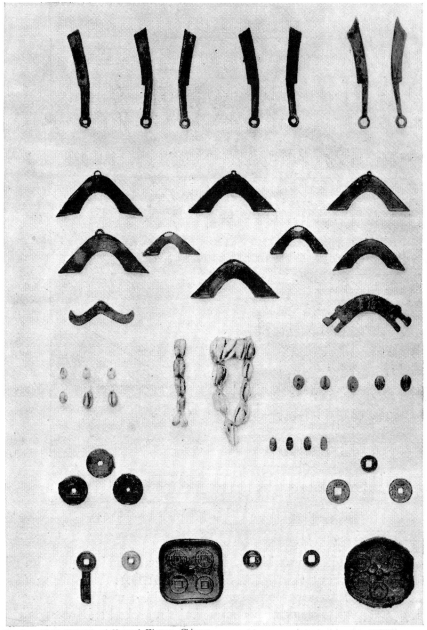

Courtesy Field Museum of Natural History, Chicago

EXAMPLES OF ANCIENT CHINESE COINS. HAN PERIOD AND EARLIER
Note cowry shells in center.

Courtesy Field Museum of Natural History, Chicago

EXAMPLES OF ANCIENT CHINESE COINS. HAN PERIOD AND EARLIER

III—24

Courtesy Field Museum of Natural History, Chicago

BRONZE MIRRORS OF THE HAN PERIOD

greatest native dynasty. Chinese still call themselves "Sons of T'ang" as they do "Sons of Han". The capital was the converging point of philosophers, scholars, and religious leaders of many faiths. At the same time the country was opened to foreigners, among them Moslems, Nestorians and Manichaeans. The Nestorians, who were a Christian sect from western Asia, came as missionaries and church builders. Persians came to China seeking aid against the Arab conquest. Simultaneously the Japanese learned much that was to raise their country out of barbarism.

After a brilliant period of progress in the arts, including poetry and music and the development of block printing, the T'ang dynasty weakened and came to an end. This dynasty is known as one in which the earliest known printed book appeared, as well as the one which first saw printed money. The T'angs left the scene in 907 A.D.

From that year to 960 there was much disorder in the country. Various factions fought amongst themselves for power, and five of them were strong enough for short periods to be granted dynastic distinction.

THE SUNG DYNASTY

The Sung dynasty, a period especially glorified by achievements in literature, philosophy, and the famous socialistic experiment of Wang An-shih, existed for over three hundred years (960-1280 A.D.). It began well but soon felt the pressure of the frontier barbarians. These included the K'itans, the Chin Tatars, and the Mongols. Genghiz Khan, one of the world's foremost fighters and military organizers, led his Mongols into North China early in the thirteenth century, and by 1214 most of the territory north of the Yellow River was in his hands. At the time of his death in 1227 still more territory had been added. Alliances between Mongols and Sung were effective for a time, but this brotherhood was most unnatural. By the year 1280 we see the last of the Sung monarchs throwing himself into the sea at the time Kublai Khan, grandson of Genghiz, became emperor of all China.

GENGHIZ KHAN

KUBLAI KHAN

THE DYNASTY OF KUBLAI KHAN

The Mongol dynasty, for all its fame in history, lasted less than ninety years. It was founded, as we have seen, by Kublai Khan, the hero of Coleridge's celebrated poem. He was in all respects as able a soldier as his grandfather had predicted. The capital was by this time near Peiping and from there he ruled not only China, but most of the sprawling Mongol empire which extended across Asia to Mesopotamia and into Europe. Military expeditions were sent also into Japan, Cambodia, Burma and Java, but these added no glory to the name of the brilliant Kublai.

Mongol power reached its peak under Kublai Khan, and the tremendous extension of influence was a great boon to trade. Consequently there was steady travel by both ship and caravan between Europe and Cathay, as China was then called in Europe. Missionary and merchant met on the high road of Asia. Among the merchants the name of Polo will ever be remembered. There were three Polos who went to China from the flourishing Venetian seaport on the Adriatic—Nicolo, Maffeo and Marco; Marco was the son of Nicolo. Marco Polo spent many years in the service of Kublai and on returning to Venice wrote the memoirs that have made him famous.

The Mongol dynasty was no exception to the rule that Chinese dynasties based upon forced military power are short lived. In fact it collapsed about ninety years after having begun so auspiciously. When this happened the outlying districts lost their protection and the trade routes became unsafe. For a while China lost contact with the west.

THE MING DYNASTY

The Ming dynasty (1368-1644 A.D.) was purely Chinese. Although it was brilliant in many respects, not much originality can be claimed for it. The third ruler moved the capital to Peiping, and the palaces and temples which are so much admired by the tourist were largely the work of this emperor. The Ming rulers sent expeditions to Java, Ceylon and even as far as the Persian Gulf. Korea was also invaded. But with the weakening of the Ming line the Japanese entered Korea and sailed as pirates up and down the Chinese coast.

As has already been mentioned, China of the Ming period was not particularly creative, even though architecture and glazed pottery had considerable charm. The China of that day was wealthy, but lacked abilities observed in earlier days.

Courtesy The Art Institute of Chicago

TOMB OF YUNG-LO, ONE OF THE MING EMPERORS, IN JEHOL

CHINESE LIMESTONE STATUE

(Late 6th—early 7th century)

During the Ming dynasty Europeans began again to interest themselves in China. The Portuguese, in the sixteenth century, sailed to India, Malacca, China and Japan; and Spanish ships landed in the Philippines, thus establishing a control that lasted until the Spanish-American war in 1898. The Jesuits soon followed and after some difficult years established themselves in China. Some of them were so highly regarded for their knowledge of astronomy and mathematics that they were put in charge of the government bureau of astronomy in Peiping. During the following (Manchu) period they were given still further duties.

THE MANCHUS

The Manchu dynasty carries China into the midst of present day relations with the rest of the world. It lasted from 1644 to 1912. The Manchus were a small Tatar tribe northeast of China who easily pushed aside the weakened Ming dynasty. They were conquerors, these Golden Tatars, but they accepted Chinese customs. Moreover, the native Chinese were eligible for office, except in their own provinces. This was the Manchu method for preventing revolt. At the same time no official was allowed to remain in one place long enough to gain a real following.

By 1700 the Manchu empire included not only China, but Manchuria, Mongolia, Tibet and Turkistan. A few years later Cochin-China and Korea were paying tribute.

The principal events of the Manchu dynasty were connected with adjustment to European influence and affairs. As we have seen, the Jesuits were in the country before Manchu times. Missionaries of other orders followed, with the result that Europe learned a great deal about the glamor, the life and especially the opportunities existing in the land of China.

During the nineteenth century increased European trade interest in China caused serious trouble and a number of grave skirmishes took place. China was subdued and practically came to believe that she was destined to serve the interests of the world. The complete downfall of the Manchus came with revolution in 1911 and since 1912 the country has been a republic.

Courtesy Field Museum of Natural History. Chicago

A TIBETAN LAMA PARTICIPATING IN A RELIGIOUS CEREMONY

TIBET—THE MOUNTAIN KINGDOM

Courtesy Field Museum of Natural History. Chicago

YAKS SERVE AS PACK ANIMALS IN TIBET

Tibet and especially its capital, Lhasa, have always spelled romance and adventure. Naturally rugged and inaccessible, the country has become even more difficult to enter because of the development of anti-European feeling. Tibet lies across the Himalayas from India and is the highest country in the world, being on the average over three miles above sea level, while its very lowest valleys are almost as high as Pike's Peak. To get into the country by any one of the passes one must climb to a height of at least three miles. The population, largely herders, is widely scattered through the mountains and has been estimated at about 3,000,000 people. Nobody knows the area of the country, and little is certain as to the natural resources of this mysterious land. But gold is to be found in most of the river beds.

[377]

POTALA
Residence of the Dalai Lama at Lhasa.

A TIBETAN DANCER, PROPERLY ATTIRED WITH ELABORATE HEADDRESS
AND BRIGHTLY COLORED HEAD FANS

WHY WE USE THE NAME "TIBET"

The Tibetan name for the country sounds something like *Bhöt*, and it was through a strange misunderstanding that our name for the country came into being. In the early days travelers went cross-country to China and India by way of the high plateau—the *Tö-bhöt*. They couldn't pronounce it correctly but they did their best, and the result was "Tibet." Thus an original misunderstanding to which was added mispronunciation produced a term which must seem queer to the ears of the peasant folk of Tibet.

LHASA—THE FORBIDDEN CITY

Few Europeans have seen Lhasa with its picturesque Potala— the early seventeenth century fortress-palace of the Dalai Lama built on a rocky hill—and the city houses stretching out below. The Dalai Lama is the spiritual and political ruler of these secluded mountain folk whose religion is a modified form of Buddhism developed through many centuries. Many have tried to reach the forbidden city but few have succeeded. However, in earlier days antagonism toward foreigners was not as strong as at present. A Christian mission was founded in the early part of the eighteenth century but finally collapsed, due not to unfriendliness, but to lack of funds.

The first Englishman to enter Tibet came in 1774, just before the American revolution, but he did not reach Lhasa. However, another of his countrymen visited the famous city in the early part of the last century and stayed five months, apparently on good terms. Shortly afterwards yet another Englishman is said to have resided in Lhasa for twelve years disguised as a Moslem. Effective exclusion of Europeans dates back only about a century. Nevertheless, the lure of adventure and the hope of gaining a new understanding of this strange country have prompted many others to make the attempt. Of these, some were killed, others saw extensive portions of the outlying districts of Tibet, but Lhasa, the goal of all, has been seen by few.

Courtesy Newberry, *Beni Hasan*

W E HAVE SEEN that many of the processes that characterized the ancient world were not simple. From primitive beginnings there arose civilizations of high merit and considerable complexity. The hunter with his easily satisfied needs learned that a better and more secure way of living could be had when he turned to farming. The process was slow but through it there came into being settlements that were forerunners of great cities. In the earliest settled communities a host of trades were soon established that never existed before. Mason, carpenter, potter, merchant, and money lender became an important part of each community, but the social structure was based primarily on the farmer and that which he produced from the soil.

Accidents in the sense of unusual men and favorable land conditions gave importance to certain localities, and accumulating wealth led in time to the formation of nations and mighty kings. Among the world's most wealthy and powerful men must be included the kings of the pyramid age. Government had its beginnings long ago and to maintain it there was taxation which more often than we may suspect served to pad the pockets of unscrupulous officials.

With the establishment of communities and roads that connected them, the merchant soon became an extremely important individual. Certain localities lacked wood, others required copper, few if any were entirely self-sufficient. The roads and seaways were soon dotted with caravans and ships bringing necessities to far away places. In this manner knowledge from one country was carried to another. Useful inventions never remained long unknown in surrounding lands. By a process of diffusion the benefits of thoughts, practices and inventions were spread afar and became so characteristic that in many instances we are unable to discover their sources. In other cases it is clear where an idea originated.

The earliest great civilizations were along the Nile and in Asia. Many centuries before Greece and Rome could be called anything but territories on the periphery of civilization there were mighty and culturally advanced states to the south and east where much that was later brought to Europe was conceived. No nation ever developed without numerous influences from foreign sources. Oriental astronomy, architecture, arts, crafts, and philosophies became naturalized on European soil and today we accept many of them as our own. But the dependence of our civilization on the labors and thoughts of generations long dead persists. The story of our civilization goes back through Europe, Rome and Greece to the Orient.

DESIGNER'S NOTE

The design and typography of this volume were executed along the same principles as in the two previous volumes of the *"University of Knowledge."*

Various maps were drawn especially for this volume under the direct supervision of the author and will greatly enhance the value of this book.

OTTO MAURICE FORKERT
Director of Design and Typography